On the Move

Lesson Plans to Accompany *Children Moving*
Sixth Edition

Shirley Ann Holt/Hale

We are children moving.
We move off of, onto, over, around, and through.
We have within us the resources for the future.
We are children
                  on
                        the
                              move!

Mc Graw Hill

Boston   Burr Ridge, IL   Dubuque, IA   Madison, WI   New York   San Francisco   St. Louis
Bangkok   Bogotá   Caracas   Lisbon   London   Madrid
Mexico City   Milan   New Delhi   Seoul   Singapore   Sydney   Taipei   Toronto

The **McGraw·Hill** Companies

On the Move: Lesson Plans to Accompany
Children Moving, Sixth Edition

Published by McGraw-Hill, an imprint of The McGraw-Hill Companies, Inc.,
1221 Avenue of the Americas, New York, NY 10020.
Copyright 2004 by The McGraw-Hill Companies, Inc.
All rights reserved.

1 2 3 4 5 6 7 8 9 0 BKM/BKM 9 0 9 8 7 6 5 4 3

ISBN 0-07-292113-7

www.mhhe.com

Dedicated to
Chase Alexander Elrod
and his love of movement

Preface

Thirty years of teaching physical education at Linden Elementary School have brought me the opportunity to teach several thousand children, many from kindergarten through sixth grade; hundreds of hours of writing lesson plans; and rewards beyond measure. This is elementary physical education.

As a beginning teacher, I spent several hours each evening writing lesson plans. After thirty years of teaching elementary physical education, I still spend considerable time developing lesson plans for my classes. The time spent writing is shorter, but the concentrated effort, time to reflect on classes and individual children, and the design of strategies to best present information and develop skills is still part of my planning each evening. Teaching is not a science to be mastered but an art to be constantly refined. The reflection and refinement are the journey. The rewards of teaching are in the journey, not in the destination.

The *National Standards for Physical Education** provide the criteria for designing learning experiences in physical education. The recently published National Teaching Standards for Physical Education† provide the criteria for accomplished teachers of physical education. The Surgeon General's Report on Physical Activity and Health‡ and subsequent reports on childhood obesity and inactivity and on increasing health risks among children provide the strongest base to date in support of quality physical education. We have the evidence to support physical education for children; we have the standards, both content and teaching, to provide the models for quality. Our task as teachers of physical education is to design learning experiences for children that assist them in developing a broad base of movement skills coupled with an enjoyment of physical activity that will translate into a physically active, healthy lifestyle after they leave the gymnasiums of our elementary schools. The lesson plans in *On the Move* are designed with those two purposes in mind.

Here are some of the highlights of this edition:

- Instructional objectives attainable within a single lesson.

- Content development with a focus on skill rather than broad exploration.

- Maximum practice of the focus skill; maximum practice for all students.

- Concentration on one cue at a time.

- Challenges throughout the lessons, not just as culminating activities.

- Both cognitive and performance assessments throughout to encourage assessment as an integral part of instruction.

- A series of physical fitness concept lesson plans.

- Sample lessons for integrated discipline activities.

- A separate section devoted to *Children Moving* Challenges written for the classroom teacher, designed for the recess or playground environment, with a focus on physical activities with minimum instruction and maximum participation for all students.

---

*National Association for Sport and Physical Education. (1995). *Moving into the future: National Standards for Physical Education.* St. Louis, MO: Mosby.

†National Board for Professional Teaching Standards. (1999). *Physical education standards for teachers of students ages 3–18+.* Arlington, VA: Author.

‡Centers for Disease Control. (1996). *Physical activity and health: A report of the Surgeon General.* Atlanta, GA: U.S. Department of Health and Human Services.

Don Chu, California State University at Chico, reminds us that physical education does what no other discipline can do. Don says, "We touch the hearts and souls of children every day." We do make a difference in the lives of children. Whether that difference is positive or negative is dependent on each of us. I hope this edition of *On the Move* will be helpful to you in your growth as a teacher of children. If I can be of assistance as you write lesson plans or develop the curriculum for your physical education program, do not hesitate to write: Dr. Shirley Ann Holt/Hale, Linden Elementary School, 700 Robertsville Road, Oak Ridge, Tennessee 37830; e-mail: sholthale@ortn.edu

Acknowledgments

Sincere appreciation is extended to the children of Linden Elementary School, who have followed my lesson plans throughout the years, and to the parents for their support of quality physical education for children. These children continue to make my teaching a pleasure and to make Monday my favorite day of the week! Special thanks to my principal, Tom Little, and to the entire staff at Linden Elementary for their beliefs in children as our present and future.

Appreciation is extended to Vicki Malinee and Carlotta Seely for their belief in another edition of the lesson plans, and to the teachers and future teachers of elementary physical education who read, adopt, and modify the lesson plans in their preparation for the teaching of children.

And finally, special thanks are extended to my husband for his belief in a mate who is both a teacher and a writer, and to my mother for her constant support and daily prayers.

Shirley Ann Holt/Hale

Contents

Part Three: Skill Themes   91

Introduction

On the Move is a collection of lesson plans to accompany *Children Moving*. They are reflective of the philosophy inherent in *Children Moving* since it was first written in 1974, teaching by themes and blending concepts and skills. The lessons are designed to introduce each concept and each basic skill from the movement framework (Figure 1) and to provide sample lessons of skill themes.

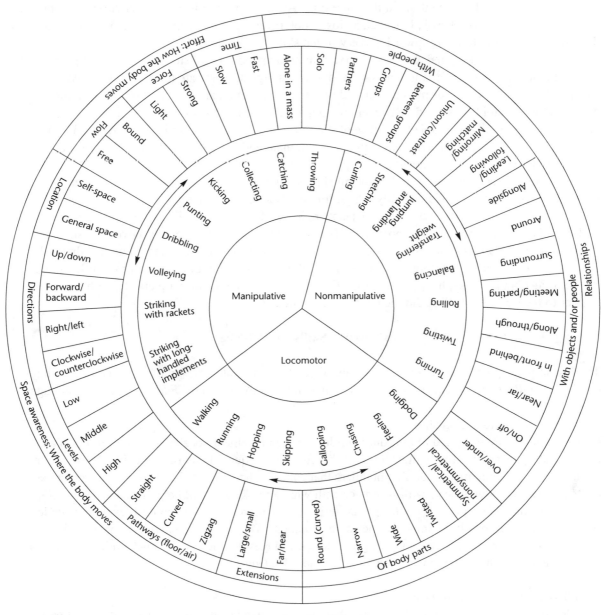

Figure 1   The Wheel

1

Two components of my personal philosophy of elementary physical education should be noted, as the lesson plans reflect both. A visitor to the gymnasium at Linden Elementary would notice the following words from the children:

We are people.
We can learn.
We can be trusted.
We can accept responsibility.

These beliefs about children and their learning translate into lessons that are child-centered and self-directed. The teacher is free to serve as a facilitator, providing the initial task and then assisting individual children as needed. A belief in trusting children and letting them be responsible, coupled with a belief in letting children learn at their own rates, translates into an environment in which children can focus on different components of a skill at the level at which each needs to be rather than perform mass drills with all doing the same thing at the same time. At first glance, this learning environment appears to be at best "organized chaos"; however, a closer look reveals a class of individuals on task, focused on the work appropriate to move toward mastery of the skill.

Lessons are also designed to provide maximum participation for all students, increased practice of the skill that is the focus of the lesson for that day, and a high success rate for each student. With the exception of the three to four minutes set aside for the introduction and the additional two to three minutes for closure, children should be actively participating for the remainder of class time—engaged in purposeful activity that maximizes practice of the skill component that is to be learned that day. Therefore, the lesson plans are written with sufficient equipment and a minimum of "down" time (taking turns, waiting in lines, and so forth).

The focus of each lesson is on developing skills and/or understanding concepts. Children have many important learning experiences in daily school life, but teaching movement skills is unique to physical education. We are partners with classroom teachers in developing responsible, contributing citizens, building character, and promoting positive self-concepts; we are *the* teachers of movement skills in the school setting. This focus places the emphasis during the physical education lesson on just that—skills. Lessons are designed as learning experiences for children; physical education is a time for learning, not a time of just being "busy, happy, and good." Concepts, skills, and themes are chosen with a positive answer to the question, "What did the children learn today?"

Concepts, Skills, and Themes

The lesson plans presented in *On the Move* are divided into six categories: movement concepts, introduction to skills, skill themes, fitness concepts, integrated activities, and *Children Moving* Challenges.

Part One: Movement Concepts
Concept lessons are designed to introduce children to the movement vocabulary and to develop an understanding of an idea that will become a subfocus in subsequent lessons. The concepts are not movements themselves but are, rather, the modifiers that enhance the quality of movement. Movement concepts provide the how, where, with whom, or with what a movement will be performed.

Most of the lesson plans for concepts are written for children at the precontrol level; their understanding is critical to skill lessons and theme development. The vocabulary and imagery used in the concept lessons have been selected for younger children; changes will need to be made in both vocabulary and examples if concept lessons are presented to older students.

Part Two: Introduction to Skills
Introducing children to dribbling by placing them in an advanced game of offensive/defensive basketball can be compared to introducing first-graders to the wonders of reading by a character analysis of

Shakespeare's *Macbeth*. When children are introduced to the basic skills of physical education, the skill should be presented in isolation, not in a dynamic multivariable situation. Introduction-to-skill lessons are designed to do just that—introduce children at the precontrol level to the skill. Remember, the precontrol level of skill execution is not age specific; older children also perform at the precontrol level when learning new skills.

The introductory lessons provide children with the mechanics of proper execution and mass practice of that skill. They will not develop mastery of the skill in one or two classes. Distributed practice of that isolated skill should be provided throughout the year. Don't rush the practice of skills for children; a great deal of practice is needed for mastery of these important basics.

Part Three: Skill Themes
A skill theme is a series of lessons emphasizing a particular skill and the concepts that enhance that skill. A basic skill introduced earlier now becomes the center of a theme. Through a series of lessons, the theme is expanded, moving from an isolated skill to a skill useful in dynamic, multivariable situations. Children are now traveling; partners are introduced. Directions, levels, pathways, and other concepts play a part in the execution of the skill. The skill themes in *On the Move* are from the text *Children Moving*, Chapters 19–30. They are written at the control level of skill proficiency. Each series of lessons shows how ideas from the progression spiral can serve as the catalyst for creating a number of lessons for children. Each skill theme provides mass practice and practice in different contexts to enhance children's mastery of that skill. Thus children move beyond performing a skill in isolation to using the skill in dynamic situations.

Part Four: Fitness Concepts
The physical fitness concept lessons are designed to introduce children to the concept of fitness and its components, as well as to provide an awareness of the importance of a healthy level of personal fitness. The lessons are designed for cognitive understanding and physical performance. Some of the lessons are planned for cooperative teaching between physical educator and classroom teacher. The fitness lesson plans included in *On the Move* are consistent with the philosophy of fitness for children in *Children Moving*. Physical fitness is the product of a quality program of physical education. At the elementary school level, its focus is the introduction to the concepts of fitness, an awareness of the components of fitness, and enjoyment of activity.

Part Five: Integrated Activities
Two series of lesson plans are presented to illustrate a thematic approach to an integrated curriculum. In the first series, the art, music, and physical education classes participate in a chosen theme; in the second series, the entire school participates in a selected theme. Both series of lessons are designed to show an approach to an integrated curriculum that does not compromise the content of specific disciplines and allows each to develop its area of expertise in relation to the chosen theme.

Part Six: *Children Moving* Challenges
The last section of the text is written for the classroom teacher. By grade level, kindergarten through Grade 4, a series of challenges is presented for the children to engage in during recess. The challenges are, for the most part, single tasks to provide children participation in meaningful physical activity when they are on the playground for their "break" during the school day. The *Children Moving* Challenges are written for minimum teacher preparation and supervision of the children, as opposed to actual teaching. Cues are given if the teacher wishes to become involved in the child's mastery of the skill beyond the initial presentation. Each set of challenges is designed for skill development with a progression between grade levels; the challenges will complement the physical education instructional program, if the school is fortunate enough to have a program in place.

The Lesson Plan

The lesson plans follow the design in *Children Moving*. Figure 2 illustrates the different components of the lesson plans that make up the body of *On the Move*.

Focus

The *focus* for the lesson is the skill or concept on which the children will concentrate during this lesson. When a skill is being developed, a series of lessons may have the same focus. The Movement Analysis Framework (see Figure 1) shows both the skills and the concepts from which curricular selection is made.

Subfocus

The *subfocus* is the concept (or skill) that serves as the modifier of the focus. A subfocus has been taught earlier as a lesson. Children should have a cognitive understanding of the concept or prior experience with the skill before it is used as a subfocus. Sometimes the subfocus will include more than one skill or concept.

Remember: the focus is an action verb; the subfocus is a modifier, an adverb.

Objectives

Instructional *objectives* are those that can be accomplished by most children in one lesson. Specifically stated, "At the end of this lesson the children will have learned to. . . ." Most of us remember the days of writing objectives in global terms, attainable after a few years of practice. For example, even though our goal may be a mature pattern of execution for an overhand throw, our objective for today is stepping forward on the opposite foot. This learning encompasses two spheres: knowledge and performance. The student will know which foot should be forward; the student will be able to perform the overhand throw with the opposite foot forward.

The objective is a statement of what the children will learn, not what activity they will do. The learning is presented as a concrete action, observable by the teacher, not an abstract concept to be grasped. For example, the children will volley the ball with an open palm or the children will swing arms back and forth in preparation for the jump.

Cues

Following a statement of the instructional objectives for skill development lessons, the *cues* are listed. The one or two cues listed are the critical cues for attaining the stated objectives of the lesson. I have found it best to focus on one cue at a time as opposed to bombarding the children with all the information needed to attain the major goal. Cues are short phrases, three to four words, that will serve as reminders for eliciting the behavior stated in the objective. For example, with the instructional objective "volley the ball with an open palm," the cue may be "flat palm" or "watch the ball."

Remember, concentrate on only one cue at a time. It will be difficult at first, but you will be amazed at how much and how quickly the children will learn.

Materials/Equipment

Materials/equipment includes those items needed to teach the lesson. Adaptations in lesson plans are often necessary based on available equipment and indoor or outdoor facilities. The sample lesson plans provided are designed for an indoor facility unless otherwise noted; they are suited for teaching outdoors with minimal adaptations.

Organization/Management

The *organization/management* section of the lesson plan is important to planning ahead and avoiding long periods of inactivity. Diagrams for stations, selection of partners, management notes, and adaptations for individual children are noted in this section.

Focus:

Subfocus:

Objectives: At the end of this lesson the children will have learned to:

CUES:

**Materials/
Equipment:**

**Organization/
Management:**

Introduction:

Content Development:

Closure:

Reflection:

Figure 2   Sample Lesson Plan

Introduction

The *introduction* comprises the first two to three minutes of the lesson. This is a critical part of the lesson as it sets the tone for the class. Introductory remarks should get the attention of the children, capture their imaginations, and make them eager participants in the lesson. During the introduction, children should be told the focus of the lesson for that day and why it is important. Relating the lesson to past and future lessons is also helpful. (If class design and facilities permit, children can enter the gym and immediately begin practice of previous skills for a few minutes before gathering together for the introduction.)

Content Development

Content development is the major part of the lesson plan. It contains the tasks and challenges that will be presented to the children. The *tasks* (T) are designed not to provide exposure to a large number of experiences but to focus on developing the instructional objective. Therefore, only a small number of tasks are given for a thirty-minute lesson. If the focus of the skill theme is on the overhand throw and the instructional objective of the lesson is stepping forward on the opposite foot, the tasks will be chosen to elicit that action.

In addition to tasks specific to the instructional objective, the lesson plan contains suggested *challenges* (C)—activities for the practice of the skill component being developed and self-testing activities for the learner. Challenges are within the instructional lesson, as well as near the end of the lesson. They provide teachers with an opportunity to observe the child's skill development and/or concept understanding in a more dynamic situation. In addition to the challenges coded with the letter "C," you will find some challenges with specific names.

In Part Three, if the lesson builds on a previous lesson, as in a series, you will find *teacher observations* following the initial task or warm-up activity. These are questions you reflect on as you observe the children's response to the task. The answers will provide feedback on both the class as a whole and on individual children.

Following the initial task, which is a review of the previous lesson, take a step back and observe the class as a whole. Using the observational questions written in the lesson plan, you will then decide:

1. to proceed with the content development of the lesson.
2. to reteach certain skills from the previous lesson.
3. to adjust the lesson to match tasks to the needs of the students.

Proceed with the lesson if the children appear to be successful yet challenged by the tasks. Reteach certain skills with appropriate cues if you observe that the class is having difficulty with one part of the skill (a negative response to an observational question). Adjust the lesson plan if the tasks are too difficult for the children, that is, if they are frustrated and have a low success rate.

This brief period of observation also permits the observation of individual children who are having difficulty with the skill. Make note and provide individual assistance to those children.

Throughout the content development section of the lesson plans, you will find examples of *assessments* that are practical, easy to administer, and readily adaptable for communication to parents. The assessments are designed as a part of, not separate from, the lesson. Children view them as an enjoyable activity, a challenge. Examples include: self-evaluation, partner observation, paper and pencil plus movement activity, videotape, computer generated presentation, group projects, and teacher observation.

Closure

The *closure* concludes the lesson for that day. During this two or three minutes, children should be reminded of the objective for the day (they tend to remember only the activity). It is a time to review important cues to skill development, to praise behavior, and so forth. Children can anticipate the next lesson by a hint of what is to come.

Examples of performance and performance/cognitive assessments are indicated by an icon.

An icon is also included for a check for cognitive understanding. These are brief pauses within a lesson that provide the teacher with a quick assessment of children's attentiveness to instruction and understanding of information presented.

The third icon within the lesson plans is for safety. It serves as an alert to the teacher that particular emphasis on safety is needed.

Reflection

The *reflection* portion of the lesson plan is completed after the lesson. It is your evaluation of attainment of the instructional objectives for that lesson and that particular class. The questions at the end of each lesson plan will guide your thinking in this area.

Positive or negative responses to these questions will also provide guidance for planning the next lesson:

Did this class meet the instructional objective?
What tasks do I need to reteach?
Was the lesson too easy or too difficult for this class or for certain children?
What tasks will be the warm-up activity for the next lesson?

Reflection also includes making notes about individual children, identifying who is having particular difficulty and who needs extra help tomorrow or when this theme is revisited.

Two final thoughts: Although my personal belief is an equal emphasis on games and sports, gymnastics, and dance, you will immediately note fewer lessons centered in creative dance and rhythms. This is not due to intentionally slighting the dance area but is a result of including a single lesson plan for each concept and each introduction to skills from the movement framework. For further discussion, please see "Notes on Dance" at the end of Part Three.

You will also note that separate activities and exercises for physical fitness are not listed within the lesson plans. This is not an indication of a lack of a belief in the importance of fitness for children but a strong belief in fitness as a product of a quality physical education program. (See "A Note on Fitness" and the lessons in Part Four: Fitness Concepts).

Teaching the Lesson

Although lesson plans are written as single units progressing from introduction to closure, it often takes more than one day to complete the tasks of one lesson plan. The lesson plans presented in *On the Move* are designed for the flow of an idea to its conclusion. The length of your class periods and the skill level of the children or classes of children will determine whether a lesson plan can be completed in one day. Mastering the skill or understanding the concept is the goal, not completing the written plan in thirty minutes. Reteach and provide practice as needed until mastery is evidenced in your response to the reflection questions.

Selection of Content

On the Move is not a curriculum guide for elementary physical education. Lesson plans are not arranged in a progression for fall to spring teaching. Concept and introduction to skill lessons represent one lesson plan for children at the precontrol level of skill development. At this level, children need a wide variety of experiences in game skills, educational gymnastics, and dance. Repeated practice is necessary to develop skills, and revisitation of concepts is needed to ensure cognitive understanding.

Children functioning at the control level and above, as evidenced by observation and assessment, are ready for skill themes. The skill themes presented in *On the Move* are a series of lessons written at the control level of skill proficiency with some extension into the utilization level. The skill themes are not in a predetermined order dictating the year's program. The selection of skill themes chosen for the year depends on your philosophy for each of the content areas (games, gymnastics, dance), the number of days per week the children have physical education, and other related factors. You are referred to *Children Moving* for planning guidelines and for a sample school year overview.

What follows are lesson plans for teaching the movement concepts and introducing the basic skills of physical education, a series of lesson plans representative of the skill themes in *Children Moving*, a series of physical fitness concept lessons, sample lessons for a thematic integrated curriculum, and *Children Moving* Challenges for the classroom teacher. I hope that these lesson plans will assist you in becoming a more effective, reflective teacher of elementary physical education.

A Note on Fitness

The children at Linden Elementary do not start each class with fitness exercises; lessons begin as written in the sample plans, with the class coming together for an introduction, time together, and an immediate emergence into the lesson—with each lesson designed for maximum participation and time-in-activity. The concepts of fitness are taught in a series of wellness lessons throughout the school year. Fitness testing consists of a fall screening, journal entries with goals established, and a spring follow-up test. Our goal for fitness is that for all movement: development of skills, coupled with a positive attitude toward movement, and enjoyable experiences in physical education that lend themselves to development of a health-enhancing, physically active lifestyle.

I am often asked to be specific about the fitness level of my students, based on this philosophy of fitness as a product of quality physical education. A recent comparison of Linden students, ages nine and ten, with the national average based on the National School Population Fitness Survey (1985) showed that the number of Linden students meeting the Fitnessgram standards for good health were more than double the national average. For us, the emphasis will continue to be "fitness through physical education."

Source: Corbin, C. C. & Pangrazi, R. P., "Are American children and youth fit?" Research Quarterly for Exercise and Sport. *American Alliance for Health, Physical Education, Recreation, and Dance (AAHPERD), 63 (2), 1992, pp. 96–106.*

PART ONE

Movement Concepts

Space Awareness

Location

Focus: Location (self- and general space)

Subfocus: Locomotor movements
                  Stretching, curling, twisting

Objectives: At the end of this lesson the children will have learned to:
                  1. locate self-space while traveling.
                  2. travel in general space without bumping into others.

> *For most children the ability to move without bumping into others requires much practice and is reviewed in lessons throughout the year.*

**Materials/
Equipment:**   Drum
                  Carpet squares (one per child)
                  Music (optional) for locomotor movements

**Organization/
Management:**   This is a lesson in organization and management wherein children learn to respond to a signal and to travel in general space without collisions. It is critical to all further lessons in physical education.

Introduction:

Today we are going to learn about self-space and general space. Both are important as you move in relation to others in games and dance and in relation to equipment in gymnastics. Scattered throughout the work space are carpet squares. Quickly move to the carpet square of your choice; it will be your home base for exploring self-space. Self-space is the amount of space you occupy when not traveling.

Content Development:

1.0   While seated in your self-space (on your carpet square), explore that space by extending your arms and legs as far from you as possible.

T   Stretch your arms and legs in all directions—high, low, in front, in back, and to the sides.

T   Stand on your carpet square. Stretch and twist to extend your space as far as possible. Remember to keep one foot on your carpet square as you stretch and twist.

T   Pretend there is a bubble surrounding you. You must stay inside this bubble, but you can extend it as far as possible in all directions: Stretch, twist, and push inside your bubble to make it as big as possible.

"The Amoebae"
 After the children have explored self-space, a favorite creative dance activity is the amoebae dance. The amoebae begin as blobs curled on the floor in self-space. On signal, they begin to move by stretching, twisting, and extending, always remaining in self-space. The dance is greatly enhanced by the use of body sacks (oversized pillow cases made by stitching together old sheets or commercially purchased ones) that cover the child but allow full range of movement in self-space.

2.0   Stand on your carpet square. On signal, begin traveling in the open spaces of the room. When you hear the drumbeat, stop wherever you are.

> *Establish the boundaries of the work space before children begin traveling. Lines on the floor and permanent or environmental structures outdoors can define the boundaries of general space. A moment of attention to this management protocol will save time and avoid problems later in the lesson.*

T   Travel throughout general space without bumping into others; avoid their bubbles.

T   Travel with your favorite locomotor action. On signal, stop in a balanced position without falling down.

> *Observe for stopping on signal and avoiding others. If children are having difficulty, use the carpet squares as home bases for stopping.*

T   Look for open spaces as you travel. Travel quickly to that open space, look for another, and move to that open space.

C   See if you can travel to all the open spaces within our work space without ever bumping another person.

T   Change directions as you travel; sometimes move to the side or backward.

T   Travel tall; travel low.

T   This time gallop like a horse as you travel. Keep one foot in front at all times.

T   Walk tall like a giraffe, jump like a rabbit on two feet, run quietly like a deer, and so forth.

> *Young children enjoy the imagery of animals. However, it is important that the emphasis be placed on the movement, not on the animal. Verbal cues provide the link: How would a rabbit move? Would a giraffe walk tall or low?*

T   Repeat traveling with skipping, hopping, and various locomotor movements.

> *Save running until last in the series of locomotors. It is children's favorite but usually lacks control at this level.*

"City Streets: Crowded Spaces"
The focus of today's lesson has been on understanding self-space and traveling safely in general space. We are going to challenge our skills of moving safely and stopping on signal by an activity called "City Streets: Crowded Spaces." (Refer to *Children Moving*, Chapter 16, "Reducing the Size of the General Space.") The boundaries for our general space will be one-half the size of our room. On signal, begin traveling as you choose, without bumping others.

T   Change the speed of your travel—sometimes fast, sometimes slow—to avoid others.

T   Now I am going to reduce the amount of general space. Continue to travel without bumping others, stopping on signal.

T   As the space becomes smaller, you may want to try moving at different levels, such as tall and very thin or curled close to the floor.

T   As I reduce the amount of space further, you may need to actually stop to avoid others—pause, then continue your travel. Remember to always look for open spaces as you move.

> *Continue reducing the activity space to the smallest amount that allows general space movement. A revisitation of this activity can include changes in rate of travel as children move in "rush hour traffic" and in response to "traffic signals."*

Closure:

We had fun today with many of our activities (refer to City Streets, Animal Imagery, or Amoebae), but what was the objective of our lesson? What were we trying to improve?

Why is traveling in general space without bumping others important?

How would you describe self-space?

Reflection:

Do the children have a cognitive understanding of self-space and general space?

Can they move in general space without bumping others?

Can they stop on signal in a balanced position?

Directions

Focus: Directions

Subfocus: Locomotor skills

Objectives: At the end of this lesson the children will have learned to:
1. name the directions of movement.
2. identify the directions when demonstrated by others.
3. move in the direction named by the teacher.

Materials/
Equipment: Drum

Organization/
Management: Movement in self- and general space

Introduction:

All movement takes place in a given direction. When I wiggle my nose (model), it moves from side to side or left to right. When I blink my eyes, they move up and down. Our lesson today is about directions—movement directions. We will try to remember them as "6+2." Let's see how many we can name. The "+2" are more difficult to guess. We will discuss these as we move.

> *For older children, link the importance of directions to games and sports skills, gymnastics, and dance; for example, in soccer they need to be able to travel not only forward as they dribble but also to the right and left and sometimes backward.*

Content Development:

1.0   Inside our magic boundaries, select your self-space. Explore that self-space by moving in as many different directions as you possibly can.

T   Move only your arms—upward, to the sides, in front, and behind you. Now move your feet and legs in as many different places as possible in your self-space. How about an elbow? Your nose? One shoulder? As you move in self-space, you are changing directions.

T   Move only your arms up and down in self-space; now right and left; now front to back. With your bottom and hands as bases of support, move your feet and legs up and down, right and left. How's that for a good workout for the abdominal muscles?

2.0   Stand in your self-space. Is there sufficient room in front of you to begin moving? Walk in the direction you are now facing; this is forward direction. Forward direction is the way each of us is facing. We will be traveling in what seems like many different directions, yet we are all moving forward.

T   March in a forward direction like a toy soldier or a robot.

T   Gallop forward. Remember, the same foot is always in front when you gallop.

T   Hop, gallop, jump, skip in a forward direction.

3.0   The opposite of forward is _____. Move backward so your back leads as you travel in general space. Look over your shoulder to avoid collisions.

T   Can you gallop backward? It's great fun.

   Our first two directions were what?

4.0   Now move from side to side like ice skaters. I should see your entire body move, not just your feet.

T   Slide-step across the work area, traveling to your right. Extend your right arm (model) in the direction you are going to travel.

T   Extend your left arm as you slide to your left through general space.

T   Traveling to the side is not always in a straight path. Move throughout general space, weaving in and out around others, as you travel to the right and to the left.

   Now you have traveled in four directions. Tell a friend the four directions we have traveled thus far.

5.0   Assume a position in your self-space like a jack-in-the-box (curled position, close to the floor, on your feet). On signal, pop up out of your box, extending your body upward (model). Get back in your box. Close the lid. Ready? Pop!

T   Have you ever seen someone on a pogo stick? They move up and down but also forward. Travel throughout general space as if on a pogo stick. Take small jumps; the action is up and down with very little forward movement.

6.0   At the beginning of class we said the movement directions were "6+2." We are now ready for the "+2." They are big words—clockwise and counterclockwise—but the movements are not difficult. Stand in self-space; spin around leading with your right shoulder. This is clockwise—the direction the hands move on a clock.

T   Now spin to your left. This direction is counterclockwise.

T   Imagine a large clock on the floor. Travel the way the hands would move, in a large circle clockwise. On signal, turn and travel the circle in the opposite direction, counterclockwise.

T   You have moved in eight different directions today. Travel in any direction you choose, but keep the same direction until you hear the signal to stop. I will observe and see if I can correctly name the direction you travel. Ready? Begin.

There is a tendency to rush through beginning skills and concepts, for example, locomotor movements and directions for children. Remember, children at the precontrol level often perform an action correctly, but not consistently. They need repeated, varied practice of the concepts and skills.

   I saw. . . . Now let's see if you can identify the directions. Brian, show us your favorite. What direction did he move? Susan, show us a different direction. (Continue with different children demonstrating the eight directions and the class identifying.) Everybody, show me your favorite.

"Malfunction in the Toy Shop" (a favorite of children)

The master craftsman has just created a new supply of toy soldiers and robots. He knows they look good, but can they move? You may choose to be a robot or a toy soldier; your stance, your movements will be as such. The first test is traveling forward. On signal, begin to move in a forward direction.

T   Make your movements angular, somewhat jerky.

T   Make sharp turns as you travel. Good, now let's see if the robots and toy soldiers can move backward. Remember to move like a robot—small steps, almost rigid leg actions.

T   These are special toys; they can extend an arm to the right or left and move in that direction.

T   The robots and toy soldiers cannot move their total bodies from high to low, but they can move body parts. Test the arms—up and down. Bend at the waist—down and up.

T   Oh, no, something seems to be wrong. There are short circuits in the robots. The toy soldiers are confused. They are all moving in circles clockwise. Now they are moving counterclockwise. Quick, turn off the power. Short-circuit—collapse in self-space!

Closure:

What was the focus of our lesson today?

Let's name the directions. I call them "6+2." Who can name them?

Put your nose up, heels down.

Extend one hand forward, the other backward.

Show me one elbow to the right, one elbow to the left.

Draw a circle in the air clockwise, now counterclockwise.

Reflection:

Can the children move in the designated directions?

Can they identify the directions?

Levels

Focus: Levels

Subfocus: Time
                    Pathways

Objectives: At the end of this lesson the children will have learned to:
                  1. move body parts at low, medium, and high levels.
                  2. travel throughout general space in the designated level.
                  3. move to different levels by rising and sinking.

Materials/
Equipment: Drum
                  Deflated balloon

Organization/
Management: Children in self- and general space

Introduction:

High, medium, and low are three movement levels. High level is above your shoulders—higher than your head. Low level is below your knees—close to the floor. Medium level is between the two—the space from your knees to your shoulders.

When you jump in the air to catch a ball above your head, you are receiving at what level? Forward and backward rolls on the mats in gymnastics are at what level? When you spin a hoop around your waist, it is moving at what level?

Levels of movement will be important later in our games, gymnastics, and dance work. Who can give me an example of levels in games, gymnastics, or dance?

Content Development:

1.0   Standing in self-space, explore all the space surrounding you at high level. Extend your arms in all directions—forward, backward, to the sides.

T   Explore all the space surrounding you at low level as if searching for lost coins in muddy water.

T   Close your eyes. Explore the space at medium level with your hands as if you are in a very dark room, unsure of your surroundings.

The tasks from Location and Extensions lessons, with an emphasis on levels, can be used to complement this lesson.

2.0   Travel throughout general space with your trunk stretched, your head high like a tall giraffe with its head in the clouds.

T   Travel at low level: a snake slithers, a duck waddles, a turtle crawls. Boys and girls can do all this and more; show me a different way to travel at low level.

T   Standing in your self-space, visually locate a spot in the room that is empty—an open space. On signal, travel quickly to that open space as if you don't want anyone to see you, medium level, almost invisible.

T   Locate another open space to which you are going to travel. On signal, quickly move to that open space traveling at medium level. When you arrive, jump high in the air, then sink to a low level position as if suddenly hiding in your secret place.

T   Assume your jack-in-the-box position at low level. On signal, pop up quickly and travel at the level you choose. When you hear the drumbeat, return to your jack-in-the-box position at low level.

T   Assume a low level jack-in-the-box position. On a four-count signal, slowly rise to medium level. Freeze in any balanced position you choose. On the next four-count signal, continue to slowly rise to a balanced high level position. Reverse from high to low for eight counts.

Expand children's learning experiences, for example, levels in self-space, combinations of loco-motors and levels.

"Rising and Sinking to Change Levels"
(Hold a deflated balloon in your hand.) Our final activity for today centers on rising and sinking to change levels, inflating and deflating like a balloon. In your self-space assume a position at low level—very flat like this balloon.

T   As I inflate this balloon, you will rise from low level. I will gradually inflate the balloon to half size. That will be medium level. When I fully inflate the balloon, you will rise to high level. (Gradually inflate the balloon to half size, then quickly deflate it.)

T   Watch the balloon closely; change levels as it inflates and deflates, sometimes slowly, sometimes quickly. Each time I stop inflating or deflating the balloon, freeze at that point of your movement. (Stop the action often to freeze balances at different levels. Repeat several times, inflating to various degrees as children rise and sink.)

T   (Inflate the balloon to its fullest as the children rise to high level.) If I turn loose of the balloon, what will happen? Correct, it will travel through general space at high level and then drop to the floor. Will it travel in a straight pathway? No, it will zigzag. Will it travel quickly or slowly? Quickly. When I release the balloon, travel quickly in general space at high level, zigzagging as you go. On signal, collapse to the floor at low level; remember, no collisions when you collapse.

This is a favorite that children ask to have repeated each year.

 Show the children a drawing with hands at high level, medium level, and low level (Figure 3). Have the children circle a figure in response to teacher directions.

Select photos from sports magazines showing the different levels; have students match photo and designated level.

Closure:

What movement concept did we study today?

Name the three levels. Define each level.

How will levels be used in gymnastics? Name a sport in which levels are important. Who can tell me why levels are important in that sport?

Figure 3 Hands at High Level, Medium Level, and Low Level

Reflection:

Can the children position body parts at different levels?

Can they travel at the designated level?

Pathways

Focus: Pathways
Subfocus: Locomotor movements

Objectives: At the end of this lesson the children will have learned to:
1. identify the three pathways: straight, curved, zigzag.
2. move in each of the designated pathways.

**Materials/
Equipment:**   Music for locomotors
Drum
Obstacle course materials: wands, jump ropes, hoops, yardsticks

**Organization/
Management:**   Children moving in self- and general space

Introduction:
Pretend you are going home from school, knowing that a plate of your favorite cookies or a new bike is waiting for you. Would you go straight home or wander around the neighborhood first? Right, you would make a straight path home. What if you are going home with what you suspect is an "unhappy" note from your teacher or to report a broken window from a softball game? Would you go in a straight path or zigzag through the neighborhood before going home?

Today we are going to learn the three movement pathways and move in each of them. These pathways will be used later in our offensive and defensive strategies for games and sports, to add excitement in gymnastics floor patterns, and to express ideas in creative dance (important link for older students).

Content Development:
1.0   In your self-space, move your hands in straight pathways up and down; now move them side to side. Follow me as we do straight pathways with our hands.

T   Now let's try straight pathways in the air with our feet and legs. Resting on your bottoms and hands, move your feet and legs in straight pathways up and down. Now move them side to side.

Can you feel the abdominal muscles getting a workout?

T   Move your hands in curved pathways—up, down, all around—making smooth curves.

T   Try the curved pathways in the air with your feet and legs—up, down, all around—but don't let them touch.

T   How about zigzags. Zigzag your hands side to side in the air. Zigzag them up and down.

T   You guessed it! Zigzag your feet and legs as you rest on bottoms and hands in self-space.

   We have moved in three different pathways in self-space. Let's name the three.

2.0   Stand in your self-space, ready to travel. The first pathway you will travel is straight. When the music starts, walk in a straight pathway. When you come to the side boundary, stop and walk backward until you come to another boundary. When you meet another person, one of you may pause and then walk in the opposite direction. Or one of you may make a bridge with your legs for the other person to travel through. Remember, only straight pathways; pretend there is black paint on your feet, leaving a straight path of footprints.

T   Walk on all the straight lines painted on the gymnasium floor (or blacktop).

T   This time, as you travel straight pathways, listen for the drumbeat. Each time you hear the drum, stop, do a one-quarter turn, and continue in a straight pathway until you hear the next drumbeat.

Children enjoy the imagery of robots or toy soldiers for this task.

2.1   The second kind of pathway we will travel is curved. This curved pathway will be made with your feet, not with your arms. When the music begins, move in slow, curved pathways like a glider plane or a soaring bird.

T   Travel in large, curved pathways.

T   Travel in small, curved pathways.

T   Stretch toward the ceiling as your feet make a curved pathway.

T   Travel close to the floor at low level as you make your curved pathway.

2.2   When a dog chases a rabbit, the dog runs in a straight pathway. To avoid being caught, the rabbit runs in what type of pathway? A zigzag. Let's move in a zigzag pathway like a rabbit.

T   When I observe your travel, some of you are traveling in a curved pathway. What makes a pathway zigzag? The sharpness of the corners when you change directions. This time really emphasize the change of directions; jump like a rabbit from side to side.

T   Glide like an ice skater, side to side.

T   Let's zigzag backward. We call this zag . . . zig!

 We have moved in three different pathways: straight, curved, zigzag. Choose one to show me, but don't tell me which one you are going to do. I should be able to watch you travel and name the pathway. (Have the children move; observe and name the pathways you see.) Now I will call the name of the pathway I wish to see; move in that pathway.

T   The letters of the alphabet (capital letters) are formed with combinations of straight, curved, and zigzag pathways. Think of the first letter of your name. Travel the pathways throughout general space that will write this letter. (Let's decide on manuscript or cursive form before we start.) Make the letter so large it takes you from one side of our general space to another.

"Obstacle Pathways"
 Against the wall are jump ropes, wands, hoops, and yardsticks. You are going to use these to create a large obstacle course of pathways. Who can tell me what an obstacle course is? This obstacle course will consist of pathways to travel. Some will be straight; others will be curved or zigzag. Decide which pathway you are going to create. Select the equipment you will need—jump rope and hoops for curved, wands for zigzag, and yardsticks for straight. Place your equipment on the floor to create straight, curved, and zigzag pathways. Connect your series of pathways with one other person's pathways to form our obstacle course. Let's decide how we are going to travel our obstacle course. Walk on the straight pathways, hop the curved pathways, and jump like a rabbit over the zigzag pathways.

21

Closure:

What was the focus of our lesson today?

What three pathways did you learn?*

Draw a _____ pathway in the air with your finger.

The basketball player uses what pathway to dribble to the basket if no one is guarding?*

The football player uses what pathway to avoid the tackle?*

The soccer player dribbles the soccer ball in what pathway as he travels through the defense?*

*These items can easily be used as a paper and pencil assessment for cognitive understanding.

Reflection:

Do the children have a cognitive understanding of the different pathways?

Were the children able to move in each of the designated pathways?

An excellent follow-up activity for the classroom or indoor quiet time is the correlation between pathways and designs or pathways and capital letters. Show the children posters that illustrate pathways (Figure 4). Ask individual children to find the pathway on the poster that you name.

Trace a capital "C" in the air; show where it is on the poster. Ask the children what pathway the letter "C" represents. Choose different letters to illustrate the three pathways and combinations of pathways.

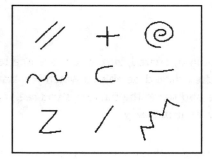 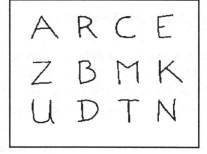

Figure 4 Pathway Posters

Extensions

Focus: Extensions

Subfocus: Time
Twisting, curling, stretching actions

Objective: At the end of this lesson the children will have learned to:
move in a way that shows the contrast of near and far extensions.

**Materials/
Equipment:**   Carpet squares (one per child)
Drum

**Organization/
Management:**   Children moving in self- and general space
This lesson is designed to be taught outdoors, using strong
sunlight for creating shadows.

Introduction:

Earlier in the year we experienced a lesson on self- and general space. One of the tasks we did in that lesson was exploring our self-space by stretching, twisting, and curling. Those actions resulted in extensions of body parts as we "pushed" the space around us. Our lesson today is designed to focus on extensions.

Sometimes in games lessons I will ask you to "pull in the ball" after a catch or "extend your arms" in a volley. In gymnastics you will make large and small balances as well as extend body parts for counterbalance. You will hear me use the words *extend* or *extensions* often. Understanding this concept will help you be more skillful movers.

Content Development:

1.0   Review the self-space tasks from the lesson plan on Location (page 11).

T   Pull all the body parts close together so you are seated in a tightly curled position. On signal, begin to slowly extend body parts away from the center. Begin with just your fingers, then your hands, arms, and legs. Complete your unfolding by being fully extended.

T   I will provide eight counts with the drum for the extension, then eight counts to pull body parts back to the curled position. Don't rush.

Use stretching, twisting actions to extend body parts, curling actions to pull body parts back to the tucked position.

2.0   Sit on your carpet square so you can see the shadow created by the shape of your body. Watch what happens to the shadow as you extend arms and legs away from your body.

T   Change the shadow by extending only your hands and fingers.

T   Change the shadow by extending your arms in different directions, close to and far from each other.

T   Get into different positions to create shadows by extensions of one foot, then both legs.

T   Explore extensions with different stretching, twisting actions to move away from the tuck, curling actions to return to the tucked position.

"Shadow Dancing"
You are going to create images by what we will call "Shadow Dancing"; that's what you have been doing. Sit on your carpet square with body parts close together. Create shadow images as you extend body parts.

T   Sometimes extend slowly, then quickly return to your curled position.

T   Sometimes twist or stretch your whole body as you extend parts.

T   Contrast the images by doing all the extensions slowly, then repeat them with very quick movements.

T   Jump, stretch, and leap in the air as you explore extensions from your carpet square.

T   As you return to the curled position each time, explore different starting positions, such as on your knees and on your feet.

Watch your shadow. This is a dance that is fun to watch!

Soft background music can "free" children for creative dance experiences. However, care must be taken in music selection so the music does not dictate the rhythm of children's movements.

"The Amoebae" (with a focus on extensions; see page 12).

Closure:

What new concept did we study today?

What does the word *extension* mean?

Why do you think we study extensions?

Reflection:

On verbal signal, can the children create extensions of body parts?

Do they stretch for a full extension?

Effort

Time

Focus: Time

Subfocus: Locomotors
Spatial awareness

Objectives: At the end of this lesson the children will have learned to:
1. move body parts slowly and quickly.
2. move in general space at slow and fast rates of speed.

**Materials/
Equipment:**   Drum
Blackboard, chalk

**Organization/
Management:** Children moving in self- and general space
Traveling without collisions

Introduction:
Today we are going to study time—the difference between moving slowly and moving quickly. When you move through the hallways at school, does the teacher want you to move very, very fast? When you hit the ball in a softball game, should you run slowly to first base or as fast as you can? Sometimes it is important to move as fast as possible; sometimes we should move more slowly.

Content Development:
1.0   Let's contrast the differences in time. Move your hands toward each other very slowly. Just at the moment before they touch, move them apart as quickly as possible. Again, together slowly, quickly apart.

T   Travel in general space using any locomotor action you choose.

T   Using that same locomotor action, travel very slowly.

T   Repeat the locomotor action, moving very quickly through general space with no collisions or loss of balance.

T   Choose your favorite locomotor action for travel in general space. When you hear the drumbeat, change the time of your travel from slow to fast or fast to slow. I should be able to identify the time you are using by watching the speed of the travel.

2.0 Let's think of action words that describe moving quickly and slowly. I'll write them on the board as you name them.

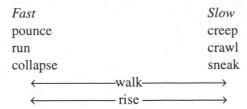

Fast   Slow
pounce   creep
run   crawl
collapse   sneak
←————————walk————————→
←——————— rise ———————→

(Refer to *Children Moving,* Chapter 17, for additional words to contrast moving slowly and quickly.)

T   Now let's combine those words into a "time" sentence, similar to the "movement" sentences you did when we practiced locomotor actions.

Movement sentences are described on page 44. If "time" sentences are introduced before "movement" sentences, follow the task progression in that lesson.

T   Pretend you are walking through a dark alley at night; move very slowly. On signal, quickly run in the opposite direction as if a mouse suddenly frightens you.

T   Begin traveling slowly in a large circle as if you are a lion stalking your prey. Make the circle smaller as you sneak up on your prey. Quickly pounce on the target you are stalking.

T   Slowly rise from low to high level as if you are stiff and unsure of every movement. On signal, quickly collapse to the low level position.

T   Travel as if you are a balloon floating slowly through space. On signal, "explode" as if pricked with a pin: travel erratically and very quickly for a few seconds, then sink slowly to the floor.

T   Run quickly in general space as if you are a distance runner "on top of the world." Decrease your speed as if you are "on your last leg" moving slowly uphill. Increase your speed as if you have a burst of energy. Slow to a steady pace, then walk.

"Slow Motion Sports"
Think of a favorite action you have seen, such as a basketball player jumping for a rebound, the punt in a football game, the swing of a bat, or the strikeout throw in a baseball game. Be very specific; choose only one action. Pretend we are seeing a video of that action; practice it several times until you can do it exactly the same way each time. Now perform the action as if the camera is set on slow motion; repeat the movement sequence three times.

T   Now perform the action as if the camera is switched to fast speed. Repeat the sequence three times so I will not miss it. The action is the same; only the speed has changed.

Just for fun, let's watch some of them and see if we can guess the sport and the action.

Closure:

What was the focus of our lesson today?

What are the two contrasts of time we studied?

Do you think you are more in control when traveling slowly or very quickly? Why?

Reflection:

Can the children move body parts and the whole body both slowly and quickly?

Can they move fast or slow in response to descriptive words of "time"?

Can they run with body control, stopping on signal, no collisions?

Force

Focus: Force

Subfocus: Spatial awareness

Objectives: At the end of this lesson the children will have learned to:
1. make body shapes that illustrate strong and light force.
2. travel with strong and light movements.
3. contrast strong and light body actions.

**Materials/
Equipment:**   Drum
Picture of sumo wrestler
Balloons (eight)
Small balls for throwing (eight)
Kicking balls, slightly deflated (eight)
Hoops (two)
Colored plastic tape for target zone

**Organization/
Management:** Children moving in self- and general space
(See Figure 5 for stations.)

Introduction:

Have you ever seen a picture of a sumo wrestler? They are really large persons. (Show picture.) What do a sumo wrestler and an ant carrying an object twice its size have in common? They both represent strong force. How about a single snowflake and a cartoon elephant in a tutu? They illustrate light movements. The focus of our lesson today is force—the contrasts between strong and light.

Knowing when to use strong force and when to use light force is important in throwing, kicking, and striking as well as in dance. We will focus on the contrasts between strong and light force today. As you become more advanced in skills, you will learn to use different degrees of force to accomplish the task.

Content Development:

1.0   In self-space, make a statue that shows strong force; make yourself look heavy and firm.

T   Repeat your statue, tightening every muscle in your body.

T   Now make a statue that demonstrates light force—so light a puff of wind would blow you away. Think of yourself as a ghost, a leaf in the wind—no tension, no tightness.

T   Let's use some contrast words to illustrate the two types of force:
Punch in the air as if boxing a heavyweight opponent.
Flick in the air as if dusting a speck on a cobweb.
Glide across the room like a skilled ice skater.
Stomp on the floor as if getting rid of the ice that builds up on your skates.

2.0   Travel in general space as if you are a single snowflake floating through the air. As the snow fall it collects into a snowball, growing in size until it becomes large. Travel as a heavy snowball.

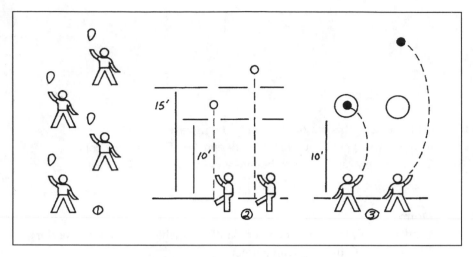

Figure 5   Stations for Strong and Light Force

T   Travel as a raindrop in a gentle spring shower. Change from a gentle raindrop into a raindrop in a
     fierce thunderstorm—so heavy it hurts when it hits.

Stations for Practice

The stations set up today are for practicing the contrasts in strong and light force.

Station 1: Punch the balloon in the air with strong movements. Strike the balloon with light movements. I should be able to identify the action as strong or light by watching you hit the balloon.

Station 2: Kick the ball so it travels completely across the general space area. Kick the ball so it
travels only to the target zone halfway across the general space area [gymnasium, blacktop, playground area].

Station 3: Throw the ball so it travels as far as possible. Throw the ball with less force so it will
land in or near a hoop.

Closure:

What was the focus of our lesson today?

Give me an example of light force. Of strong force.

Why do you need to be able to use different amounts of force in physical education activities?

Reflection:

Can the children identify strong and light movements?

Can they move with both strong and light movements?

Can they kick, throw, and strike with a contrast between strong and light force?

Flow

Focus: Flow

Subfocus: Spatial awareness

Objectives: At the end of this lesson the children will have learned to:
1. move in a way to contrast bound- and free-flow movements.
2. move a pizza circle with bound- and free-flow movements.

**Materials/
Equipment:**   Drum
Cardboard pizza circles (one per child—available at local pizza parlor)
Music: "Sea Gulls," by Hap Palmer

**Organization/
Management:**   Children moving in self- and general space

Introduction:

Today we introduce a movement concept called flow. When we think of the word *flow,* we usually think of free-flowing water. Actually there are two types of flow in movement—bound and free. A movement that is stoppable at any point is bound. The baseball player executing a bunt checks his or her swing for the soft tap. A movement that is unstoppable is an example of free flow. The swing of the baseball player with full power is not stoppable at will; it continues until it is completed.

There are times in games, gymnastics, and dance when we need bound-flow movements and instances when we need a free-flow movement. The combination of bound- and free-flow movements adds excitement to gymnastic routines and heightens the expressiveness of creative dance.

Content Development:

1.0   Stand in self-space. Raise one arm high in the air, stopping the action each time I count 1-2-3-4. Hold the arm high in the air; on signal, let it drop to your side. The first action was bound flow; the second was free flow. What was the difference in the two actions?

T   Walk across the room as if you are carrying your lunch tray with a "too-full" bowl of soup.

T   Travel in general space as if you are a cloud or a balloon floating, or perhaps an eagle soaring in the sky.

2.0   What do I have in my hand? A pizza circle. We are going to use the circle to demonstrate free and bound flow. Hold your circle on your open palm. Explore moving the pizza circle over, under, and around your body.

T   As you move, experiment with bound and free flow. Try some moves that you can stop at any time; try some moves that you cannot stop without dropping the pizza circle.

T   Hold the circle at high level. Quickly turn your palm down and sweep the circle in an arch to low level, then back upward (model).

T   Make curved pathways in the air as you move the circle. These are free-flow movements; if you stop the action, the circle will fall to the floor.

T   Try the free-flowing movements in front of your body, then to the side, as you turn in self-space.

"Pizza Circle Dances"

Combine the free- and bound-flow movements into a sequence. Pause. Begin a new series of movements with the circle. Pause. Begin again. These movements all together will form our "pizza circle dances." The music will provide a soft background for your work.

Stay within two to three feet of your self-space for this expressive activity. The music will be two minutes in length. Continue your sequence of bound and free movements throughout that time period. As the music ends, slowly sink to the floor with your circle. (Allow several minutes of practice on bound- and free-flow movements and the sequencing.)

When you are comfortable with your creative work, I will videotape the class.

Closure:

What was the focus of our lesson today?

What are the two types of flow? How do they differ?

Can you name examples of bound and free flow from a favorite game, gymnastics, or dance activity? (Older students)

Reflection:

Can the children demonstrate both bound- and free-flow movements?

Can they identify both when demonstrated by the teacher?

> *The cognitive understanding of the concepts often precedes the ability to apply that concept; for example, children can identify and describe bound and free flow before they can use flow in activity. Therefore, the lessons at this level focus on the contrasts within the concept and children's understanding of that concept. The purposeful application of concepts, such as force and flow, is critical following basic skill mastery.*

Relationships

Shapes

Focus: Body shapes

Subfocus: Spatial awareness
Stretching, curling actions

Objectives: At the end of this lesson the children will have learned to:
1. make the basic shapes (wide, narrow, round, twisted) with the body and body parts.
2. identify the basic shapes and body parts contributing to the shape.

**Materials/
Equipment:**   Drum
Electronic music for "Transformers"

**Organization/
Management:**   Children moving in self- and general space

Introduction:
What do a pretzel, a piece of spaghetti, a playground ball, and the opened mouth of an alligator have in common? They represent different shapes: a pretzel is twisted, spaghetti is narrow, a ball is round, and the open mouth of the alligator is very wide. These are the four basic body shapes we use in our themes of study. Let's say them together.

Content Development:
1.0   Make a very narrow shape, long and thin like a piece of spaghetti. Stretch your body so you are as narrow as possible.

T   Make a different kind of narrow. If you were standing, now be at low level near the floor; if your feet and hands were touching the floor, now use different body parts as bases of support.

     Remember, the position of your legs and arms makes the narrow shape; keep them close.

2.0   The opposite of narrow is _____. Show me a very wide shape with arms and legs extended far to the sides.

T   Sit down in self-space and make a wide shape.

     Remember, arms and legs create a wide shape.

3.0   Make a rounded shape like a playground ball, an apple, or an orange.

T   Curl your spine to make a round shape.

T   Stand on one foot and curl your body toward your knees. Tuck your chin and pull your arms close to your body.

32

4.0 Twist your body like a pretzel. Twisting is rotating a body part around a stationary axis, not crossing over (model with arms and legs).

T Extend your arms outward; twist one forward, the other backward. Twist your legs inward. Twist your head. Twist your trunk. Hold that position. Now look at everyone else. Aren't we a silly lot?

5.0 I will name one of the body shapes. Show me the shape I name:

Wide . . . .

Remember, extend free body parts for a really wide shape.

Narrow . . . .

Keep body parts close together and s-t-r-e-t-c-h.

Round . . . .

The key body part for creating a round shape is your spine; curl it forward.

Twisted . . . .

Don't forget: arms, legs, head, and trunk.

 The tasks in 5.0 can easily serve as an informal assessment as children demonstrate the shape named by the teacher. They can also provide the verbal response to these questions: What body parts create narrow shapes? What creates wide? What body part creates a round shape? Twisted?

T Make your favorite shape—wide, narrow, round, or twisted. The shape should be so clear that I will be able to name it as I walk by you.

Continue children's learning experiences with body shapes, levels, and bases of support.

"Transformers"

We are going to combine body shapes and actions to do an activity called "Transformers." The word *transform* means to change from one thing to another, thus the name of the activity. You are going to be a transformer that changes shape four times. Your shapes may be wide, narrow, round, or twisted. You may also be a combination of shapes, such as wide legs and narrow arms. The movement of body parts will change you from one shape to the next.

Make the first shape of your transformer. On signal, move your arms, legs, trunk, and head to change to the second shape of your transformer. Move slowly as you change shapes; I will give eight counts of the drum to help you change slowly.

You have now changed into the second shape of this magical, wonderful transformer. Hold that shape.

Now slowly change into the third shape. Make your shape very clear.

Change to the fourth and final shape of the transformer.

Let's repeat the transformation; then we will give them names.

"Dance of Shapes"
Let's combine the shapes we learned today with travel in general space to create a "Dance of Shapes."
Create a wide shape. Hold 1-2-3-4-5-6-7-8.
Create a narrow shape. Hold eight counts.
Create a round shape. Hold eight counts.
Create a twisted shape. Hold eight counts.

Remember to make the shape very clear with the extension of free body parts.

Walk toward me. 1-2-3-4-5-6-7-8.
Pivot clockwise for a quarter turn and change the locomotor movement; continue your travel forward for eight counts.
Pivot clockwise for a quarter turn and travel forward eight counts.
Pivot clockwise for a quarter turn and travel eight counts.
In self-space, combine body shapes and actions for a sixteen-count dance.

Remember to make the shape very clear before each action.

Repeat the shapes from the beginning segment (eight counts each).
Repeat the shapes (four counts each).
Repeat the shapes (two counts each with quick changes).

Choose an ending shape from the four basic shapes. Hold four counts.

Closure:

We had fun today being transformers (doing our "Dance of Shapes"), but what were we studying? What was the objective of our lesson?

What are the four body shapes?

Which of the shapes does a defensive basketball player use in a guarding position?

Which shape does the gymnast use for forward and backward rolls?

 Show the children pictures of the different body shapes in sports or physical activity contexts. (Watch for photos of local athletes in the newspaper.) Have the children identify the body shape of the "in action" photo.

Have the children match the body shape to the sport or physical activity action in Figure 6 (older students).

Reflection:

Can the children use their whole bodies and body parts to make each of the shapes?

Can they identify each of the shapes when demonstrated or when seen in photos of athletes in sports, gymnastics, or dance?

Name:_____   Homeroom: _____

Date: _____

Matching Shapes and Actions

Match the following sports or physical activities to the body shape used for the action:

1. Jumping for a rebound in basketball   wide

2. Defensive guarding position in basketball   narrow

3. Batter executing a power hit in baseball   curled

4. Forward and backward rolls in gymnastics   twisted

Figure 6   Matching Shapes and Actions

Actions

Focus: Stretching, curling, twisting actions

Subfocus: Body shapes

Objectives: At the end of this lesson the children will have learned to:
1. twist, curl, and stretch in self-space.
2. twist, curl, and stretch to move into the four shapes.

**Materials/
Equipment:**   Drum
Chalkboard, chalk
Paper, pencil
Music: free flowing, 4/4 count as background for "Partner Statues"

**Organization/
Management:**   Children moving in self- and general space

Introduction:

Stretching, curling, and twisting actions lead us into the four body shapes: wide, narrow, round, twisted. The ability to stretch that extra inch often determines which player in the game intercepts the pass, gets the rebound off the board, or successfully receives the pass. Curling into a tightly rounded shape is essential for good rolling in gymnastics. Twisting helps us fake the opponent or avoid being tagged in the game. Stretching, curling, and twisting actions convey messages in our creative dances.

Content Development:

1.0   From a standing position in your self-space, extend your arms as far from you as possible, stretching your entire body. Don't forget to stretch your fingers also.

T   Stretch upward, in front, to the sides. Feel the stretching action in your trunk as well as in your arms and fingers.

T   Sit down in your self-space and stretch arms and legs in the space surrounding you. Feel the stretching action in all free body parts, that is, in all parts not touching the floor.

T   Repeat the stretching action while seated; point your toes like a dancer or gymnast as you stretch.

Stretching actions can make both wide and narrow shapes. Explore both wide and narrow shapes as you stretch.

2.0   Seated in your self-space, curl your spine as you move slowly into a rounded shape. Concentrate on feeling each vertebra curl as you move slowly into the rounded shape.

T   Slowly curl your spine to one side, creating a curled shape; return to an upright position and curl to the other side.

T   Carefully curl your spine backward, creating an arch. This curling action is often seen in gymnastics when we do bridges (balances) and walkovers (weight transfers).

3.0   Standing in your self-space, twist your trunk to your right, to your left. Twist your legs by rotating them inward and outward. Twist your arms forward and backward. Remember, when you execute a twisting action, the body part rotates.

Let's name the body parts that can do the twisting action—legs, arms, trunk, head.

T   Let's combine the body shapes we have learned with these three actions: Make a wide shape. Slowly pull your arms and legs toward your body as you curl your spine into a rounded shape. Hold the round shape with body parts close together. Slowly stretch your arms and legs into a narrow shape. Really stretch so you feel the muscles extend. Make a wide shape by stretching body parts away from the base of support. Slowly twist into a new shape.

  Stretching actions create what shapes?
Curling actions create what shape?
Twisting actions lead to what shape?

"Partner Statues" (upper elementary)
Let's combine the body shapes of wide, narrow, round, and twisted with the three actions of stretching, curling, and twisting. You will need a partner for this activity.

Partner #1, make a statue that shows either a wide, narrow, round, or twisted shape; concentrate your focus on one body part. Be sure your statue has a secure base of support.

Partner #2, add to the statue by touching two body parts to Partner #1. Your statue should show a different body shape. If your partner chose a wide shape, you can be either narrow, round, or twisted. The statues do not support each other; you are touching the partner but can balance without his or her support.

After a four-second count, I will give the signal for the next action. On signal, Partner #1, use either twisting, curling, or stretching actions to move away from the statue created by Partner #2. Pause, focus on your partner. Travel around Partner #2; make another statue by touching two body parts to Partner #2. Again, hold the touching statue four counts.

Make either a narrow, round, twisted, or wide shape with your statue. On signal, Partner #2, use either twisting, curling, or stretching actions to move away from the statue created by Partner #1 (four counts). Pause, focus on your partner and his or her statue. Travel toward your partner; make another statue by touching two body parts to Partner #1. Hold the joint statue.

Continue changing by adding and taking away shapes. I will give you the four- and eight-count signals for holding the statues, and for moving away from and back to your partner. Remember, the statues will show shapes; the travel will begin with either stretching, curling, or twisting actions.

"Colors, Shapes, and Actions" (primary and upper elementary)
We have studied body shapes and actions. Quickly share with the person next to you: The four body shapes are . . . . The three actions are . . . .

I am going to name a color. When I say the color, think of the first thing that enters your mind. Think of it, but don't say it aloud. The color is red.

Do you have the image clearly in your mind? What shape is it? We have studied four shapes—wide, narrow, round, and twisted. Make the shape that best represents what you thought of when I said the color. I will move throughout the group to see if shapes are clear and to help if you have a difficult one.

The shapes are well defined. Now for the next question: How does it move? Does it stretch, curl, or twist? If it cannot move by itself, how do you think it would move? Would it roll, hop, bounce, or swing? Would it be heavy or light, fast or slow?

Make the shape of your "object" again. On signal, move as it would move. (Repeat two times. Divide the class into three groups to watch others.)

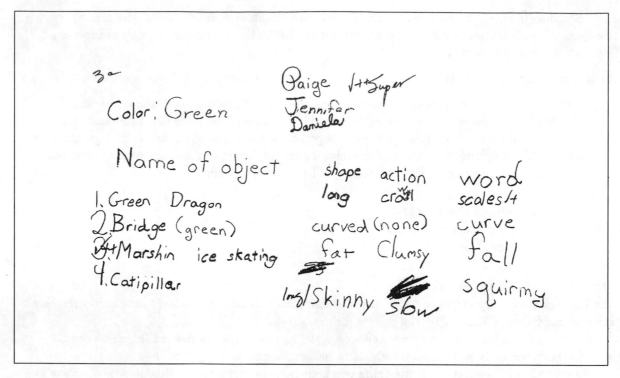

Figure 7 Children's Example of Colors, Shapes, Actions

Move to the chalkboard with me. You have made shapes for the color red. You have moved like red. Now think of a word to describe the movement you just did—a descriptive word, a nonsense word. Let's record them, using the following guidelines:

Color: Red

Object	Shape	Action	Descriptive Word
ball	round	curl	roll, bounce

Johnny, tell us about your object. What was its shape? How does it move? What word would you use to describe it? (Select several examples, then ask children to record their colors, shapes, and actions on paper. Figure 7 shows one group's depiction of the color green.)

Young children usually recall concrete objects to represent a color. Red is a playground ball that bounces, a worm that wiggles, or red paint that splashes. Older children often describe emotions with colors. Red is anger that explodes. Its shape is twisted; it darts, pounces, and thrusts into space.

The lesson can be revisited using another color; the children can be assigned different colors for group representation or be permitted to choose their color. I have found this group interpretation to be an excellent interpretive dance experience.

An excellent resource for a movement study in colors is the classic Hailstones and Halibut Bones *by Mary O'Neill and Leonard Weisgard.*

Closure:

What was the focus of our lesson today?

How do the actions of stretching, curling, and twisting differ from the body shapes wide, narrow, round, and twisted?

Reflection:

Do the children understand the actions of stretching, curling, and twisting as movements, not stationary shapes?

Do they stretch free body parts for full extensions rather than just moving the body part away from the body?

Do they actually curl the spine when moving into the round shape?

Do they rotate body parts for a twisting action rather than crossing them?

PART TWO
Introduction to Skills

Traveling

Focus: Traveling

Subfocus: Spatial awareness

Objectives: At the end of this lesson the children will have learned to:
1. travel in general space without bumping others.
2. travel in general space in a variety of ways.
3. identify the basic locomotor movements (gallop, skip, hop, jump, run, slide) when they are demonstrated by the teacher or another student.

CUES: Heads up (Keep your head up to avoid collisions with others)
Balanced stops (Stop without falling down when you hear the drum)

**Materials/
Equipment:**   Chalkboard
Drum

**Organization/
Management:**   Children moving in general space

Introduction:
If I watched your class during free time on the playground, how many different ways to move would I see? I would see walking, running, hopping. . . . These are ways to travel called locomotor movements; they are used in games, gymnastics, and dance.

Earlier in the year we focused our attention on moving without bumping into others and stopping on signal. Those two things will be very important today as we work on our locomotor movements in general space. (Establish or review the boundaries for general space.)

Content Development:
1.0   Travel in general space any way you choose; stop on signal in a balanced position without falling down.

2.0   Begin traveling in general space. Each time you hear the drum, change to a different way of traveling. (Repeat traveling four or five times, exploring different ways.)

Remember to keep your head up to avoid collisions with others as you travel.

T   Travel on your hands and feet; travel with stomach up, then with stomach down.

T   Travel on three body parts.

T   Travel on two body parts other than your feet.

T   Travel in a way that is so unique no one else in class will have thought of it.

43

3.0   Let's travel using specific locomotor movements. Walk throughout general space without bumping anyone. Walk fast; walk slowly. Walk forward; walk backward. Walk with giant steps; walk with tiny steps. Walk in a way that says "This is me."

T   Gallop in general space; remember, keep the same foot in front at all times. Now lead with the other foot.

T   Hop on one foot five to six times, then switch to the other foot. Continue hopping, alternating feet after each five hops. Hop backward; hop as you turn in a circle clockwise, then counterclockwise.

T   Skip in and out, around the room; the skip is a light, airy, step-hop. Lift your knees high in front as you skip.

Do not push for a mature pattern of skipping with young children. The correct skipping pattern will come with repeated opportunities, minus pressure, to enjoy the movement.

T   Extend one arm at shoulder height; turn your head to look in that direction. Slide across the room (model).

Yes, this slide is different from the slide in baseball and the slide you do "just for fun" at the end of a run. It is also different from the slide used in sports to move quickly from side to side. This slide creates a moment of being airborne, with both feet off the floor. Repeat the sliding action, concentrating on the light, airborne feeling as you go.

Practice sliding to your right and then to your left.

T   Now for the real challenge. Can you move by running throughout general space without bumping another person? Cover as much area as you can before the drum is hit.

Remember, heads up; balanced stops.

Run quietly, like Indians moving swiftly on a hunt, like deer through the forest. Be sure all of your foot touches the floor, not just your toes.

Look for the "open spaces" as you run; travel quickly to an open space. Pause momentarily to find another open space, then run quickly to that space.

"Movement Sentences"
Let's put together some of the locomotor movements we have practiced by making a "Movement Sentence." I will write the first one, then we will write one together: Walk, hop, skip. What does a comma mean when you are reading? Right, it means to pause. The drum will be our signal to pause. Ready? Walk . . . , hop . . . , skip.

Excellent, now let's do one together. Mark, how would you like us to travel first? Mary, what next? Susan? Our sentence is: Gallop, run, slide? Show me a body shape and expression that illustrates questioning. Good, use that ending.

Repeat with different combinations and endings. (Action words such as collapse, deflate, drop, and flatten can be used as endings. Refer to Children Moving, *Chapter 17).*

Observation of children during this type of activity can provide an authentic assessment of individual abilities to execute the identified locomotor skills. Remember, some children may execute a skill incorrectly, due not to their inability to do the skill but to an incorrect cognitive understanding of the skill.

Children enjoy manipulative activities like dribbling or jumping rope in each lesson; they also benefit from the distributed practice of all skills. A station format for practice of manipulative skills can follow concept lessons that do not involve the basic manipulative skills.

Closure:

What was the focus of our lesson today?

I will ask different persons to demonstrate a way to travel, and we will see if we can name the locomotor movement they are demonstrating.

Reflection:

Can the children travel in general space without bumping others?

Can they stop on signal in a balanced position?

Which children, which classes, need concentrated practice on the various locomotor movements?

Jumping and Landing

Distance

Focus: Jumping and landing—distance

Subfocus: Extension of body parts

Objectives: At the end of this lesson the children will have learned to:
1. swing their arms back and forth in preparation for jumping forward.
2. bend their knees in preparation for jumping.
3. land with bent knees.

CUES: Swing and spring (Swing your arms and bend your knees
  in preparation for jumping)
  Squash (Bend your knees for soft, quiet landings)
  Heads up (Keep your head and shoulders erect as you jump)

**Materials/
Equipment:** Drum
  Large mat with tape line each six inches
  Yardstick or tape measure
  Jump ropes (one per child)

**Organization/
Management:** Sufficient space for jumping without collisions
  (See Figure 8 for stations.)

Introduction:
Today we are going to practice jumping forward for distance. Some of you may choose to be long jumpers on your middle and high school track teams. For now, however, you are jumping just for fun.

Jumping is somewhat like throwing and catching; we cannot practice jumping without also practicing landing. So although our emphasis today is on jumping, we will also practice landing correctly.

Stand on the yellow sideline facing me. Place your hands on your hips; if your elbows touch the person next to you, find a new space. You will need room to swing your arms freely when jumping.

Content Development:
1.0   Stand with your feet shoulder-width apart. Bend your knees as if your legs were coiled springs. Swing your arms back and forth as you bend your knees (model).

T   Swing and spring; swing and spring; 1 . . . 2 . . . 3 . . . jump! (Repeat two or three times.)

T   When I observed your first jumps, I noticed some of you doing a stepping action, almost a leap from one foot to the other. Let's all jump from two feet to two feet. Ready? Swing and spring; swing and spring.

T   When you land, be sure to bend your knees to absorb the force (model). Squash! (Repeat the jumping action several times giving the verbal cue: swing and spring, swing and spring, swing and spring. Jump! Squash!)

Observe for swinging arms and bending knees in preparation and on landing.

T   Continue to practice jumping on your own, returning to the starting position on the line before each jump. Try to jump even farther each time.

One of the biggest temptations when introducing skills to children is to give them all the cues they need for mastery of the skill in the first lesson. I have found, however, that children need to focus on only one cue at a time, in this instance swinging the arms, then bending the knees. Remember, the lesson is only thirty minutes in length.

2.0   Select a jump rope; stretch it in a straight line on the floor. Jump over your rope to show me a proper landing with bent knees.

T   Place your rope in a "V" shape. Standing at the smallest part of the rope, jump over and land correctly with bent knees. Turn so you are at the midsection of your rope; jump over. Stand at the widest part of the "V"; now jump over your rope.

As you increase the distance of your jump, swinging the arms becomes very important. Remember the cue: Swing and spring! Swing with vigor to the front for good distance.

T   Do you need to make your rope wider or smaller? Adjust the width of the rope and continue. Be sure you have enough room to jump without bumping someone else or their rope.

Remember, swing and spring; squash.

T   When you can successfully jump over your rope at its widest part, reshape the "V" to make the rope wider. When we make our ropes wider, it is a temptation to approach with a run and leap over the rope. Remember, we are taking off on two feet and landing on two.

T   Lie down beside your rope. Stretch the rope until it is as tall as you are. Can you jump that distance?

T   Many of you are really getting distance on your jumps. I can see you swinging your arms and bending your knees in preparation. As you begin to jump greater distances, we need to introduce a new cue: heads up! This cue helps us do several things. We focus on the target distance for our jump. We avoid collisions with others. We are balanced when we land. Continue to jump for greater distances, keeping your head and shoulders erect as you jump and land.

 Before we begin our practice stations today, let's review the cues for good distance jumping. Tell the person beside you the cues for jumping and landing.

Stations for Practice
Four stations are set up for continued practice of our jumping for distance.

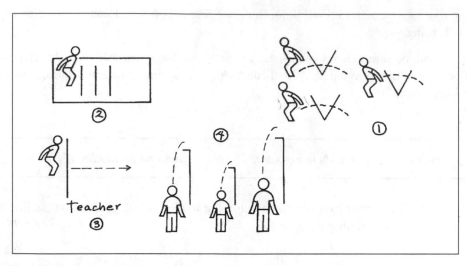

Figure 8 Jumping and Landing (Distance)

Station 1: Practice of "V" ropes as before. Remember, two-feet take offs and two-feet landings—no running.

Station 2: Stand on the mat, with toes behind the first tape mark. Coil the spring, swing the arms. Swing and spring, swing and spring, swing and spring . . . jump. After you land, look behind you and count the number of tape marks you jumped over. Quickly return to the starting line for another jump.

Station 3: Record student's jump in feet and inches. (Teacher record.)

 This station serves as teacher observation of the cues that are the focus of the lesson.

Students thoroughly enjoy trying to better their individual scores when the theme is revisited and seeing their progress from one year to the next. This one-on-one situation also provides time for individual evaluation of the jumping pattern and correction of mechanics as needed.

Station 4: Measure your height by stretching a rope from your forehead to the floor. Place the rope on the floor showing that height. Stand at one end of the rope and jump to the other end of the rope.

Closure:

What skills were we trying to improve today?

What should you remember about your arms and legs in preparation for jumping?

What should the knees do for a good landing?

Reflection:

Do the children swing their arms back and forth in preparation for jumping?

Do they land with knees bent to absorb force?

Height

Focus: Jumping and landing—height

Subfocus: Extension of body parts

Objectives: At the end of this lesson the children will have learned to:
1. swing arms back and forth in preparation for jumping.
2. bend their knees as they swing their arms.
3. swing their arms upward when jumping for height.
4. land with bent knees.

                CUES: Swing and spring (Swing your arms and bend your knees in preparation for jumping)
                         Squash (Bend your knees for soft, quiet landings)

**Materials/
Equipment:**   Large mat, milk crate (box filled with large empty cans from school cafeteria or packed with paper)
Stretch rope with balloons suspended
Six-inch strips of masking tape
Magic marker
Music: "Jump Jim Joe"

**Organization/
Management:** Children scattered in general space
(See Figure 9 for stations.)

Introduction:
During our last lesson on jumping, we practiced jumping for distance. We learned that our arms swing back and forth and our knees are bent in preparation for jumping. We also learned to bend our knees when we land to absorb the force of the landing.

    Today you are going to jump for height. Your arms still swing back and forth in preparation, but this time your arms swing upward as you jump. Let's all try it together. Swing and spring, swing and spring, swing and spring . . . jump!

    What is the same about jumping for height and jumping for distance? What is different?

Content Development:
1.0   Repeat jumping for height several times with verbal cues: swing and spring, swing and spring.

T   This time jump really high—reach for the ceiling. Stretch your entire body upward.

T   Continue to practice your jumping for height, this time focusing on your landings. A proper land-

---

Continue children's practice of vertical jumping for several minutes, observing the class as a whole and individual children for mastery of cues (extension upward and soft landings with knees bent) and providing individual assistance as needed.

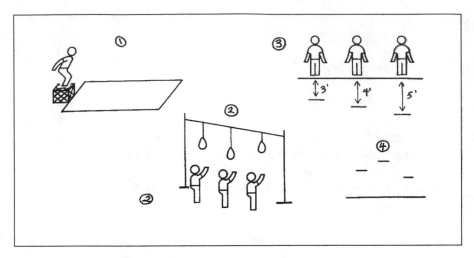

Figure 9   Jumping and Landing (Height)

ing is crucial when jumping for height because you are looking upward. Remember: squash!

Stations for Practice

The stations today focus on landing correctly from the jump, jumping for height, jumping for maximum distance, and jumping the distance of your height.

Station 1: Stand on the milk crate; ask the person behind you to hold the crate steady when you jump. Jump off the crate, landing on the mat.

The temptation is to just step off the crate. Jump high in the air as you take off from the crate.

Don't jump for distance. Focus on a good landing with knees bent to absorb the force.

Station 2: The balloons are suspended at different heights. Choose the one you wish to jump for. Stand slightly behind the balloon. Jump and tap the balloon. When you are successful, try a higher balloon.

The temptation here is to run and jump with a one-foot takeoff; use a two-feet takeoff to jump upward.

Balloons suspended in this manner have a built-in increased challenge. As the child hits the balloon, the string holding it wraps around the rope, raising the balloon. Each successful jump creates a higher one. The stretch rope can also be angled higher or lower by adjusting one end of the rope where it is attached to the pole. This enables the teacher to match the challenge to the student.

Stretch upward as you jump.

Station 3: Practice jumping for distance. Stand behind the sideline, jump to the first tape line, which is a distance of three feet. When you are successful, try the four-foot distance. The last one is really far—five feet.

Remember, swing and spring; squash.

50

Station 4: Pieces of tape are on the wall. Lie on the floor with your heels at the sideline. Ask a friend to place a piece of tape on the floor just above your head. Stand on the sideline and jump toward your tape line. When you can jump that far, write your name on the piece of tape.

The folk dance "Jump Jim Joe" is an excellent follow-up or revisitation activity.

Closure:

Stand with your feet together, legs straight, arms at sides. Model as you ask the following questions and as the children give their responses.

Am I ready to jump? What do I need to do with my arms? My knees? What will I need to remember when I land?

What is different with my arms when I jump for height as compared to jumping for distance?

Is jumping upward needed in gymnastics, dance, or games and sports? How? Why?

Reflection:

Do the children swing their arms back and forth in preparation for the jump and then upward for height as they jump?

Do they land with knees bent to absorb the force?

Balancing

Focus: Balance, understanding the concept

Subfocus: Extension of body parts

Objectives: At the end of this lesson the children will have learned to:
1. balance on one foot for several seconds as an example of static balance.
2. maintain balance while walking a low balance beam and on small surfaces as examples of dynamic balance.

                CUES: Stillness (No wiggles, no wobbles—hold very still)
                          Extend arms (Extend your arms outward for good balance)

**Materials/
Equipment:**   Walking cans
Stick figure drawings of various static balances (choose drawings that use the extension of arms or legs to maintain good balance)
Large mat
Stepping blocks
Small balance beams (two)
Low bench (if available)
Hoops (two)
Standards to hold hoops (four)
Beanbags (four to six)
Plastic tape

**Organization/
Management:**   Children scattered throughout general space
(See Figure 10 for stations.)

Introduction:
Today we are going to study balance. What does balance mean? (Stand on one foot, lean forward with arms waving.) Am I balanced now? (Stand on one foot, arms extended outward from the body, not moving.) Am I balanced now? Balance is _____.

    Why do I put my arms out? Correct, to help me stand still to maintain balance.

    Balance is one of the major components we will study in gymnastics. It is also important for all our game skills, for example, kicking, receiving a pass slightly off balance, or dodging and faking opponents. Good balance helps us stay in control and continue to move quickly.

Content Development:
1.0   Stand on one foot in your self-space. Try to stay balanced until I count three seconds. One-thousand-one, one-thousand-two, one-thousand-three. Extend your arms for good balance.

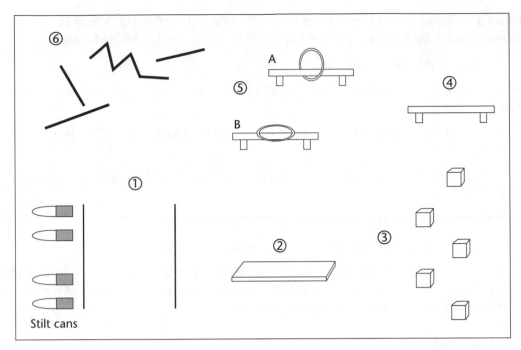

Figure 10   Stations for Static and Dynamic Balance

T   Now let's try the other foot. It will also help to focus your eyes on one spot on the opposite wall or a spot on the floor (playground).

T   An even more difficult test of our skill is to balance on one foot with eyes closed. You choose which foot to balance on first. Ready? Begin.

T   Repeat the challenge on your other foot. Being able to stand on one foot without arms waving in the air or the other foot touching is an example of static balance—holding our balance in self-space (Grade 2+). We will study static balance when we create balances on different bases of support at one of our stations today.

2.0   Hop up and down on one foot five times. Don't move forward, just up and down. This is dynamic balance—maintaining balance while moving (Grade 2+). This is the type of balance most often used in game situations.

Stations for Practice

Our station work today focuses on these two types of balance: holding a stationary balance without tumbling over or waving our arms and legs, and maintaining our balance as we travel (model).

Station 1: Walking cans (refer to *Children Moving,* Chapter 23). Balance on the cans; count to three. Walk forward to the tape line; turn and walk to the starting line.

Station 2: Balance on one foot; count to three.
    Balance on the base of your spine.
    Balance on two knees and one elbow with the free arm extended.
    Create a new balance that you can hold stationary for a count of three.
    Look at the stick figure balances posted on the wall; try these.

Station 3: Stepping blocks (scrap pieces of two- by four-inch lumber cut in four- or five-inch lengths; glue felt on bottom to prevent sliding). Walk on the blocks without falling off.

Walk backward. Walk sideways.

Station 4: Low bench (or beam). Walk forward on the bench. Focus on the end of the bench as you walk.

Very carefully, walk backward. **Remember, eyes focused on the end of the bench as you walk.**

Station 5: Balance beam. Walk the beam, going through a vertical hoop without touching the floor or touching the hoop.

Walk the beam, stepping in and out of (over) the hoop.

Station 6: Tape pathways. Walk on the different pathways without losing your balance.

Walk with a beanbag balanced on the back of your hand, on your elbow, your shoulder, your head. The cues are very important now: arms extended, eyes focused forward as you travel with the beanbag balanced on your head.

 "Balance Task Sheet"
We have practiced improving our balance today while standing and while moving. The balance task sheet (Figure 11) lists the skills we have just completed plus some additional ones. For each skill you can successfully do, give yourself a smiling face. You may return to any station for added practice, and you may try the new stations before marking your sheet.

Closure:

What did we study today?

What is the difference between static and dynamic balance?

Why is good balance important?

Reflection:

Can the children balance on one foot in self-space for several seconds?

Can they walk a low beam and/or bench without extraneous arm motion and losing their balance?

Do they use their arms as needed for balance?

Name: _____ Homeroom: _____

Task Sheet for Balance

	I can balance on one foot for 5 seconds.
	I can balance on the other foot.
	I can balance on one foot with eyes closed.
	I can balance on my feet and hands.
	I can balance on knees and elbows.
	I can balance on:
	I can walk the beam forward.
	I can walk the beam sideways.
	I can walk the beam backwards.
	I can go through the hula hoop and not lose my balance.
	I can walk the balance pathways.
	I can walk the stepping blocks without falling off.

Comments:

Figure 11   Balance Task Sheet

Transferring Weight, Rolling

Focus: Rolling

Subfocus: Actions, shapes

Objectives: At the end of this lesson the children will have learned to:
1. curl the spine and tuck the chin into a rounded shape in preparation for rolling.
2. transfer weight onto the back for the rolling action.

> **CUES:** Chin tucked (Tuck your chin onto your chest)
>   Round back (Curl your spine like the letter "C")
>   Bottoms up (Raise your bottom and tip over, placing your shoulders on the mat as you roll)

**Materials/
Equipment:**   Small, individual mats (one per child)

**Organization/
Management:**   Established protocol for response to signal, listening position
                 Mats scattered throughout general space with sufficient space
                     between for working safely

Prerequisites to the lesson on rolling are the lessons on actions (curling) and shapes (rounded).

Introduction:
Today we are going to learn one of the basic skills of gymnastics—rolling with a curled spine. Sometimes in our lessons we do log rolls with stretched, narrow shapes, but today we will roll with curled, rounded shapes. We will use this rolling throughout our gymnastics work.

Content Development:
1.0   Stand at the back of your mat facing me; the length of your mat is in front of you. With your weight balanced on both feet, tuck yourself into a rounded shape. Place your hands on the mat in front of you.

Curl your spine for a truly rounded shape.

Tuck your chin toward your chest to complete the rounded, tucked shape.

Watch as I do the three steps in preparation for the rolling action:

1. hands on the mat
2. round the back
3. tuck the chin

Now I am ready to roll across the mat (model).

T   Only one final step is needed. Did you notice what I did just before I rolled across my mat? I raised my bottom upward to begin the transfer. Let's all do the actions together. Ready position: hands down, round the back, tuck the chin. All together: bottoms up and roll!

Keep your rounded shape as you roll across your mat.

T   Let's try one more roll all together. Assume the ready position for rolling. Say the cues with me:

    1. hands down
    2. round the back
    3. tuck the chin
    4. bottoms up and roll.

 Tucking the chin is critical for safe rolling actions. Children should never be forced to roll over their heads if they cannot tuck the chin, are uncomfortable with the roll, or cannot support their body weight momentarily with their hands.

T   Practice the rolls on your own. Say the cues aloud each time to help you remember. They are very important.

C   See if you can do three forward rolls with your back rounded when you begin and rounded when you complete the roll.

T   If you are staying in a rounded shape, tucking your chin, and remembering to place your hands on the mat, you may want to attempt returning to a standing position after the rolling action. The key is to push with your hands as you transfer weight to your rounded back.

Remember, the ready position is the same.

Don't rush the rolling action; push with the hands.

C   As I observe the next few minutes, you may choose to roll returning to the standing position or without the stand. Try to do five rolls that the Olympic judge would give a score of "10."

2.0   This next type of forward roll is called a straddle roll. For some of you it will be easier than the tuck roll. You will still be rolling forward, but the starting position is very different. Stand behind your mat facing me. Spread your feet apart in a very wide shape. Stretch your arms upward above your head in a narrow shape (model).

T   Stretch arms upward, bend over, and place your hands flat on the mat (model).

Spread your feet far enough apart for an easy reach to your mat.

Place your hands at the edge of the mat, almost between your feet. Don't reach forward toward the middle of the mat.

Watch the next step of our rolling action. Stretch arms upward, place hands flat on the mat, tuck your chin to your chest, and slowly roll across the mat (model).

T   Let's do the steps all together. Ready position?

    1. feet apart, stretch toward the sky
    2. hands flat on mat
    3. tuck your chin, and slowly roll

When you finish this roll, you should still have your legs in the wide shape, seated on your mat.

T   Say the cues with me as we do the straddle roll together.

> stretch arms
> stretch arms, hands flat on mat
> stretch arms, hands flat, tuck chin, and roll

 What touches the mat first when you begin the rolling action? Correct: your upper back; your chin is tucked on your chest.

T   As I observe your straddle rolls, a few of you are rolling toward the side of the mat rather than forward across the mat. Concentrate on hands flat on the mat until you roll over. Continue your practice.

Remember, tuck the chin, roll slowly.

C   Class is almost over. Choose the roll you like better—the tuck or the straddle. As a final check for today, execute four rolls with rounded backs and tucked chins. Yes, you may do two of each if you prefer.

> *Which to teach first—the tuck or the straddle? The advantage of the straddle is there is no fear of going over. The child is so close to the mat, due to wide legs and lowered hips, that the rolling over is easy and safe. The tuck roll places the emphasis on the rounded back—critical for forward and backward rolling actions. Either way, I have found that having the children recite the steps (cues) is a major key to successful, safe rolling.*

Closure:

What was the focus of our lesson today?

Should the back be rounded or straight for rolling? Show me.

Who can tell me the four steps for a tuck roll?

What is the difference between a tuck and a straddle roll?

Why is it important to keep the chin tucked when doing forward rolls?

Reflection:

Do the children round their backs and tuck their chins in preparation for forward rolls?

Do they maintain the curled spine as they roll across their mats?

Kicking and Punting

Focus: Kicking (and punting)

Subfocus: Spatial awareness
Force
Accuracy

Objectives: At the end of this lesson the children will have learned to:
1. kick a stationary ball from a stationary position so it travels along the ground.
2. approach a stationary ball and kick it along the ground.
3. drop a ball and contact it (kick) after one bounce.

CUES: Watch the ball (Watch the ball until it leaves your foot)
Shoelaces (Contact the ball with your shoelaces or Velcro)
Nonstop approach (Run, run, run . . . kick; don't stop)

Kicking and punting are merely introduced in this first lesson; mastery of the skills is not the intent of the lesson. I find it most successful to teach the first lesson as an introduction and to follow with a second lesson on kicking from a stationary position and with an approach. Punting is taught later in the series, usually as a revisitation and after mastery of basic kicking—along the ground and in the air.

**Materials/
Equipment:**   Kicking balls* (one per child)
Plastic tape
Hoops (five to six)
Empty plastic bottles, liter size
Large, colorful target (vaulting box)
Rope suspended ten to twelve inches from floor, colorful streamers

---

*After a year or two of use, plastic balls are no longer good for dribbling and bouncing. They become partially deflated and cannot be reinflated. They are excellent for kicking. Mark each with a large "K," so the children know these balls are for kicking practice.

**Organization/
Management:**   Safety rules for kicking
(See Figure 12 for stations.)

Introduction:

Today we are going to do a special lesson, a lesson on kicking. You will learn to kick balls along the ground and in the air. Can you think of a game or sport that has kicking as one of the skills? Soccer players kick the ball along the ground and in the air. Football players learn to punt and to place kick. Kicking is an important part of a playground game of kickball. It is a skill everyone needs, both boys and girls.

Content Development:

1.0   Select a ball from one of the hoops near the wall. Place the ball about ten feet from the wall; stand behind the ball, facing the wall. On signal, kick the ball to the wall. Retrieve the ball and kick again.

 Be aware of others when you are retrieving the ball and when you are kicking.

T   As I observed you kicking, I noticed some of you were contacting the ball with your toes, some with the inside of your foot, and some with the top of your foot. This time when you kick, concentrate on contacting the ball with the top of your foot—your shoelaces or the Velcro. Kick, retrieve the ball, position it, kick again . . . .

T   Sometimes the ball is traveling along the ground; sometimes it is traveling through the air. Let's focus on kicking so it travels along the ground. The key is to make contact *behind the ball,* not under it. Practice on your own, kicking the ball so it travels along the ground to the wall.

> *Allow several minutes for practice, as children experiment and refine the skill. Observe and provide individual and/or class assistance as needed.*

T   Kick the ball hard enough for it to travel to the wall and then rebound back to you after it hits the wall.

Remember, watch the ball; shoelaces.

T   Remember when we talked about extending our arms for good balance. As you begin to kick harder, you may want to extend your arms for good balance. Continue your practice of kicking, extending your arms as you kick the ball really hard to the wall.

T   (Place a series of plastic tape markers along the wall, three feet from the floor.) Kick the ball so it contacts the wall below the tape line.

C   See if you can kick the ball five times so it travels straight to the wall.

 Have a friend observe your kicking for the following:

1. Are you watching the ball?
    2. Are you contacting with shoelaces?
    3. Are you contacting behind the ball so it travels along the ground?

T   If your friend can say "yes" to all these questions, take two giant steps backward and kick again. You are now kicking from a distance of approximately fifteen feet from the wall!

T   When you kick at a greater distance, you must kick harder for the ball to travel to the wall. However, nothing has changed. Remember our cues! Continue to practice your kicking; you select the distance this time.

> *You are ready to introduce the next part of the lesson, approaching a stationary ball and kicking it along the ground, when you observe individual children who have mastered kicking from a stationary position (intratask variation) or when the majority of the class has mastered the skill. (Refer to* Children Moving, *Chapter 11.)*

2.0   Place the kicking ball ten to twelve feet from the wall as before. Take three giant steps back from the ball. Approach the ball and use the instep of your foot to kick it to the wall. Don't forget, watch the ball until it contacts your shoelaces.

T   As I observe your kicking, I noticed some of you are approaching the ball, stopping, then kicking. It is time for our new cue: run, run, run . . . kick. The kick will now be a continuation of your approach; don't stop.

      Remember, contact the ball directly behind center. What happens if your kicking foot gets on top of the ball? Right, you may fall down.

T   Place the kicking ball ten to twelve feet from the wall as before. Begin traveling in general space. On signal, approach your kicking ball and send it forward to the wall. The kicking action is an extension of your travel; don't stop before you kick.

      Remember, kick with the instep.

T   Continue traveling in general space. On your own, approach your kicking ball and send it forward to the wall. When you kick, your eyes should be focused on the ball, not the wall. Remember the cue: Watch the ball.

T   Select a partner with whom you would like to practice your kicking. Place the ball three to four feet in front of you; approach the ball and kick it along the ground, sending it to your partner. Your partner will then place the ball on the ground, approach it from three to four feet, and kick it to you.

      Remember, nonstop approach; behind the ball.

C   You may choose to kick the ball to your partner from a stationary position or with the approach we have just practiced. You may choose to be f-a-r from your partner or closer. See if you can kick the ball ten times to your partner so it travels along the ground and so your partner does not need to move more than one to two steps to collect the ball.

3.0   The next type of kicking you will do is just for fun. We will practice this kick later in the school year. This kick is called the punt. It is more difficult than the two you have learned, but so much fun. Stand about fifteen feet from the wall, holding the kicking ball in both your hands (model). On signal, drop the ball and let it bounce one time, then kick it toward the wall. For this kick, contact the ball underneath so it will travel in the air.

T   Watch again as I punt the ball. Do I toss the ball in the air or drop it? Right, simply release both hands to drop the ball; don't toss it. Continue to practice your punting, releasing the ball as in a drop.

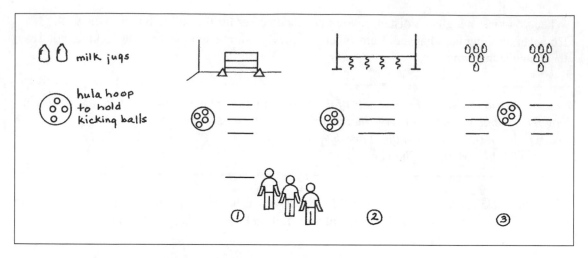

Figure 12 Stations for Kicking and Punting

T   When I observed your punting, I noticed the ball sometimes went forward, sometimes back over your head, and sometimes it didn't go anywhere. Remember our cue from before: Watch the ball until it contacts your shoelaces. Let's try again.

T   If you are really brave and if you can punt a ball after it bounces, you may want to try contacting the ball for the punt before it bounces. This is really hard, so don't feel frustrated!

T   Practice on your own either the stationary kick, the approach kick, the drop/bounce punt, or the drop punt. You may practice by yourself, kicking toward a wall, or you may practice with a partner, kicking to each other across the open space.

Stations for Practice

The stations today are designed to practice kicking a stationary ball along the ground, approaching a ball and kicking, and punting. The colored tape marks give you a choice of distance. You may wish to kick from the mark nearest the target or one at a greater distance. At each station, quickly retrieve your kicking ball after your kick and return to the end of the line for another turn.

Station 1: Soccer target. Place the ball on the line from which you wish to kick. Approach the ball with three to four running steps. Kick the ball toward the wall so it hits the target between the marker cones.

Station 2: Over the clothesline. Drop the ball and punt it so it travels over the rope. You may choose to let the ball bounce or to contact the ball before the bounce.

Station 3: Kicking bowling. Stand behind the kicking ball at the tape line. Kick the ball along the ground so it travels to the jugs. See how many jugs you can make fall over.

Closure:

What was the focus of our lesson today?

What two types of kicking did you practice?

Place your hand on the part of your foot that should contact the ball for the kick.

Where on the ball do you contact for a kick along the ground?

Reflection:

Can the children kick a stationary ball from a stationary position, sending it along the ground?

Do they contact the ball with the top of the foot—with the shoelaces?

Can they approach a stationary ball and kick it along the ground?

Based on the kicking skills observed today, will the next lesson on kicking focus on continued practice of approaching a stationary ball for kicking along the ground, approaching a stationary ball for kicking in the air, approaching a rolling ball for kicking along the ground or in the air, or punting?

Throwing

Underhand

Focus: Throwing—underhand pattern

Subfocus: Spatial awareness
Extensions

Objectives: At the end of this lesson the children will have learned to:
1. toss an object (underhand pattern) forward, toward a target.
2. toss an object (underhand pattern) with arm/foot opposition.

                    CUES: Opposite foot forward (The foot opposite your throwing arm should be
                                forward for a good throw)

**Materials/
Equipment:**   Yarn balls (one per child)
Beanbags (one per child)
Plastic tape
Large geometric forms as wall targets
Hoops (eight)
Bucketball targets or two large boxes
"No-bounce" balls

**Organization/
Management:**   Sufficient space for working safely
Established protocol for throwing/retrieving balls
(See Figure 13 for stations.)

Introduction:
Our work today will focus on one type of throwing—the underhand throw. We will throw for distance and at different stationary targets. Some of our throws will arch like a rainbow; others will travel in a straight pathway to the target. The underhand throw is used in several game situations and is the only throw permitted by the pitcher to the batter in softball.

Content Development:
1.0   Select a yarn ball from a basket and stand on the side boundary facing me. Stretch your arms to the side to be sure you have sufficient space; if you touch someone when you stretch, find a new space. On signal, throw the ball with an underhand pattern so it travels across the gym (model). Retrieve the ball and get ready for the next throw.

T   Some of your throws went toward the ceiling, a few went back over heads, others traveled to the side, most came forward. Swing your throwing arm from back to front. Release the ball in front of you so it will travel forward. Ready? Throw. Practice several throws. Is the ball now traveling toward the target?

T   When I observed your first throws, I noticed some of you were standing with both feet on the sideline, others had the right foot in front, and some had the left foot in front. Our best throwing action comes with one foot in front and one foot in back of the line. How do we know which foot should be in front? If the ball is in your right hand, your left foot should be in front of the line—opposite foot forward. That is our cue for today: opposite foot forward. Check your feet and throw again.

When trying to teach young children "opposite foot forward," I have found it easier for many to understand "same foot back." We now begin all our lessons in which we need the opposite foot forward with the cue: same foot back. Young children's cognitive understanding and application of the cue have been much better. Try it with your classes!

 Continue practicing your throwing action. Each time before you throw, check to see if the foot opposite your throwing arm is in front of the line (if the same foot and arm are behind the line).

If you observe children still having difficulty sending the ball forward, give them the cue for determining the direction of the ball: Remember, release in front so the ball will travel forward.

T   On signal, throw the ball with the underhand pattern as far as you can across the room. Before you retrieve, notice how far you threw the ball, then retrieve and get ready for the next throw. Each time you throw, try to make the ball travel farther across the gym.

T   Yarn balls are fun to throw, but they really don't travel very far across the gym. Exchange the ball for a beanbag and get ready for the underhand throw.

   Remember, opposite foot forward (same foot back).

T   (Use plastic tape to mark three distance zones at intervals of approximately ten feet, fifteen feet, and twenty feet from the side boundary.) Throw the beanbag so it lands in the first distance zone.

C   How many times can you make the beanbag land in the first zone with five tries?

T   Practice your throwing for the middle distance zone. Now you must decide how hard or how easy to throw; the beanbag should land in Zone 2.

T   Repeat for distance Zone 3. Now you will need to throw much harder.

2.0   You began the lesson standing with the opposite foot positioned in front of the line. When you try to throw with increased force, you will probably want to be in ready position with feet side to side, then step forward with the opposite foot as you throw. Practice throwing and stepping forward on the opposite foot (stepping back on the same foot as your throwing arm in preparation for the throw).

   Remember, step forward.

T   Practice five throws for each distance zone. Mentally note how many successful throws you had for each zone.

At which zone do you need to step forward on the opposite foot? At which zone do you stand with opposite foot forward? What determines which one is needed?

T   Stand in distance Zone 1 facing the wall with the tape Xs. Throw the yarn ball with the underhand pattern so it travels to the wall.

When we were throwing at a target on the floor, the ball or beanbag could travel in an arch, like a rainbow, through space. When we throw to targets on the wall, the ball or beanbag should travel in a direct, straight pathway to the wall. We achieve this direct, straight pathway by extending our throwing arm toward the target.

Remember, extend toward the target.

T   Continue your practice from distance Zone 1. When you feel comfortable with this distance, move to Zone 2 and continue your practice trying to hit an X on the wall.

Remember, for Zones 2 and 3, step forward on opposite foot.

Stations for Practice

The stations today are all designed for practice of the underhand throwing pattern. One station will focus on the direct/straight pathway through the air to the target; the other two stations will focus on the arch/rainbow throw to the targets. Our goal at all three stations is throwing with the opposite foot forward.

Station 1: Continue your practice throwing at the Xs on the wall. Choose your distance zone from the wall, then decide which X you will attempt to hit when you throw the ball or beanbag. Give yourself one point if you throw with the opposite foot forward, an additional point if you hit the X.

Alternate: Throw at the geometric targets posted on the wall. Before you begin your throw, say the name of the geometric figure—circle, square, triangle—that you are trying to hit. Give yourself

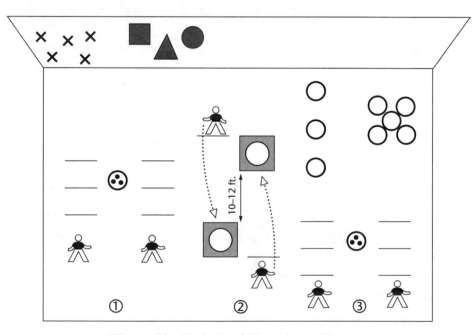

Figure 13   Underhand Throwing at Targets

one point if you throw with the opposite foot forward, an additional point if you hit the target you chose.

Station 2: (Arrange the two bucketball targets approximately ten to twelve feet from each other; use the "no-bounce" balls for this station.) Toss the beanbag or the "no-bounce" ball so it travels through the air and lands inside the box or bucket.

You will probably need the arch/rainbow toss for this station. Give yourself one point for opposite foot forward, one point if the ball or beanbag lands inside the box, two points if it lands inside the bucket.

Station 3: (Place one set of hoops in a three-in-a-row formation, another set in a "clover with center hoop" shape; the skill of the children will determine whether the hoops should be in distance Zone 1 or Zone 2. Hoops should be at sufficient distance to provide challenge but not beyond the children ever being successful). Throw the beanbag using the underhand pattern so it lands inside one of the hoops. Again, you receive one point for arm/foot opposition. The first hoop is worth one point (outside clover hoops); the second hoop is worth two points (inside clover hoop). The hoop farthest from you is worth three points.

Add all your points as you rotate from station to station.

Stations for Revisitation

Station 1: Horseshoes
Using rubber/indoor horseshoes, establish the targets approximately twelve to fifteen feet apart.*
Focus on the arch/rainbow aerial pathway, stepping forward on the opposite foot.

Station 2: Bowling
Using empty plastic bottles and playground balls, set the "pins" in bowling fashion approximately twelve feet from the starting line.* Focus on point of release and arm extension.

Station 3: Squiggle Balls (a favorite)
Place two tape lines on the floor approximately twelve to fifteen feet apart.* Standing behind the starting line, each child throws or rolls the ball toward the line, attempting to be the ball nearest the line.

*Determine distance to targets by skill level and physical size of children.

Closure:

What type of throw were we learning today?

In what sport or game is this throw used?

What is important to remember about our feet when we do this throw?

Reflection:

Can the children execute the underhand throw with arm/foot opposition?

Does the object travel in the desired forward direction when the children throw? (Is the arm extended toward the target?)

Special thanks to James Greene, a Linden parent, for the bucketball invention.

67

Overhand

Focus: Throwing—overhand pattern

Subfocus: Spatial awareness
Extensions
Twisting action

Objectives: At the end of this lesson the children will have learned to:
1. throw an object (beanbag, ball) with an overhand throwing action.
2. throw an object stepping forward on the opposite foot.

    CUES: Side to target (Side to target in preparation for the throw)
           Arm and foot back (Step back on the same foot as the throwing arm in
                preparation for the throwing action)

**Materials/
Equipment:**   Yarn balls (one per child)
Wall targets (geometric figures, colors, cartoon characters)
Stretch rope, hoops (two), Frisbees suspended by string (two)
Inflated balloons suspended by string (two)
Tennis balls (two)
Nerf balls (two)
Whiffle balls (two)
Plastic tape
Frisbees to hold balls (three)

**Organization/
Management:**   Sufficient space for working safely
Established protocol for throwing and retrieving balls
(See Figure 14 for stations.)

Introduction:
Earlier in the year we learned to throw balls and beanbags with an underhand throwing pattern. All our work today will focus on another type of throw—the overhand throwing pattern. This skill is used in many games for distance and accuracy, for throwing to a partner and at targets. We will use the overhand throw today for throwing at stationary targets.

Content Development:
1.0   Select a yarn ball and stand on the side boundary facing me. Stretch your arms to the side to be sure you have enough space; if you touch someone when you stretch, find a new space. On signal, throw overhand (model) so the ball travels across the gym. Retrieve the ball and get ready for the next throw.

T   In our first lesson on throwing we focused on arm and foot opposition—having the opposite foot forward for the throw. I am pleased to see so many of you have remembered that important cue. Let's throw again, being sure the opposite foot is forward when we throw.

T   Let's move a step closer to a mature throwing pattern—throwing like the big guys! Stand at the side boundary with the yarn ball in your throwing hand. Stand with your side toward the target—

68

the wall. Pull your throwing arm back toward the wall behind you (same foot and arm are back); extend your free arm toward the wall in front of you (model). Practice several throws with this starting position.

Remember, put your side to the target.

T   Throw the ball toward the opposite wall. Note the distance of your throw each time before you retrieve the ball. Each time you throw, try for greater distance.

T   When we practiced our underhand throw for maximum distance, you stepped forward on the opposite foot as you threw the ball or beanbag. Practice your overhand throws, stepping forward on the opposite foot as you throw. Let's do the sequence together: side to target with same foot back as throwing arm, free arm extended toward opposite wall; step forward on opposite foot as throwing arm moves forward; throw!

Remember, step forward on opposite foot.

2.0   (Stand across the gymnasium or outdoor area at a distance from the children, just beyond their throwing range.) Now you will have a target at which to aim—me! Stand at the sideline, side toward the target. Pull your throwing arm back in preparation for the throw. Ready? Aim. Throw! Retrieve the ball and get ready for the next signal.

T   As I observed your throwing, some of the yarn balls were landing on the floor not far from your feet; some were traveling at an extremely high level, far above the target. Let's do a pretend throw in slow motion. Side to target (same foot and arm backward; extend free arm toward target). Ready? Aim. Throw as you step forward on the opposite foot. Your throwing arm should now be extended toward me.

T   Repeat throwing toward target several times.

Stations for Practice

Today you have practiced the overhand throwing pattern. You learned earlier in the year that the opposite foot should always be forward; for really hard throws you step forward on that opposite foot. Today you have learned to stand with your side to the target in preparation for the throw.

Our stations today are designed for practice of the overhand throw toward stationary targets. At each of the stations, choose your distance line, throw, and retrieve the ball quickly, then return to your group for another turn.

Station 1: The Shooting Gallery
(Large laminated targets inside tape rectangles on wall; two nerf balls.) Stand at the distance zone of your choice, side to target. Throw the ball at the target inside the rectangle. Give yourself one point if you remember to throw with the opposite foot forward (same foot and arm back), an additional point if the ball hits inside the "box," two more points if you hit the target inside the box.

Station 2: Gong Show
(Suspend two Frisbees inside hoops from a stretch rope.) Throw the whiffle ball at the Frisbee in the center of the hoop. Give yourself one point for arm/foot opposition, one additional point if the ball goes through the hoop, two additional points if you hit the Frisbee.

Station 3: Balloon Throw
(Suspend two balloons from strings. Tape them to the wall at slightly different heights appropriate for children.) Throw the tennis ball at the balloon. This station really tests your memory of what we have learned today: side to target, step forward on opposite foot, throw really hard!

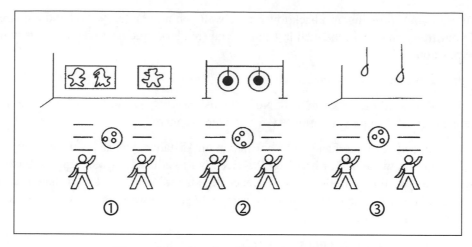

Figure 14   Overhand Throwing at Targets

These throwing stations are favorites of children, K–6. The built-in challenge of targets within targets and the varying distances at each station provide for different skill levels.

Closure:

All our work today focused on what skill?

How do I know which foot to put forward when I throw?

Show me the position for a good overhand throw.

Reflection:

Do the children throw with an overhand action?

Do they step forward on the opposite foot?

Do they stand with side to target in preparation for the throw?

Do they release in the direction of the target?

With a skill such as overhand throwing, it is very difficult for us as teachers to focus on a single cue. So many things can be wrong, and we want to provide feedback on all the mistakes. It takes great discipline to focus on the single cue, for example, opposite foot forward. The rewards of doing so in terms of student learning and expediency of student learning are tremendous.

Catching

Focus: Catching

Subfocus: Spatial awareness
                   Underhand throwing

Objective: At the end of this lesson the children will have learned to:
                   move their arms in front of the body (elbows flexed) in preparation for catching the
                   ball or beanbag.

                   CUES: Watch the ball (Watch the ball until it touches your hands)
                              Hands ready (Bend your elbows slightly in readiness for the catch)

**Materials/
Equipment:**   Various types of large, lightweight balls (plastic, beach, nerf)
                   Tennis, whiffle, small nerf, yarn balls for stations
                   Net, approximately six feet by eight feet
                   Small inclined surface with sides (plastic slide from jungle gym or long box with top
                       and ends removed)

**Organization/
Management:**   Children scattered throughout general space with sufficient space for working safely
                   Response to signal (proper placement of catching balls during teacher directions)
                   (See Figure 15 for stations.)

Introduction:
The skill we are working on today is actually one half of a two-part skill—throwing and catching. We are going to focus on catching the ball with hands only. The skill of catching is important in many games we play as well as in middle school and high school sports like basketball, football, and softball.

Scattered around the room are different types and sizes of balls. Some are large, some are small, but all are lightweight so they will not hurt if they hit you when you are trying to catch. Spread out in general space and begin to toss the ball to yourself and catch it.

Content Development:
1.0   As I observed you warming up, I noticed several of you were having trouble tossing the ball upward. Some balls were going far from your space; others were going back over your heads. Let's focus on the tossing action for just a moment.

Hold the ball slightly in front of you with both hands. Toss the ball by lifting your arms upward, stopping the lifting with your arms at eye level.

T   Continue to practice, tossing the ball only slightly above your head.

T   The toss looks much better. Now we are ready to concentrate on the catch. Try to catch with your hands only. Sometimes it helps to let the ball bounce one time before you catch it (model). Toss, bounce, catch. Let's all do that together. Ready? Begin.

Remember, watch the ball until you see it touch your hands.

Bend your elbows slightly to avoid having your arms stiff as you are getting ready for the catch (model).

C   Try for ten without a mistake. Toss, bounce, catch.

T   As I observe your catching, I see elbows slightly bent in preparation and eyes focused on the ball. I think you are now ready to toss and catch without the bounce. Toss the ball slightly above your head and catch with hands only.

If you are having trouble with the ball hitting your chest instead of your hands, try reaching for the ball. Don't wait for it to come to you.

Children at the precontrol level of catching will spend considerable time on mastering the catch with hands only as opposed to a cradle catch against the chest. They need practice catching with hands only in a variety of contexts before focus is placed on the next cue, that is, reach and pull.

2.0   Stand approximately six to eight feet from the wall. Remember the bubble of your self-space and your neighbor's—don't stand too close. Toss the ball to the wall and catch it after it bounces one time.

T   Throw the ball just hard enough for it to rebound to you. Too much force will send it over your head.

Remember, watch the ball; hands ready.

Practice several more catches as I observe the readiness of your arms and hands.

T   You are getting your hands and arms in excellent ready position for catching the ball. Now focus on reaching out for the ball. Don't wait for it to come to you.

T   You appear to be ready to catch the ball as it rebounds from the wall without the bounce. When you feel comfortable, try this skill.

Remember, keep arms and hands ready; the ball will come quickly.

3.0   Return to your self-space scattered about the room. Toss the ball upward and catch it before it bounces.

Remember the key to the toss—release the ball at eye level. Toss only slightly above your head.

C   See if you can catch the ball five times with hands only.

T   See if you can catch the ball above your head by reaching for the ball rather than waiting for it to come to you. This will be the focus of our next work on catching: reaching for the ball.

C   I will time you for thirty seconds. Try to toss and catch in your self-space without dropping the ball. Focus: hands only for the catch. (Older students: If you are successful as a class, I will not hear a ball touch the floor.)

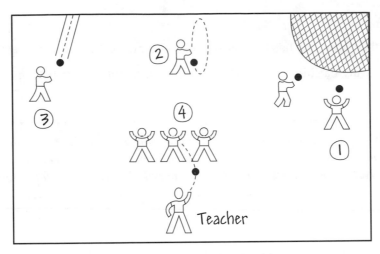

Figure 15 Stations for Catching

Children at the precontrol level of skill development need mass practice and revisitation to the theme often. Station practice as revisitation will be enjoyable and beneficial.

Stations for Practice

Four stations are set up for practice of the skill we have been learning—catching with hands only. The stations are for fun but will give us additional practice of our catching. Even professional athletes spend lots of time practicing the skill of catching.

Station 1: (Suspend a net approximately six feet above the floor, with the back corner higher than the front edge so the ball will roll off. One 8-1/2-inch plastic ball.) Toss the ball above the net. It will slowly roll down the net and drop off. Catch it with hands only before it bounces.

Station 2: (Use tennis balls, whiffle balls, yarn balls, nerf balls.) Select a ball. Toss and catch it five times; you may let it bounce if you wish. After five catches, try another type of ball. Continue until you have practiced with each type of ball.

Station 3: (Use slide with raised edges or a long box with top and ends removed, back against wall, slight incline; playground or plastic ball.) Toss the ball up the slide. It will come back toward you quickly. Catch it first after one bounce, then before the bounce.

Station 4: Teacher-student toss. Stand facing me. I will toss the ball for you to catch. We will first catch after a bounce and then without the bounce. When you are successful three times, you may take one step backward if you wish.

 Use this station to note individual visual tracking of the ball, hands/arms in ready position, and catching with hands only.

Closure:

Our lesson today focused on throwing and catching. Which skill were we concentrating on today?

Do we catch with hands only or against the chest?

Show me the correct arm position for catching: correct, arms extended with elbows slightly bent.

73

Reflection:

Do the children get their arms and hands in ready position in preparation for catching the ball?

Do they extend their arms, catching with hands only, or do they still trap the ball against the chest in a cradle catch?

Future lessons: When the answers to the reflection questions are positive, the children are ready for a focus on thumbs together for high catches, thumbs apart for low level catches, and pulling the ball to the body. See the lessons on catching in the skill themes section for details.

Volleying

Focus: Volleying

Subfocus: Force
                    Spatial awareness

Objective: At the end of this lesson the children will have learned to:
                    volley a balloon with an open, flat palm.

            CUES: Watch the balloon (Watch the balloon until it touches your hand)
                   Flat palm (Keep the palm open for a flat surface)

**Materials/
Equipment:**   Deflated balloon
                    Inflated balloons (one per child)

**Organization/
Management:**   Safe use of balloons
                    Lesson designed for indoors

Introduction:
I have hidden in my hand what we are going to use in physical education today. Can you guess what it might be? (Several responses from children) It is a balloon. We are going to learn the skill of volleying—striking the balloon to keep it in the air. For that purpose we will need round, inflated balloons. I have those ready for you.

Content Development:
1.0   Select a balloon and quickly find a self-space with sufficient room to work. Strike the balloon upward, keeping it in the air. Try not to let it touch the floor.

    Remember, watch the balloon.

T   Strike the balloon with an open, flat palm (model).

T   Try to stay in your self-space as you volley. Strike the balloon directly underneath so it will travel upward, not forward. This will help you stay in your self-space.

C   See if you can volley the balloon five times in your self-space.

C   Count how many times you can volley the balloon in the air.

C   On signal, begin to volley the balloon in your self-space. Try to keep the volley going until you hear the drumbeat to stop. How many of you never let the balloon touch the floor? Let's try again.

T   Now volley the balloon with your other hand.

    Remember, flat palm.

2.0   Most of you are pretty good at volleying with your right and your left hands. Let's explore striking with different body parts.

T   Volley the balloon first with one hand, then with a different body part. Return to a volley with your hand each time you need more control.

T   Volley with an elbow, with one shoulder, then with your nose. Volley with your knee, then with your foot.

T   Alternate the volley from knee to foot to knee. This is like a soccer skill.

Keep the body surface flat for the volley, just like you did your palm.

C   Just for fun, see how many different body parts you can use to volley the balloon.

Remember, watch the balloon; flat surface.

3.0   Strike the balloon so it travels forward, away from you. Contact the balloon behind center rather than underneath for this volley.

In what other skill have we talked about contact behind the ball to travel forward versus contact underneath to travel upward? Right, kicking a ball along the ground or in the air.

T   Walk forward as you volley the balloon in front of you.

Tap the balloon easy. Trying to volley really hard only sends the balloon in a crazy pathway.

T   Travel across the gym volleying the balloon as you go.

Adjust the speed of your travel to the force of the volley; don't get ahead of the balloon.

"I Can"

For the next few minutes practice volleying with the balloon. You may practice the skills we have introduced today, or you may think of new tricks. The only rule is that the trick must use the skill we learned today, the volley. After several minutes of practice we will come together and list the skills on our "I Can" volley chart.

For younger children it saves time if you record the skills for the children. Have each child tell his or her favorite skills; record them on a legal pad. Later, chart the skills on a large poster board for display on the wall. The skills become a challenge for others to try during revisitation practice time.

Closure:

What new skill did we introduce today?

What is different about volleying in self-space and volleying as you travel?

When do you think we will use the skill of volleying?

Reflection:

Can the children visually track the balloons until they touch their hands or other body parts for the volley?

Do they volley with flat, open palms?

If reflection answers are positive, the next lessons on the volley can then focus on an underhand pattern; striking a variety of lightweight balls such as beach, nerf, and plastic balls; and moving feet quickly to always be in position for contact.

Dribbling

Focus: Dribbling

Subfocus: Spatial awareness

Objective: At the end of this lesson the children will have learned to:
dribble a ball with finger pads.

> **CUE:** Pads, pads, push, push (Push the ball with the finger pads for a good dribble; don't slap)

Materials/ Equipment: Drum
8-1/2-inch playground balls (one per child)
Hoops (to hold playground balls)
Music for dribbling, 4/4 beat

Organization/ Management: Response to signal (hold playground ball in both hands; place playground ball on floor between feet)
Organization for equipment placement (hoops placed around perimeter of work area to hold balls)

Introduction:

One of the skills we learn with a playground ball is to dribble. Dribbling is a skill you will use in physical education throughout elementary school. It is also a main skill of basketball. How many of you have seen a basketball game? Can the players hold the ball and run down the floor? No, they must dribble.

Content Development:

1.0   Select a playground ball from a hoop near you. Stand in a self-space far enough from others so you will not interfere with their work—your playground ball will not bump them if it gets away from you.

T   Bounce the ball in front of you with both hands and catch it after each bounce: bounce, catch; bounce, catch.

Remember, push the ball with your finger pads (model). Don't slap the ball.

Press the fingers and thumbs of your hands together; your fingerpads are touching. These are the parts that should touch the ball when you dribble.

T   Continue your bounce-catch sequence. Stand with your feet shoulder-width apart so you will not bounce the ball on your toes.

C   Bounce the ball and catch it five times without moving from your self-space. Bounce, catch, one; bounce, catch, two; continue to five.

T   Let's bounce the ball two times before we catch. Ready? Bounce, bounce, catch. Bounce, bounce, catch.

T   Bounce the ball hard enough so it will rebound slightly above waist height. What happens if you bounce the ball too hard? It will go over your head. What happens if it is not hard enough? It won't come back up. Continue to practice your bounce, bounce, catch with the ball bouncing to hip height. This will become an important cue later in our dribbling lessons.

T   This time bounce the ball in front of you without catching it after each bounce (model). This is called a dribble. Ready? Begin. See how long you can keep the dribble going.

Remember, pads, pads, push, push.

C   Practice until you can dribble five times with no mistakes. When you reach five, try for ten.

2.0   When you are ready, begin to dribble the ball with one hand like a basketball player. Dribble as if you were going to dribble all day—push with the finger pads.

> *Beyond kindergarten the stance for the dribble is changed to a front/back stance—opposite foot forward/same foot backward. This creates the pocket for the dribble, to the side and slightly in front, which is needed for travel and games play.*

T   Let's all dribble with one hand ten times. Ready? Begin.

Some of you may find it easier to keep the dribble going if you move your feet slightly as you dribble.

T   Do you think we can go for twenty-five? Yes, let's all begin together.

C   Count the number of times you can dribble without losing control or moving from your self-space. (Time for one minute.)

T   Let's all say the alphabet as we dribble—one bounce per letter. Ready? A, B, C. . . .

> *Expand/continue children's learning experiences with dribbling. The skill of dribbling itself presents constant challenge for young children; they enjoy the practice.*

3.0   A really good basketball player is able to dribble not just with the preferred hand but with either hand. We are going to repeat some of the tasks while dribbling with the nonpreferred hand—just for fun. As we become more skilled at dribbling, we will be able to do all the skills with either hand. (Based on the skill mastery of the children, repeat several tasks.)

C   When the boys and girls in grade _____ (next higher grade) are working on a new skill, they test themselves for thirty seconds to see if they can do the skill successfully. I'm going to put on the music; while it is playing, you may choose to practice one of the skills we introduced today, or you may choose to test yourself to see if you can dribble for the thirty seconds in self-space without losing control. Ready? Begin.

I observed some of you practicing the bounce-catch, some dribbling with two hands, and some dribbling with one. If you did not lose control of the ball or lost it only one or two times, give yourself a "pat on the back."

The final thirty seconds of music is for fun dribbling. You may choose to dribble in self-space, dribble and travel, or dribble while walking the lines painted on the floor. This dribbling and traveling we will study later.

 Have each student trace or outline his or her hand on a piece of paper. Ask them to color the part of the hand that should be used for dribbling. (Primary)

Closure:

Today we worked on one type of dribbling—dribbling with fingerpads. What sport uses this type of dribble?

What is the cue for a good dribble?

With what part of the hand should you contact the ball for the push?

How do you avoid dribbling on your toes?

Show me the proper stance for dribbling with the right hand. With the left hand. (Beyond kindergarten)

Reflection:

Do the children push the ball with fingerpads rather than slapping it?

Can they dribble with sufficient control to stay in self-space rather than following the ball all over the area?

Future lessons: When the answers to the reflection questions are positive, the children are ready for a focus on dribbling at waist height, forward/back stance, dribbling while traveling, dribbling with eyes focused over, not on, the ball, as well as continuing practice with the nonpreferred as well as the preferred hand.

Rackets and Paddles

Focus: Striking with rackets and paddles

Subfocus: Spatial awareness

Objectives: At the end of this lesson the children will have learned to:
1. strike an object with a racket or paddle.
2. position themselves with arm/foot opposition for the striking action.

     CUES: Watch the ball (Watch the ball until it touches your racket)
     Flat surface (Contact the object with a flat face on the racket)
     Arm/foot opposition (Racket back, opposite foot forward)

Materials/ Equipment:
Inflated balloons (one per child)
Beaver tail rackets (half hose over extended coat hangers)
Wooden, Plexiglas, or Ethafoam paddles
Small nerf balls
Yarn balls
Hoops to hold equipment (or similar protocol)

Organization/ Management:
Response to signal (hold paddle and balloon still)
Position hoops around perimeter of work area to hold equipment
(See Figure 16 for stations.)

Introduction:
Earlier you were introduced to the skill of volleying; during that lesson we practiced striking a balloon with different body parts and with an open palm. Today we will learn to strike an object with a racket or paddle. The racket actually becomes an extension of your arm. The skill is very similar to the underhand volley we studied earlier.

Content Development:
(Place balloons and beaver tail rackets at different locations outside the working area; this will eliminate crowding as children select equipment. Balloons can be stored in large garbage bags for use in later lessons.)

1.0   Select a beaver tail racket and one balloon. Strike the balloon in the air so it does not touch the floor.

     Watch the balloon until it touches your racket. Strike the balloon with a flat surface. Have you heard those cues before? Yes, when we did volleying with an open palm.

T   As I observe, some of you are having trouble with the balloon traveling all over. You may be hitting the balloon too hard; tap it gently as you continue your practice.

81

C   In your self-space, see how many times you can strike the balloon before it touches the floor.

T   Strike the balloon so it travels upward; again try to stay in your self-space.

Keep your racket flat, not at an angle.

T   When we worked on volleying with a flat palm, we discovered the difference in where the balloon would go if we contacted directly underneath or behind the balloon. Where do we contact to send the balloon upward? Continue your volleying of the balloon, contacting directly underneath to send it upward.

T   Strike the balloon so it stays in front of you as you travel forward in general space. Now the contact is behind the balloon.

T   See if you can travel and strike the balloon forward as you travel from one side boundary of our general space to the opposite side boundary.

Always watch for others when you travel.

2.0   Exchange your balloon and beaver tail racket for a nerf or yarn ball and a paddle. Be sure the balloon is in the bag; they can become airborne quickly. Strike the ball with the paddle, sending it upward. Collect the ball after each hit and begin again; don't try continuous hits just yet.

The ball travels much faster than the balloon; watching the ball until it touches your racket will be even more important now. Continue your practice, concentrating on watching the ball.

T   Hold the ball at shoulder height and the paddle at waist height. Drop the ball and hit it upward with the paddle (model).

Remember, hit the ball gently. Pretend it is an egg; don't break it.

T   Can you stay in your self-space and do single hits? Drop, hit, collect.

C   See if you can do five single hits without moving from your self-space.

T   Turn so you are facing a wall; you should be approximately four to five giant steps from the wall. Strike the ball so it travels forward to the wall.

T   Remember the hand/foot opposition we learned earlier; it is needed here. Let's get our feet in proper position before we begin: racket in right hand, right foot back. Single hits: drop, hit, bounce, collect.

T   If I want the ball to travel forward to the wall, will I contact the ball directly under to send it upward or slightly behind to send it forward? (model) Continue your single hit practice to the wall: drop, hit, bounce, collect.

Remember, racket/foot opposition.

 As I walk around and observe your striking with the racket, I will watch for two things: racket/foot opposition and flat surface for contact.

This assessment allows individual assistance as well as class observation for extension of skills or continued practice with group cues for refinement.

C   Try for five single hits; when you are comfortable with five, try for eight.

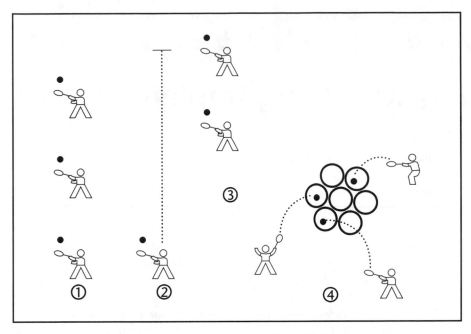

Figure 16   Stations for Striking with Rackets

Stations for Practice

Our stations today are designed for practice striking balloons and balls upward and forward.

Station 1: Balloons and rackets in general space. How many upward hits can you do with no mistakes? Count them.

Station 2: Balloons and rackets with forward travel. Travel across the gymnasium striking the balloon forward with the racket.

Station 3: Nerf balls and paddles in general space. Can you do five single upward hits without moving from self-space? Try continuous hits upward. How many?

Station 4: Balls and paddles in clover. (Yarn balls, paddles, and hoops positioned in clover design on floor.) Strike the ball so it travels forward and lands in a hoop. Each time you are successful, increase your distance by taking a giant step backward.

Closure:

What was the focus of our lesson today?

Show me the correct way to hold the racket or paddle for striking the balloon or ball. What is the cue for this position? (flat surface)

Which was easier—balloons or balls? Why?

Reflection:

Are the children successful at striking balloons with rackets?

Do they appear to visually track the balloons or balls until contact is made?

Can they send the balloons or balls upward and forward rather than back over their heads?

Striking with Long Implements, Bats

Focus: Striking with long implements, bats

Subfocus: Locomotors
Spatial awareness

Objectives: At the end of this lesson the children will have learned to:
1. stand in readiness for striking with side to the target.
2. strike a ball, sending it forward.

    CUES: Side to target (In readiness for batting, stand with your side to the target)
            Bat pulled way back (Pull the bat way back in readiness to strike the ball)
            Watch the ball

**Materials/
Equipment:** Batting tees or tall marker cones
Whiffle balls (many)
Large plastic bats
Carpet squares
Whiffle balls suspended on strings/stretch ropes, standards

**Organization/
Management:** Arrangement of batting tees, suspended balls
This lesson is designed for outdoors, with sufficient space for striking with bats.

Introduction:

Today we will introduce a very important skill of softball or baseball—batting. We did striking with body parts and the open palm when we volleyed the balloons. We practiced striking balloons, yarn balls, and nerf balls with beaver tail rackets and paddles. Today we will learn striking with a bat.

    Remember, I asked you to think of the paddle as an extension of your arm. Now the extension is much farther from your hands, and the bat is much heavier. Keeping your eyes on the ball will be very important when practicing this skill.

Content Development:

(Arrange batting tees outdoors with sufficient space for swinging; arrange them so all balls are traveling in the same direction. Place a carpet square beside each tee, to be moved from side to side depending on whether each individual child is left- or right-handed. A second carpet square placed four to five feet behind the tee for children who must wait a turn will be an asset for safety!)

1.0   Stand on the carpet square beside the batting tee on the side opposite your writing hand. Hold the bat with your nonwriting hand near the end; the hand you write with should be just above so they almost touch. Hit the ball off the tee, sending it across the field (model). Place another ball on the tee and hit again; you have three balls to hit. Each of the three persons in your group then quickly collects a ball and the next person has a turn.

Remember, side to target; bat pulled way back.

Standing on the carpet square will help you always remember to have your side toward the target—in this situation, the open field where the ball is to go.

A couple of cues are very important as you continue to practice batting from the tee:

1. **Watch the ball at all times.** You should see the ball touch the bat. In how many different lessons does Mrs. Hale say "watch the ball"? A lot. It is a critical cue for catching, striking, and batting.

2. **Bat way back/swing through.** Pull your bat way back in preparation for the hit; swing through, not down (model).

Allow several minutes practice, observe and give individual assistance needed for level swing and side to target.

C   See if you can make contact with the ball for each of your three swings.

2.0   (Divide the class into two groups. One group remains at the batting tees; the second group moves to the suspended balls for practice. Suspend whiffle balls from stretch ropes with yarn or string. Stretch the ropes across the practice area attaching them to volleyball standards, basketball posts, and so forth. Refer to *Children Moving*, Chapter 30).

T   Stand beside the ball you are going to hit. Swing the bat, sending the ball forward. Striking a ball suspended from a string may be more difficult than striking a ball placed on a batting tee. The balls move slightly; watch them closely.

T   As you begin to swing harder at both stations, your front foot will feel as if it should step forward. Do so as you continue to practice; the stepping forward will give you more power.

C   Can you hit the ball three times in a row for a perfect batting average? At the batting tee, this means contacting all three balls on the first swing. At the suspended balls, stop the ball after each hit.

"Hit and Run"
Select a partner and return to the batting tees. This activity will combine batting, running, and collecting the ball. Partner "A," stand on the carpet square at the batting tee as before. Partner "B," stand on a carpet square twelve to fifteen feet from the batter.
    Batter, side to target. Partner "A," strike the ball off the tee, sending it as far as possible. Immediately run to the carpet square and back to the batting tee. Partner "B," as soon as the ball is hit, collect it and run to replace the ball on the tee. Switch positions.

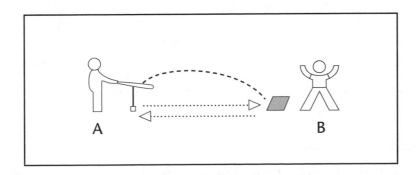

Batter, be sure you drop the bat before you run; don't throw it. Both partners are running; be careful.

If partners are equally matched in skill, they may choose the challenge of keeping score. If the batter gets home first, one point; if the fielder gets the ball on the tee before the batter touches home, one point.

Revisitation after much distributed practice:

"Hit, Run, Throw"
(Divide the children into groups of three, placing children with similar skills together. Organization is as above with three bases added in diamond formation.)

This activity adds two more skills to batting and running—the skills of throwing and catching. Partner "A," stand at the batting tee as before. Hit the ball really hard, then run the bases as if you hit a home run. Run all the bases; don't stop.

- Run as fast as you can.
- Remember to tag all the bases.

Partner "B," collect or catch the ball, then throw it to home base where partner "C" is waiting to catch it. Partner "B," you must stand behind the midfield carpet square until the ball is hit. Partner "C," as soon as you collect/catch the ball, place it on the batting tee.

- Even if the fielder catches the ball, the action is the same: fielder throws the ball home; batter runs all the bases.
- Batter, if you get home before the ball is on the tee, give yourself a point.
- After each play, the catcher becomes the batter, the batter moves to the field, and the fielder comes to the safety square (home base) behind the tee.

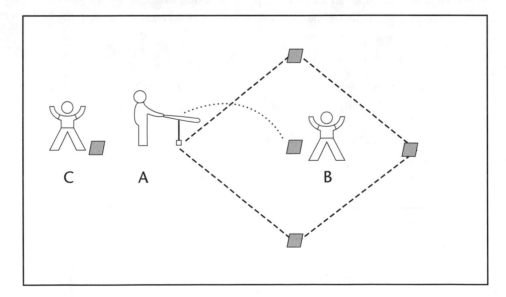

Closure:

What new skill did we introduce today?

Show me how to stand in readiness for batting. How do I hold the bat? Where do I focus my eyes?

How will the ball travel if I swing level? (model)

Where will the ball travel if I am a "wood chopper"? (model downward swing)

Reflection:

Do the children stand with side to target in readiness for batting?

Do they pull bats way back in readiness as opposed to resting bats on their shoulders?

Can they contact the ball off the batting tee?

On the Move and the *National Standards for Physical Education*

The *National Standards for Physical Education* provide the framework for all curricular decisions. By defining "what students should know and be able to do" they answer the question, "What will my students learn today?" The *National Standards* are inclusive of grades K–12; they are described briefly here for elementary physical education.

1. Demonstrates competency in many movement forms and proficiency in a few movement forms.
2. Applies movement concepts and principles to the learning and development of motor skills.

The lesson plans found in *On the Move* are centered around the *National Standards for Physical Education.* All lessons are designed to develop children's movement skills and concept understanding and application. These skills and concepts are identified in *Children Moving,* adapted from the work of Rudolph Laban. The skill base is the foundation for the development of competency in a broad range of movement forms.

3. Exhibits a physically active lifestyle.
4. Achieves and maintains a health-enhancing level of physical fitness.

Physical fitness as a process and a product of physical education is my personal philosophy and the philosophy of the authors of *Children Moving.* The *National Standards* for elementary-age children emphasize enjoyment of physical activity, an understanding of the components of fitness, and development of a positive attitude that will lead to adoption of a health-enhancing, physically active lifestyle.

5. Demonstrates responsible personal and social behavior in physical activity settings.
6. Demonstrates understanding and respect for differences among people in physical activity settings.

Physical education is the richest of environments for the development of responsible personal and social behavior, as well as understanding and accepting differences and likenesses among people. Cooperative projects, creative dances, folk dances from different cultures, and the interaction of children in physical activity provide a multitude of opportunities for teaching these standards. These goals for children, like fitness, are not left to chance—for teachable moments only. Lesson plans are designed with opportunities for this development throughout.

7. Understands that physical activity provides opportunities for enjoyment, challenge, self-expression, and social interaction.

An elementary physical education program that provides children enjoyment, challenge, self-expression, and positive social interaction, coupled with skill development and concept understanding, is a physical education program that links children forever to a world of movement. Children on the move today are adults on the move tomorrow!

Source of standards: National Association for Sport and Physical Education. (1995). *Moving Into the Future: National Standards for Physical Education.* St. Louis, MO: Mosby.

Responsible Personal and Social Behavior

Sometimes careful attention to responsible personal and social behavior and understanding and respect for others (*National Standards 5,* 6) seem too difficult to teach with all we are trying to do in the thirty-minute lesson. As a result, these critical learnings for children are left to chance, with a focus only during teachable moments, or are omitted altogether. Sandy Coble (Bloyis, CA) suggests focusing on a single sense with a "Visual T" when asking children to explore these concepts.

Discussion during Set	*Discussion during Closure*
What will I SEE today that will show me: responsible behavior? respect for others?	What did I SEE today that showed me: responsible behavior? respect for others?

The trick is the focus on a single sense only. The children are not permitted to explain; they must provide examples only of what I as the teacher will see, did see. The same approach also works well with the sense of hearing in the "Auditory T":

What will I HEAR today that will show me respect for others?	What did I HEAR today that showed me respect for others?

PART THREE
Skill Themes

Traveling

Lesson 1

Focus: Traveling, with changes in direction

Subfocus: Spatial awareness, locomotors, directions

Objective: At the end of this lesson the children will have learned to:
change directions while traveling.

                 CUES: Heads up (Keep your head up to avoid collisions with others)
                           Balanced stops (Spread your feet and lower your hips slightly to maintain
                                your balance when you stop)

---

*This lesson assumes different locomotor movements as a prerequisite. If you observe that children
have not mastered the different locomotor skills during the early tasks, do not proceed to a focus
on directions; focus instead on locomotor movements.*

**Materials/
Equipment:**   Drum
                Music of different rhythms (4/4, 3/4) selected to accompany the locomotor movements
                Country hoedown-type music with strong beat for "Follow Me"

**Organization/
Management:**   Children moving in general space

Introduction:
Today we begin one of our "connector" themes, a theme that we concentrate on by itself for a short
period of time, but a theme that fits into many others.

    The focus of our lesson today is a part of almost every lesson we do; it is traveling. We use it in
games, gymnastics, and dance, as well as in everyday physical activities. We will begin our lesson with
a review of our basic locomotor skills and then add different concepts: directions, speed, and so forth.

Content Development:
1.0   Travel in general space any way you wish other than running. On signal, stop in a balanced position.

Repeat three to four times, observing children for traveling with no collisions and balanced stops.

As I observed you moving, I noticed some of you are having difficulty stopping without falling down. This time, as you travel, focus on lowering your center of gravity by bending your knees for a balanced stop.

T   Move again throughout general space with your favorite locomotor movement.

2.0   I'm going to designate the locomotor movement. By this time, you should be pretty good at all the basics.

T   Gallop throughout general space.

Now lead with the other foot.

CUE: Same foot forward (keep the same foot always in front)

T   Slide to your right as you travel.

Now slide to your left.

CUE: Buoyant landings (light, "springy" actions as you travel)

Remember to raise your arms to shoulder height and turn your head to look in the direction you are traveling.

T   Skip as you travel in general space. Move as if you are very light and airy.

CUE: And hop, and hop, and hop (step, hop through general space)

T   Do a series of buoyant jumps—one jump leads into another; don't stop in between. Pretend you are on a pogo stick.

CUE: Boing, boing (boing, boing . . . just like Tigger the Tiger)

T   Hop on one foot.

Now try the other foot.

CUE: Up, up, light, light (light, quick actions as you hop)

Hop five times on one foot, then five on the other. Continue this pattern.

T   We have one more jumping pattern in our locomotor movements for today—taking off on one foot and landing on the opposite foot (model). Do you remember what this is called? A leap. Travel in general space with a not-too-fast run. After three or four running steps, leap in the air. When you land, continue the pattern: run, run, run, leap.

CUE: Arms up . . . stretch (lift your arms; stretch arms and legs as you leap)

Remember, soft landings.

Teacher Observation:

Do the children demonstrate correctly the different locomotor movements?

Do I need to reteach specific ones?

3.0   I have saved your favorite way to travel—running—until last. Travel in general space by running at a speed you can control. Run swiftly but quietly like deer in the forest.

CUE: Light on your feet (light, buoyant landings for quick steps)

4.0 Run throughout general space. Each time you hear the drum, quickly change directions by turning to the right or left and continue running.

> **CUE:** Check your speed (slow your speed slightly so you will be balanced when you change directions)

> **Remember to keep your body centered over your feet to maintain balance.**

T This time when you hear the drum, execute a half turn and continue traveling.

> **Quickly look for others when you turn, so you will not bump into someone when you begin to run.**

T In all our tasks thus far you changed directions but always traveled forward. This time when you hear the drum, run, slide, or gallop a few steps to the right, to the left, or backward before you continue running.

T Travel throughout general space using your favorite locomotor movement. Each time you meet another person, change the direction of your travel and continue moving.

> Change only the direction of your travel, not the locomotor movement you are using.

T Create your own pattern of traveling forward, backward, to the right, and to the left as you run. Only you will know the pattern, but I can almost see you thinking as you move.

"Follow Me"

Let's combine our locomotor skills with keeping the beat of the music in self-space. The activity is called "Follow Me." Spread throughout general space, facing me. I'll move to the right, the left, forward, and backward. You will mirror my direction. If I go left, you will go right; if I go forward, you will go backward. I'll hop, jump, gallop, slide, walk, and move in various ways. After each locomotor phrase, we will stop in self-space and do rhythms such as touching hands to knees, nodding our head forward and backward, or crossing our knees as in the Charleston. You will only need to watch and follow me.

> *Keep all actions in a count of eight, that is, eight slides to the left, eight to the right. Clap 1-2-3-4-5-6-7-8. (Taken from* Children Moving, *Chapter 19.)*

"Dance of Locomotors"

Let's combine our locomotors into a dance that demonstrates locomotors and changes in direction. You may choose to do the dance alone, with a partner, or in a small group (no more than five). Your dance must include three different locomotor movements; you may do more if you wish. Choose a leader for your group; that person will lead the first locomotor.

Each time you change to a different locomotor movement, change directions and change leaders.

Create an interesting floor pattern as you travel.

Practice your Dance of Locomotors until you can perform it exactly the same way (order of locomotors, directions, and floor pattern) three times. We will then watch each of them.

Criteria for Evaluation:
> Inclusion of at least three locomotor movements
> At least three changes of direction
> Ability to repeat order of locomotors, directions, and floor pattern

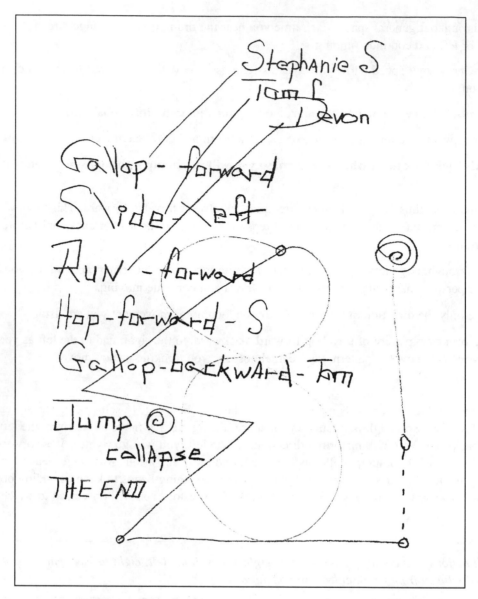

Figure 17 Children's Example—Dance of Locomotors

This is not the time to evaluate mastery of locomotor movements; it is the time for children to enjoy the dance. Figure 17 shows one group's dance pattern.

Closure:

What was the focus of our lesson today?

Name the different locomotor movements you used for your travel.

Name the directions you traveled.

Why do you need to be able to change directions as you travel?

	Locomotors					Dribble						
	gallop	skip	hop – r	hop – l		pads, pads	stance		height		travel/control	
Anderson, Mary	+	+	≈			⁻ ⁺ ⁻	+		⁻ ⁺			
Bates, Brianna	+	≈ ⁼	+			⁺ ⁻	+		+			
Becker, Tom	+	⁻ ⁺	+			⁺ ⁺	+		+			
Cagle, Angie	+	+	+			⁻ ⁺ ⁺	+		+			
Harris, Daniel	+	+	−			⁻ ⁺	+		+			

Figure 18 Sample Checklist

Reflection:

Have the children mastered the basic locomotor skills reviewed today?

Can they combine traveling with changes in direction?

 Teacher Checklist

On a checklist list the basic locomotor movements as well as the major cues for each skill (Figure 18). Periodically observe the children as they perform the locomotor movements, coding the checklist when they demonstrate mastery of the critical cue as well as a mature pattern of overall skill execution. *Checklists can be rather simple, with a "+" for mastery, or they can be more complex, including the date of mastery.* It is important that skills be assessed more than one time. Remember, children at the precontrol level can perform skills correctly but not consistently.

97

Lesson 2

Focus: Traveling, with changes in speed

Subfocus: Spatial awareness, locomotors, speed, directions

Objective: At the end of this lesson the children will have learned to:
travel at fast and slow speeds.

                 CUE: Check your speed (Slow the speed of your locomotor movement)

**Materials/
Equipment:**   Music with 4/4 and 3/4 beats to accompany locomotors

**Organization/
Management:** Children moving in general space

Introduction:

The focus of our lesson today is traveling with changes in speed. Changes in the rate of travel add excitement to gymnastic sequences, provide different expressive qualities to dances, and are a measure of high skill in games situations. (*Give specific examples according to the age of the children.*)

Content Development:

1.0   (*Begin the lesson with a review of the basic locomotor skills from Lesson 1; observe again for correct execution of the traveling pattern, ability to move with no collisions, and ability to stop in balanced position. Reteach as necessary.*)

2.0   Travel throughout general space with your favorite locomotor movement. On signal, slow your speed for a moment, then change to a different locomotor movement. This is "checking" your speed.

T   Travel in general space, moving as quickly as you can yet with control. On signal, continue traveling but at a lesser speed. Each signal will mean an increase or decrease in speed. Try to move the entire time with no stops and no collisions.

T   Travel in general space by running your best speed, moving very fast but able to stop on signal.

Remember, when traveling this fast, it is easier to stop in a balanced position if you lower your center of gravity by bending your knees.

Who can tell me the cue we learned earlier? Let's try again, focusing on balanced stops.

T   Hurriedly walk in general space as if looking for a friend or the younger brother Mother told you to watch. Move among other people quickly with no collisions.

3.0   Let's combine changing speeds with changing directions as you travel. On signal, "check" your speed, then change the directions of your travel—to the right or to the left.

Remember to check your speed slightly before you change directions.

T   Run as if someone is chasing you. Zigzag to the right and to the left, changing directions to avoid this imaginary tagger.

T   Travel as if you are chasing someone. Pretend they are far from you; just as you reach them, they flee in the opposite direction. They are very good at avoiding a tagger.

T   Travel throughout general space at a fast speed; when you meet another person, change directions and change your speed to moving very slowly. Each time you meet someone, switch directions and reverse speed from fast to slow or slow to fast.

T   Standing in your self-space, visually target a person across the area. Walk at a moderate pace toward that person as if he or she is a good friend you have not seen in a long time. Just as you reach the person, you realize you do not know him or her; walk quickly away.

"Cat and Mouse"

Look around the room and locate the person who will be your target for Cat and Mouse. On signal, travel quietly at moderate or slow speed toward that person. When you are close enough to touch him or her, *run* as far away from that person as possible. Sneak, retreat; sneak, retreat. This *meeting and parting* is the game of Cat and Mouse.

Remember, the person you are pursuing is probably pursuing someone else.

"City Streets, Crowded Spaces"

City Streets and Crowded Spaces will be a challenge to your ability to move in and out of crowded spaces with changes in directions and speed.

Establish the boundaries for travel with a reduction in general space; divide the class into two groups.

On signal, begin walking in general space, avoiding others as if on a crowded street. On signal, increase the speed of your walking as if you were in a hurry.

Change from walking to a different locomotor movement; you may choose running. Now travel in this confined space with no collisions.

(*Reduce the amount of general space.*) Now let's really challenge your control while moving in general space. Again, start slowly as you travel in and out among other travelers—no collisions. You may wish to change directions as well as increase or decrease your speed to avoid collisions.

Continue reducing the amount of general space. The challenge becomes greater as the amount of space becomes smaller.

Group 1, stand very still in your self-space. You are the tall buildings in the city; you may be tall and wide or just tall. Group 2, travel throughout general space without bumping other travelers or the buildings. Listen for the signal to designate "Red Light" or "Traffic Jam." (*Switch the groups after thirty seconds.*)

Closure:

We added what new concept to our theme of traveling today?

Do you always travel at your fastest speed in games? Give me an example of traveling at a moderate or slow speed in a game or sport.

Reflection:

Do the children travel with no collisions when moving at a fast speed?

Can they still stop on signal in a balanced position when moving fast?

Can they change speeds while traveling?

Lesson 3

Focus: Traveling, in different partner relationships

Subfocus: Spatial awareness, locomotors, pathways

Objectives: At the end of this lesson the children will have learned to:
1. travel in two partner relationships—side-by-side and lead-follow.
2. mirror the actions of a partner.

CUES: Heads up (Keep your head up to avoid collisions with others)
Balanced stops (Spread your feet and lower your hips slightly to maintain your balance when you stop)

Materials/ Equipment:
Four-by-six-inch index cards
Country hoedown music with a strong beat for "Follow Me"

Organization/ Management:
Relationship/action tasks written on cards
Method for selection of partners

Introduction:
We are continuing our work today on the theme of traveling. Thus far, we have reviewed the different locomotor movements and learned to travel with changes in direction and speed. Today our focus is on relationships with people as we travel. We are progressing toward combining the theme of traveling with chasing and fleeing, a fun situation in games.

Content Development:
1.0 (*Begin the lesson with a review of the different locomotors. Observe for correct execution of the traveling pattern, ability to move without collisions, and ability to stop in balanced position. Code teacher observation checklist during this introductory movement time.*)

2.0   Select a partner whose running skill is comparable to your skill; the speed, control, and ability to change directions are very similar. When you find a partner, sit beside that person. Persons standing still need a partner; select one quickly. You established the first partner relationship we are going to learn today when you sat beside a partner. Side-to-side is one of the relationships we study.

Travel throughout general space maintaining this side-to-side position. Partner "A" is now the decision maker; he or she chooses how to travel. On signal, partner "B" gets to make the decisions.

T   Continue traveling, changing directions as you go.

T   Vary your speed—sometimes fast, sometimes slow.

Remember, all your actions are in relation to your partner: side-to-side.

3.0   Stand behind your partner, with partner "B" as the leader. You are now in a lead-follow relationship. Partner "B," think of the locomotor movements you wish to use on the pathways you will follow. As the leader, begin to travel in those pathways. Partner "A" will follow, matching your locomotor movements and pathways. On signal, switch positions. Follow your partner approximately three to four feet behind for no collisions.

101

T   Leader: change the speed of your movements as you travel—sometimes very slow, sometimes very fast.

T   This time let's travel in phrases like the song "Dueling Banjos." Stand in the lead-follow position with partner "A" in front. The leader will travel, combining directions, pathways, and speed as he or she chooses for fifteen seconds. When you hear the drum, stop. Partner "B" will then follow, copying the actions. On signal, partner "A" begins a new sequence of travel.

T   Let's increase the length of the phrases to twenty-five seconds.

4.0   Return to self-space and stand facing your partner with about three feet separating you. This partner relationship is called mirroring. Remaining in self-space, contrast the actions or shapes of your partner by doing the following:

Partner "A," move arms quickly in slashing action; partner "B," move arms slowly and smoothly.

Partner "A," make a wide body shape; partner "B," make a narrow body shape.

Partner "A," move at high level; partner "B," move at low level.

The actions of partners will now mirror each other. Stay facing your partner and move as if you are looking in a mirror. A mirror reverses the left-right image. If partner "A" lifts his or her left arm, partner "B" will lift the right arm.

T   Now that you are rested, we are ready to travel in general space again. Face your partner to mirror actions as you travel. Partner "B" is the first leader. You may move right, left, forward, and backward. Partner "A" will mirror your actions while he or she stays facing you. On signal, switch positions as leader.

Remember when we did the activity "Follow Me" earlier in our lessons on traveling? That was a mirroring relationship: When I moved forward, you moved backward; when I moved to my left, you moved to your right. You are now doing the same action/relationship with your partner.

Can you mirror the positions and actions of arms while you travel?

"Action/Relationship Tasks"
(*Divide the class into small groups, three to five students per group.*) In our study of traveling you have worked alone and with partners. We have learned to travel side-to-side, mirroring a partner, and with a lead-follow relationship. These same relationships exist for groups.

On the card I will give each group is written one or more of the concepts we have learned today. Do not tell persons outside your group the key words. As a group, put together a short series of actions and travel to demonstrate these words. After a few minutes of practice, we will look at each group action to see if we can identify the relationship word printed on your card.

Print cards with one or two of the following:

Relationship	Action
side-to-side	unison
facing	mirror
lead-follow	matching
	contrasts

Some cards have both a relationship word (side-to-side, facing, lead-follow) and an action word (unison, contrast, mirror, match). I will ask you to tell us if you are showing action or relationship or both when you demonstrate.

Remember, use traveling with directions, time, level, and shapes to demonstrate the relationship word.

Closure:

What was the focus of our lesson today?

Show me a side-to-side relationship with a partner. Show me lead-follow. Show me the position for mirroring.

Why do you think you learn different partner/group relationships? When will you use what you learned today?

Reflection:

Can the children travel in side-to-side and lead-follow positions with partners?

Can they mirror the actions of partners in self-space, that is, left-right image?

Lesson 4

Focus: Dodging

Subfocus: Twisting, turning actions

Objective: At the end of this lesson the children will have learned to:
twist and turn as ways of dodging.

                  CUE: Quick actions (Twist and turn quickly)

**Materials/
Equipment:**   Drum

**Organization/
Management:**   Method for selection of partners
Sets of partners scattered throughout general space

Introduction:

In our theme thus far we have learned to travel with changes in speed and directions, to travel in relation to others. You practiced chasing in an imaginary game by running very fast; you avoided being "tagged" by running faster and by quickly changing directions.

    Today we add the last element to our study of travel to successfully play the games of chasing and fleeing. That element is dodging. In dynamic games situations, players often dodge the opponents by twisting, turning, and changing directions quickly. Sometimes they even jump in the air to avoid being tagged or hit. Learning to dodge effectively is important for runners in baseball and for ball handlers in basketball and football.

Content Development:

1.0   We are going to practice the skill of dodging by being participants in "Karate Dancing." You will need one partner for this activity.

T   Stand facing your partner at a distance of four to five feet. Pretend you are receiving a "punch" to the right shoulder. Keeping your feet firmly planted in self-space, quickly twist your trunk, leading with the right shoulder, to dodge the hit.

      A "kick" is coming to the chin; twist, then turn in self-space, moving to a lower level.

      A punch is coming to the stomach. Side step and turn to avoid the contact. A kick is aimed at your lower legs. Quickly jump in the air.

      Remember, dodge by twisting, turning, jumping, and stepping to the side.

T   Alternate pretend punches and kicks with your partner; work only on the twisting action.

      Make all punches and kicks as if in slow motion.

T   Continue to alternate punches and kicks, practicing the turning actions.

T   Alternate pretend punches and kicks with your partner. Partner "A," execute a slow-motion kick or punch. Partner "B," dodge the action. Partner "B," return a punch or kick; partner "A," dodge. Continue for an exchange of six punches or kicks.

      Remember, these are pretend punches only—no contact.

You will need to tell your partner which body part you are going to "punch" or "kick" so the partner can twist, turn, or jump as needed. Say "to the shoulder," "to the feet," for example.

Don't forget, the action is slow motion; the dodge is fast.

"Karate Dance"
Put a series of pretend punch and kick actions with dodging reactions into a sequence. This sequence will be a "Karate Dance." You and your partner will alternate pretend punches and kicks as you have practiced. After six to eight actions and reactions, complete your dance with a "double knockout"—both partners deliver a punch simultaneously; both forget to dodge. Sink slowly to the floor for your ending shape.

Remember, no contact!

The emphasis is on dodging. Make your reactions to punches and kicks very clear.

> *Allow sufficient practice time for children to develop dance sequences. Monitor the class, providing verbal cues and individual assistance.*

 Videotape the children's Karate Dance sequences. Have the children do a self-assessment of their twisting and turning actions by (1) coding the number of times they twisted in the sequence and the number of turns they completed; (2) evaluating the twisting, turning actions against a mature pattern; (3) recording their feelings about the dance itself.

Criteria:
At least three twisting actions
A minimum of three turning actions
Clear beginning and ending
No physical contact
A series of pretend punches and kicks

Closure:

What was the focus of our lesson today?

What ways did you learn to dodge?

Why do you need to develop the skill of dodging?

Reflection:

Can the children twist the upper trunk to the left and to the right while in self-space?

Can they turn to the right and to the left?

Is there a difference between their twisting and turning?

Lesson 5

Focus: Traveling, chasing, fleeing, dodging

Subfocus: Directions, twisting and turning actions

Objective: At the end of this lesson the children will have learned to:
use chasing, fleeing, and dodging in a games situation.

                 CUE: Quick actions (Twist and turn quickly)

**Materials/
Equipment:**   Drum

**Organization/
Management:**   Large open space for chasing, fleeing activity
Class divided into groups of six with a balance of running skills within each group

Introduction:

Today is the day when it all comes together. We began our study of traveling with a review of different locomotor movements and traveling quickly with control. We focused on partner and group relationships, an essential part of games play. You practiced running to chase and to flee.

We then focused on learning the different skills of dodging. Changing directions quickly, twisting, turning, and even jumping were the ways you practiced to avoid being caught by the chaser. The activity we are going to do today combines the skills of chasing, fleeing, and dodging into a game situation.

Content Development:

1.0   Before we begin the game situation, let's review the skills we need for successful participation. Run quickly throughout general space, avoiding others. On signal, stop in a balanced position.

     CUES: Heads up
               Balanced stops

T   Run quickly in general space, changing directions each time you hear the drum.

     Create your own change of directions by zigzagging to the right and to the left.

     CUE: Quick actions

T   Run as fast as you can with control, "check" your speed to a moderate run each time you meet another person. Alternate fast and moderate as you travel.

T   Twist, turn, or jump as you come close to others.

T   Pretend someone is chasing you. Run fast, with changes in directions as you go.

T   Pretend you are chasing someone who is very clever at dodging. Can you catch them?

     As I observe the class I see you running very well. You are dodging others who are suddenly too close, you are stopping on signal without falling down or sliding across the floor. I think you are ready to put the skills in a game situation. We will try the game for three or four minutes, evaluate our situations to see if we need to make changes, and then continue.

"Freeze and Count Tag"
(*Divide children into groups of six, each group with a space approximately the size of a quarter of a basketball court.*)

This chasing and fleeing game will really make you work hard on the skills we have been practicing. There are six people in your group, with a designated space. Make sure you know the boundaries for your space; other groups are also working.

Two people will start out as chasers—you decide who they will be. The other four people are the runners. On signal, the chasers have one minute to try to catch all the runners. If tagged, a runner has to freeze and then count to ten aloud before starting to run again. The object is for the taggers to catch all the runners at the same time. After the first minute, change taggers and begin again. (Taken from *Children Moving*, Chapter 21.)

Hints: Taggers work as a team. It may help to talk about your strategy before you begin.
    Runners, try different things to avoid being tagged: changing direction, varying speed, twisting, dodging, jumping.

Closure:

Compare your skills at chasing and fleeing. Do you use the same skills?

What skills did you use to dodge? Which skills were easiest for you? Most difficult?

Reflection:

Can the children travel swiftly in a games situation with no injuries?

Can they dodge chasers rather than just outrunning them?

Playing a game such as "Freeze and Count Tag" provides an excellent opportunity to teach the cardiovascular fitness component. Before activity begins, teach the children to take their own pulse rate—two fingers beside the esophagus on neck, count as you time for six seconds, then add a zero. This is the resting pulse. Discuss cardiovascular fitness, heart rate, and what will happen with vigorous activity.

Play the game for several minutes. Retake pulse. Discuss difference between pulse rate before and after activity. (Children are amazed at the difference.) Discuss ways to improve cardiovascular fitness and why it is so important for good health.

Dodging

Lesson 1

Focus: Dodging

Subfocus: Use of self-space

Objective: At the end of this lesson the children will have learned to:
move up, down, left, or right to dodge imaginary objects.

**Materials/
Equipment:**   Drum

**Organization/
Management:** Children in self-space

Introduction:

Today we will begin a study in dodging, which is a quick change of direction. You use this skill in many activities every day. Sometimes it is done with very little effort on your part. This morning when you were getting off the school bus you may have needed to use this skill to avoid bumping into a schoolmate. During class today, we are going to work on your dodging skills in a more dynamic setting. Often during the playing of a game you are required to make many decisions to avoid getting hit or tagged. You are able to accomplish this by changing directions quickly. Who can tell me a sport that requires the players to be able to dodge opponents? (basketball, football, soccer)

Content Development:

We are going to practice the skill of dodging in self-space using your imagination. You will need to find a self-space to begin class today.

Once you have found your self-space, practice moving either up and down or left and right quickly on your own. Remember, all of your movements must be done in your self-space.

1.0   This time we are going to pretend that the gym is full of seagulls that have been trained to get tangled in your hair on the sound of the drum. Remember, we are working on the skill of dodging, which means that your movements need to be quick.

T   I noticed that when you heard the drum some of you jumped into the air to avoid the seagulls. This time I would like for you to dodge the gulls by making a quick downward movement. This is like ducking.

T   Now I would like to see if you can dodge the gulls by quickly ducking down and then moving to the left or right before standing up again.

T   Make all of your movements in slow motion until you hear the drum.

2.0   Let's change the direction in which you need to move while dodging. All of the seagulls have left the gym and have been replaced with crabs from the beach.The crabs have been trained to attack when they hear two quick drumbeats. Remember, the crabs love to bite on tennis shoes.

T   We need to make some adjustments to the way you are dodging the crabs. Most of you are jumping straight up and down to avoid the crabs. This time can you jump in a way that you will land in your self-space but not on the same spot? That is right. You will need to jump either left, right, forward, or backward to avoid the crabs.

T   On your own I would like to see you dodge the crabs in your self-space. Remember, there could be several crabs trying to get a bite out of your tennis shoes.

3.0   Now we are going to practice dodging using both the seagulls and the crabs. Remember the seagulls will try to fly into your hair if they hear one drumbeat, and the crabs will move to bite your tennis shoes when they hear two quick drumbeats. Your movements need to be quick, and then you need to recover to get ready for the next challenge.

T   Now I would like for you to pretend you are taking a nice slow walk on the beach at night. As you walk, every once in a while a crab will come out of the sand to try and bite your toes, and the seagulls will fly down and try to get into your hair. Remember, your walk is slow and your reaction to the crabs and seagulls is quick.

After sufficient practice you might want to have the children practice the above dodging ideas while traveling about general space. Observe the class, giving verbal cues and individual assistance.

 Can you cut out a picture from a magazine of a person dodging someone or something by class next week? I will display the pictures you bring on the bulletin board.

Closure:

What was the focus of our lesson today?

Who can tell me what it means to dodge something or someone?

In our introduction, Christine mentioned that dodging opponents was important in football. Why is it important for a running back in football to have great dodging skills?

Reflection:

Can the children change direction in response to a signal?

Can they move quickly to the right and to the left?

Can they move quickly down and then recover?

Lesson 2

Focus: Dodging

Subfocus: General space

Objective: At the end of this lesson the children will have learned to: move with short quick movements on signal.

**Materials/
Equipment:**   Drum

**Organization/
Management:**   Children moving about general space

Introduction:

The last time we studied the skill of dodging, we practiced using our imagination. I limited your movements to moving quickly up, down, left, or right in self-space. Your understanding of how to dodge in such a small space was great, so today we are going to focus on dodging while traveling in general space. This will allow you to practice dodging in a dynamic situation where you will need to avoid your classmates as you move.

Content Development:

1.0   I would like for you to begin the lesson today by traveling slowly about the general space using your favorite locomotor movement except running. Be sure to use all of the general space and avoid your classmates.

T   Try moving about the general space again, and this time think more about staying away from everyone else.

T   That is much better. Now we can begin to work on your dodging skills. The gym is now filled with big green slimy ghosts that have been trained to cover you with purple slime every time they hear a drum beat. Move slowly about the general space until you hear a drumbeat, and then make a quick movement to dodge the ghost. Remember, when moving forward you must either move to the right, left, or backward. Ready? Go.

T   This time I would like for you to limit your dodging to moving backward on the drumbeat. Keep in mind that your movement needs to be quick.

T   That looks awesome. Now let's focus on dodging either to the left or the right. If I strike the drum more than once, be prepared to make two or more quick dodging movements.

T   I would like for you to travel slower this time to make it easier for me to see your quick dodges.

Well done! On the count of three everyone puff your breath really hard and rid the gym of all the ghosts. One, two, three!

2.0   Oh no! Look, the seagulls are back. Can you move about the general space this time dodging the seagulls? Remember, you need to duck down quickly to avoid them. Ready? Go!

Don't forget to use all of the general space. Look for open spaces.

T Your movements to dodge the gulls need to be sharper. Try not to hesitate when you hear the drumbeats. Continue your dodging actions with really sharp movements.

That's magnificent! I see sharp, dodging actions.

"Ghosts and Seagulls"
We will finish up today by combining the ghosts and the seagulls. The ghosts have been trained to cover you with purple slime every time they hear a drumbeat, and the seagulls will attack when they hear two beats.

I would like for you to finish up today by moving slowly about the general space and making really quick short movements to dodge our imaginary friends.

 Who would like to show me how well you can dodge on my signal?

Closure:

What directions could you move in to dodge someone if you were traveling forward?

If you were trying to cross a street and a car suddenly appeared, in what direction would you choose to move to dodge the car?

Reflection:

Can the children move about the general space and dodge each other?

Did the children choose to dodge moving forward, backward, left, right, and down?

Lesson 3

Focus: Dodging moving obstacles

Subfocus: Movement through general space
                       Pathways

Objective: At the end of this lesson the children will have learned to:
                       dodge classmates while traveling through general space.

**Materials/
Equipment:**   Drum
                       Pinnies (one pinnie for every two children)

**Organization/
Management:** Selection of partners
                       Response to signal
                       Movement through general space

Introduction:

This week we are going to be working on the skill of dodging. So far you have been trying to dodge only imaginary ideas. Today we are going to focus on dodging your classmates while traveling through general space. It will be like playing tag without a person being it.

    Earlier in the year we focused our attention on traveling without bumping into others and stopping on signal. Those two things will be very important today as we work on dodging while moving about the gym.

    Before we begin the lesson today, I would like for you to get into pairs without standing up. The person on the left side of your pair will pick up a pinnie before finding a self-space. You will be working by yourself during the lesson today.

Have the children begin moving slowly. Gradually increase the speed as you observe the children traveling confidently and without collisions.

Content Development:

1.0   How well can you travel about the general space without touching anyone else? You may travel any way you desire other than running.

    I noticed that some of you experienced some difficulty stopping without falling down. Remember to stop balanced on both feet.

T   Move about the general space this time using a different locomotor movement. No running.

    This time I'm going to specify the type of locomotor movements. You should be pretty good at all of them by now (skip, gallop, jog).

T   As I observed you moving about the gym, I noticed that almost everyone is traveling in a circle. This time see if you can travel through the general space using a straight pathway.

T   Let's continue using a straight pathway for a while. This time those students wearing the pinnies are to travel slowly in a straight path the length of the gym. The rest of you are to travel slowly in a straight path using the width of the gym. On my signal, try to get to the other side of the gym without touching anyone else.

It is important that you spread out before beginning to travel across the general space. Remember, you don't want to bunch up.

T   Change the locomotor movement you are using to travel on your straight path. Remember, the focus of the lesson is on dodging moving obstacles.

T   This time those students wearing the pinnies are to travel the width of the gym while the rest of you are to travel the length of the gym. When you get to the far side of the gym, turn around and continue moving back and forth across the general space.

T   Follow the same path this time but travel backward. Remember, you are trying not to touch anyone else.

T   Let's have those wearing the pinnies travel backward this time and the rest of you travel forward through the general space. Remember, the object is to get to the other side without touching anyone else.

T   I'm going to make it harder this time. Travel in the same direction on your straight path but a little faster than before. When you get to the far side of the gym, turn around and continue moving back and forth across the general space.

T   I like the way that Bill, Adele, Wyatt, and Teigha are dodging each other. As they move across the general space, watch how they change the speed of their movements when they get close to someone else. Let's see if all of you can change your speed at the right time to avoid touching anyone else.

T   Fabulous! That was perfect. I am really impressed with how much space you are able to keep between you and your classmates. Now it is time to change your task again. I wonder if you are able to skip about the gym using a curvy path to avoid each other?

As I observed your movements about the gym, I noticed that the corners are not being used. Brandon, Sarah, Emily, and Jeff, show your classmates how you use all of the general space. Let's all try to use the entire general space.

T   See if you are able to dodge everyone while jogging. Remember to travel using a curvy pathway.

T   This time those of you wearing the pinnies are to jog forward while the rest of you jog backward. Remember, you may need to change speed or direction quickly to stay away from your classmates.

Teacher Observation:

    Do the children demonstrate the ability to travel in general space without touching anyone else?

    Do I need to reteach the use of all the general space?

2.0   I have saved the most difficult task until last. It is your favorite way to travel—running. Let's see if you can dodge each other while running about the general space at a speed you can control.

T   Run this time, and try to use all of the gym. Remember, you are working on dodging each other. Don't let anyone get close to you.

T   Practice changing your speed as you run about the general space to avoid each other.

T   Run as if someone is chasing you. Use either a zigzag or curvy path to avoid this imaginary tagger.

C   We will make a game out of it this time. I'll time you for one minute. See how fast you can run about the general space without touching anyone else. Each person begins this game with ten points. You lose one point every time you are touched by or touch a classmate. Remember to keep track of your points. Ready? Go.

T   Show me how many points you still have using your fingers. If you have less than eight, I want you to slow down this time. If you had nine or more, try to increase your speed as you travel about the general space dodging your classmates. Good luck!

 Have all or a select number of students complete this assessment. Limit the amount of time to about two minutes. Those students involved with the written assessment can complete the task during closure.

Please circle your answer.

---

1. I am a good dodger: Yes No

2. Of the three pathways listed below, circle the one you find to be the most difficult to use to dodge your classmates.
a. Straight
b. Curvy
c. Zigzag

3. Which pathway do you like to use the best while moving to dodge classmates?
a. Straight
b. Curvy
c. Zigzag

Closure:

What skill do you need to work on today?

Is it easier to avoid your classmates using a straight path or a curvy one?

Reflection:

Do the children move about the general space safely?

Do the children use all of the general space?

Are the children able to travel about the general space without colliding?

Lesson 4

Focus: Fleeing

Subfocus: Self-space
                  General space

Objectives: At the end of the lesson the children will have learned to:
1. flee a partner in a confined space.
2. flee a partner while moving in general space.

                   CUES: Quick movements
                                Eyes on your partner

Materials/
Equipment: Drum

Organization/
Management: Selection of partners
                   Students working in pairs in self-space
                   Students working in general space
                   Response to signal (stop like a statue)

Introduction:

How many of you enjoy playing games of tag with friends? During your game of tag, you need to be able to run, change directions, change speeds, chase, and flee. Today we are going to focus our attention on only one part of the game of tag. Who can tell me what it is called when you move away from someone really fast? That's right! It is called fleeing. Can you think of any sports that require you to be able to move fast to flee another person? That is right, Alexis, football is a very good example of a sport that requires some of the players to be able to move quickly to flee an opponent. Before we begin, I would like for you to find a partner without standing up. I will give you six seconds to complete this task.

Content Development:

1.0   With your partner find a self-space and stand facing each other. I will know you are ready when I see that you and your partner are standing still.

> Let's begin with you and your partner standing about four giant steps apart. I would like for the person on the left in each pair to walk forward slowly toward your partner until you're as close as you can be without touching. Then suddenly jump backward, as if you're scared, and walk backward to your starting position. After you have had six tries, let your partner do the same thing. Remember to move forward toward your partner slowly and to flee by moving quickly.

Be sure both students get an equal opportunity to practice fleeing during the lesson.

> This time try to keep your eyes on your partner at all times, especially when you are returning to your starting position.

T   Now, instead of jumping backward and walking fast away from your partner, try jogging. Remember to change places after six tries.

I noticed that a lot of you are moving forward toward your partner in a very relaxed manner. Do you remember how Jack was afraid of the giant in *Jack and the Beanstalk*? Think of your partner as the giant and approach him with great caution (model). Giants, you can only scare your partner this time by saying boooooooo!

T Now let's have the giants jump and try to tag Jack when he gets real close. Approach your giant with great caution and be ready to flee so he can't tag you. Remember, you are working on fleeing quickly in order not to be tagged.

> (*Pinpoint.*) *I like the way Bob and Allison are approaching their partners with caution and then fleeing quickly away from them. Let's take a moment to watch how carefully they approach their partners and then quickly flee at the last second.*

2.0 Giants, this time you are allowed to move after your partners. Remember to wait until they are very close to you before you move to tag them.

C Now I want to give you a chance to see how clever you are when you try to flee from your partner. You can earn one point every time you are able to flee your partner without getting tagged. Giants, you must tag your partner before he or she leaves your self-space. After six tries change places with your partner (model).

While I observed you, I noticed that some of you are turning your back to your partner as you flee. Remember to keep a close watch on your partner.

Wow! What a difference watching your partner makes in the quality of your fleeing movements. Let's take a minute to watch Patrick, Kim, Jenny, and Dolores. Watch their eyes as they flee.

T Let's all try fleeing our partners again. Continue to practice keeping your eyes on your partner.

C We are going to finish up today with this challenge. I want you to practice fleeing your partner with a little different twist. As long as you don't get tagged by your partners, continue practicing fleeing. When you get tagged, you and your partner must change places. You will know you are getting better when you are able to avoid being tagged.

 I would like for you to study the four pictures of children fleeing a partner that I have placed on the bulletin board. How many of the pictures show the proper way to flee someone?

Closure:

What new skill did we work on today?

At what speed do you need to move to flee without getting tagged?

What should you look at while fleeing your partner?

Reflection:

Do the children move quickly when fleeing their partners?

Are the children able to quickly flee their partners without falling down?

Do the children keep their eyes on their partners in order to avoid the tag?

Lesson 5

Focus: Dodging using faking moves to avoid a chaser

Subfocus: General space

Objective: At the end of this lesson the children will have learned to: use fakes to avoid being tagged.

**Materials/
Equipment:** Pinnies
              VCR

**Organization/
Management:** Free movement about general space

Introduction:

Today we are going to continue to work on the skill of dodging. I am really pleased with how you are now able to move about the general space without colliding with any of your classmates. Can you think of any sports that you might play in middle school or high school that would require you to be able to avoid other players? We are not going to play those sports, but we are going to try to avoid classmates today while moving about the gym. Remember that you should use all of the general space and travel about the gym, not around it.

Have the children begin moving slowly. Gradually increase the speed as you observe the children traveling confidently and without collisions.

Content Development:

1.0   Let me see how well you are able to travel about the gym without touching anyone else.

T   Now, everyone jog about the gym without letting anyone else get close to you.

Teacher Observation:

    Do the children demonstrate the ability to travel in general space without touching anyone else?

    Do I need to reteach the use of general space?

T   Slow down your movements so I can see your fakes. As you travel throughout the general space, when you hear the drumbeat, pretend that you're going in one direction and then quickly change and go in a different direction.

     What you just did is called a fake. This is what we are going to be working on today. I would like for you to watch Za and Cam as they make their faking movements in response to the drum.

T   Continue to travel slowly about the general space and practice faking on your own.

T   I have observed that some of you are trying to fake but continue to move in the same direction.

Remember, to dodge or to fake someone or an object you must make a quick change of direction.

T   This time as you travel, see how close you can get to a classmate, and then pretend you're going to go one way but go another.

T   Most of your fakes so far are either to the left or to the right. This time try to go backward.

T   Great! Now I am seeing a lot of you changing directions when you get close to a classmate. Let's try it with jogging this time.

T   Some of you are using only your head to try and fake out a classmate. You need to get all of your body into the fake. Without leaving your self-space, see if you can lean to the left and then quickly push off your left foot to the right when I hit the drum.

T   Stay in your self-space and on your own practice leaning to the left and right and pushing off of the correct foot to make your fake.

T   Awesome! It's time once again to travel about the general space and practice your fakes. Remember to travel slowly and make your fakes quick.

T   I am really pleased with how well you are making your fakes. This time jog about the gym and practice faking when you get close to a classmate.

T   Now I think you are ready to try faking each other while running. Remember to use all of the gym.

2.0   Find a partner and come over and sit down with me. You are now ready to try playing a game of tag that will really make you work hard. You are going to have to use your fakes or you will be tagged. There will be two groups, and each group will have one half of the gym. Two people will start out as chasers. The rest of you are runners. I will give the chasers one minute to try and tag all of the runners on their side of the gym floor. If you are a runner and get tagged, stand still and count out loud to twenty-five, and then start running again. The object of the game is to use good fakes so you do not get tagged.

T   Along with good fakes, try moving at different speeds, changing directions, and looking at the chaser while you move in the space.

This is only one of many games of tag that can be used to practice faking. Check the speed of the game and make adjustments as needed to ensure that the children are playing under control.

We have observed that when children tag each other they can be rough. Explain to the children that the tags are to be only a touch and should be on the shoulder or below.

 I would like for you to watch this short video I made of Mrs. Harkrader's class and softly say, "yes" every time you see a good fake made by the student wearing the yellow shirt.

Closure:

Today we continued to work on the skill of dodging. Who can tell me the name of the movement you practiced today to help you avoid a classmate?

What directions could you use to fake an opponent if you were traveling forward toward him or her?

Reflection:

Are the children able to travel safely throughout the general space?

Are the children making a quick change of direction to fake out an opponent?

Do the children tag the runners gently?

Are the children able to play the game of tag within the boundaries?

Lesson 6

Focus: Fleeing

Subfocus: Use of general space

Objective: At the end of the lesson the children will have learned to:
flee a partner while traveling through general space.

                          CUE: Eyes on partner

**Materials/
Equipment:**   Drum
Pinnies (one for every two children)
VCR

**Organization/
Management:**   Selection of partners
Movement through general space
Response to signal

Introduction:

Today we are going to return to the skill of fleeing that we worked on earlier in the week. What does it mean to flee someone or something? That's right, Dena, it means to travel quickly away from a pursuing person or object. Who remembers a sport that requires a player to flee an opponent? Great answer, Jordan. Some players on a rugby team need to be able to flee an opponent. Can you think of anything in your neighborhood that you might need to flee? How about if you were in the woods?

Content Development:

1.0   I would like for you to find a different partner than you had the last time. You have five seconds to choose your partner without standing up. Sit close to your partner so I can see your pairs. Today we are going to begin our lesson using self-space and see if you are able to flee your partner safely.

The person on the left in each pair will pick the self-space you are going to be using, and the person on the right will pick up a pinnie and put it on. Those wearing the pinnies will practice fleeing first. Remember to stay in your self-space and change roles after you have had six tries to flee from your partner.

I am really impressed with how well you are keeping your eyes on your partner and how you are able to move quickly without falling down. It looks like you are almost ready to begin practicing fleeing about the general space. First of all, let's take time to revisit the idea of traveling about the general space without touching anyone else or falling down. Let's begin with you skipping about the gym.

 It is important that the children are able to move safely through general space before moving quickly to flee a partner.

T   This time let's jog using all of the general space.

T   When you are trying to flee from someone, sometimes you need to travel quickly. This time pretend you are fleeing a big bear.

> Do the children use all of the general space? Do I need to reteach the idea of moving through general space?
>
> Do the children travel safely—no collisions, stopping in a balanced position? Do they stop on signal?

Super! I liked the way you are able to travel quickly about the general space without touching anyone else.

Now you need to find your partner. Move slowly to your partner and together find a self-space. I will know that you are ready to begin when you and your partner are standing still in a good self-space.

T   I would like for the taller person in each pair to move across the gym from your partner. When I signal, the person wearing the pinnie will try to flee his or her partner. Everyone be ready to stop on my signal. Remember, we are working on learning how to flee.

T   This time the person not wearing the pinnie will work on his or her fleeing skills first. Be ready to stop when you hear my signal. Ready? Go.

T   As I observed you fleeing your partner, I noticed that some of you are beginning to bump into classmates. You need to be aware of everyone in class, not just your partner. Slow your speed slightly so you are able to travel without touching anyone else. Let's try it again.

I like the way you are now using all of the general space and are able to flee your partner without touching other classmates.

> *Be sure that both students get an equal opportunity to practice fleeing.*
> *Give feedback and assistance to the children as they work.*

T   I have noticed that some of you are having trouble keeping track of your partner while fleeing. How many of you remember talking about the need to keep your eyes on your partner when you were working in self-space? Terrific! The same thing applies when you travel about the gym. This time I am going to watch to see if you are able to keep your eyes on your partner while fleeing.

Now it's time for me to give you another clue to help you improve. When you are fleeing, try not to get caught in the corners of the gym.

2.0   Who remembers what it means to dodge someone? That's right, Alexis. It means a quick change of direction.

Use your dodging skills to help you flee your partner. Remember that you need to make quick directional changes to avoid your partner (model).

Why is it important to keep your eyes on your partner while fleeing him or her? Yes! You are right, Jacob, it helps you to decide when to change directions so you can avoid being tagged.

T   Let's try it again. Remember to keep your eyes on your partner and use your dodging skills as you flee. Ready? Go.

T   You are doing a great job of fleeing your partner and avoiding each other, so I would like to make your task more difficult. This time when I hit the drum, you and your partner are to switch tasks. If you are fleeing, you will become the chaser; and if you are the chaser, you will need to flee your partner. Remember to listen for the drumbeat and be ready to change tasks quickly.

"Partner Tag"

Put away all the pinnies and sit beside your chosen partner. The game of "Partner Tag" will really test all the skills of chasing and fleeing you have been working on thus far in our traveling lessons. Decide who will be the first fleeing partner and who will be the first chasing partner. On signal, the chaser begins a count to five; this gives the fleeing partner time to "get away" before the chase begins. If you tag your partner, stop, begin a new count of five, and begin the chase again. You will switch from being the person fleeing to the person chasing only when I give the signal. *(Give the signal to switch roles every thirty seconds.)*

Before we begin, let's review all the things we have learned for success in games of fleeing and chasing:

Chasing: Run really fast
    Heads up to avoid collisions
    Tag the person gently on the shoulder

Fleeing: Run even faster
    Heads up to avoid collisions
    Look for open spaces
    Change directions and speeds
    Twist, turn, dodge, fake your opponent (the chaser)

Remember, everyone else is running as you and your partner are chasing and fleeing. Be aware of others, but remember you can chase only your partner.

 Videotape the class chasing and fleeing with partners. Have the children watch a segment of the videotape and analyze their actions based on the above cues.

Closure:

To flee your partner, does it help if you can see him or her as you move about the gym?

What skills, other than running fast, are important to be successful when fleeing?

Why are dodging, faking, and changing directions important?

Reflection:

Are the children able to move without touching anyone else?

Are the children able to use all of the general space while fleeing their partner?

Are the children watching their partners while trying to flee?

Dribbling

Lesson 1, Part 1

Focus: Dribbling

Subfocus: Self-space

Objectives: At the end of this lesson the children will have learned to:
1. dribble with a front/back stance, in self-space.
2. dribble in self-space with knees bent.

A Note About Cues: Although several cues are listed below, it is important to focus on only one cue at a time. When you observe that the class has mastered that cue, then focus on the next one.

CUES FOR SELF-SPACE:
Front/back stance (Position your opposite foot forward for dribbling)
Waist high (Dribble the ball at a height between your knees and your waist)
Bent knees (Bend your knees in readiness to move)

REVIEW CUE: Pads, pads, push, push

**Materials/
Equipment:**   Drum
Playground balls (one per child)
Music with a 4/4 count for dribbling

**Organization/
Management:**   Established protocol for response to signal (stop dribbling; hold playground ball in
        hands or between feet)
Children scattered throughout general space

Introduction:
Today we begin our study of the skill theme of dribbling. We call it a theme because there will be a series of lessons and different concepts will be introduced. You learned to dribble in self-space earlier, but we did not add any concepts, such as directions or pathways. All these dribbling components are combined in the dribbling skills required for the sport of basketball, for the Harlem Globetrotters, and for ball gymnastic routines.

Content Development:
1.0   Scattered around the sides of our work area are the playground balls you will be using today. When you get the ball you are to use, select a space and begin to practice dribbling within that self-space. I will observe to see if you have remembered the cue for a good dribble that you learned earlier.

T   As I observed your dribbling, I noticed some of you were having trouble keeping the ball under control. Remember, push with your fingerpads for a good dribble. Dribble again in self-space, concentrating on the push.

T   Pads, pads, push, push was the first cue we learned for dribbling. As you continue to practice your dribbling in self-space, say those words softly aloud: pads, pads, push, push. I will walk among you; I should hear you saying them as I pass. The words actually create a rather nice rhythm for the dribble.

2.0   Now let's concentrate on the height of the ball for the dribble. How high do you think a basketball player should dribble the ball? Does a six-foot-six-inch player dribble the ball higher than a first-grader? What is the correct height? Waist high. This time as you dribble concentrate on dribbling the ball at waist height.

C   Now you have two cues for a good dribble in self-space. See if you can dribble until the music stops without losing control or moving from your self-space.

I am impressed! I don't see anyone slapping the ball; I saw correct use of the finger pads for good dribbling. That was our first cue for dribbling.

T   We need one other cue before we begin traveling in general space as we dribble today. When playing any games that involve dribbling, you need to always be ready to move. Being ready means never standing with "stiff" legs (model) but keeping the knees bent in readiness to travel. Continue your dribbling in self-space with knees bent.

T   Let's add one more component "just for fun." It's called "Hot Feet." Dribble in self-space with your feet constantly moving. You are not traveling; you are just moving your feet quickly in self-space.

Remember, hot feet—keep 'em moving.

Children at the control level of dribbling and beyond need to be equally skilled with the preferred and nonpreferred hand. Repeat tasks throughout with the nonpreferred hand.

3.0 Just for fun, let's see what happens when you travel as you dribble. On signal, begin traveling in general space, dribbling with your preferred hand.

> *Allow brief periods (thirty seconds) of dribbling in general space, stopping as needed for safety and review of cues.*

Closure:

What happens to our skill level when we switched from dribbling in self-space to traveling? Right, we reverted to an out-of-control level. Nothing has changed in the dribbling cues. What were our cues today?

> Pads, pads, push, push
> Bent knees
> Waist high

We will continue to work on dribbling and traveling tomorrow.

Reflection:

Have the children mastered dribbling with control in self-space?

Do certain critical elements need reteaching?

Is the class ready for continued work on traveling and dribbling?

Each dribbling lesson begins with a review and practice of dribbling in self-space—a broadening of the children's dribbling skill base. Throughout the theme, tasks (one per day) may be selected from the following during the warm-up and review portion of the lesson. The tasks provide additional practice for the children with enough challenge to prevent their becoming bored with "just dribbling."

1. Dribble the playground ball with your body in different positions.

2. Dribble the ball in different places in relation to your body—front, sides, back, between legs, around the body, and so on.

Older boys and girls enjoy the challenge of the following ballhandling tricks:

1. Dribble between your legs, making a "Figure 8" pathway with the ball.

2. Dribble around your body, making a circular pathway with the ball.

3. Hold the ball at low level between your legs, one hand in front and one hand in back; switch your hands from front to back without dropping the ball.

4. Keeping the ball at low level between your feet, dribble two times with your hands in front, then two times with your hands behind you. The dribble is: front—left, right; back—left, right.

5. Dribble two playground balls at the same time. Switch the hand you're using to dribble each one without losing control of either dribble.

Lesson 1, Part 2

Focus: Dribbling

Subfocus: General space

Objective: At the end of this lesson the children will have learned to:
dribble while traveling.

> **CUES FOR TRAVEL:** Eyes over the ball/heads up (Focus your eyes forward, not down at the ball)
>
> Ball to the side (Dribble the ball slightly to one side, not directly in front of you)

> **CUES FOR SELF-SPACE:** Front/back stance (Position your opposite foot forward for dribbling)
>
> Waist high (Dribble the ball at a height between your knees and your waist)
>
> Bent knees (Bend your knees in readiness to move)

> **REVIEW CUE:** Pads, pads, push, push

Content Development:

1.0   (Review self-space tasks with preferred and nonpreferred hand.)

2.0   When you were first learning to dribble, many of you watched the ball. Now we must begin to change that. Basketball players and persons really good at dribbling actually look over the ball, not down at the ball. This will be very important when we begin traveling and dribbling. Dribble in your self-space looking over the ball.

> **Remember, eyes over the ball/heads up (focus your eyes forward, not down at the ball).**

C   I will time you for thirty seconds; see if you can dribble without looking directly down at the ball until you hear the signal to stop.

T   Without moving from your self-space, visually locate a person in the room who will be your visual contact for the dribble. Keep eye contact with that person as you dribble in self-space. If your contact looks down at the ball, say his or her name to remind them to look at you.

> **Remember, heads up!**

T   Continue to dribble in self-space looking over the ball, and I will move throughout general space. I should always be able to see your eyes watching me. If I say your name, it is a reminder to look up, not down at the ball.

> You may wish to turn in your self-space as I travel in and out so we will always be able to maintain eye contact.

3.0   As I observed your dribbling in self-space, I noted that you are keeping control of the ball, you are dribbling at waist height, and you are bending your knees. As I traveled, I saw eyeballs everywhere. That tells me our practice last lesson and today was very good. You are now ready for dribbling while traveling. Travel throughout general space, dribbling as you go.

T   It is critical that you look over the ball to avoid collisions with others. Travel again, avoiding collisions with others.

Repeat travel and dribble several times.

T   When you worked on traveling, we practiced traveling to "open spaces," always looking for the open space in general space. Continue your practice of dribbling, looking for the open spaces as you travel.

T   You are pushing with fingerpads and looking ahead, but several of you are still losing control of the playground ball as you travel. Adjust your speed—travel at a slower pace.

When children first begin to dribble and travel, the skill often reverts back to a precontrol level. Stop the activity if children become careless, the majority are losing control, or collisions are occurring.

4.0   Much better control. When we first practiced dribbling in self-space, we learned a front/back stance—standing with the opposite foot forward. Show me the front/back stance that is correct for you. Excellent, those of you who dribble with the right hand have your left foot forward; those of you who dribble with the left hand have your right foot forward. This creates a "pocket" for the ball slightly to the side. This is very important when traveling and dribbling. On signal, travel throughout general space, dribbling with the ball "to the side." When you hear the drum, stop to rest for a moment as you switch to the other hand for dribbling.

Don't forget: front/back stance and knees bent in readiness for the travel-dribble; ball to the side and heads up when you travel.

C   When the music begins, dribble as you travel throughout general space. Your goal is to maintain control of the ball and of your body, no collisions. Continue your travel and dribbling until the music stops. How many of you never lost control of the ball? I trust there were no collisions.

C   Each of you has 100 points. When the music starts, begin dribbling and traveling. If the ball gets away from you, subtract 10 points. If you have a collision with another person, subtract 25 points. Your goal is to finish the game with the original 100 points.

Stop the activity after one to two minutes of continuous dribbling or if you observe children in unsafe situations.

How many of you finished with all 100 points? How many kept at least 80 points? That will be our goal in dribbling—to always have a score of 80 percent or better when practicing or testing ourselves.

Repeat the task after answering any questions for understanding. Ask how many improved their scores from last time or maintained the full 100 points.

Closure:

What skill were we trying to improve today?

Where do you keep your eyes focused when dribbling and traveling?

Should the ball be positioned in front or to the side when dribbling and traveling?

Reflection:

Do the children dribble in self-space with fingerpads and at waist height?

Can the children dribble in self-space looking over the ball rather than looking down at the ball?

What happens when the children travel and dribble?

Is the class ready to move forward, or do I need to reteach certain components?

> *This lesson is purposely divided into two parts to illustrate a very important part of teaching skills to children. Very often, children do not master critical elements as fast as we anticipated; more practice is needed. When a large leap is made, such as the switch from dribbling in self-space to general space, the loss of control is very evident. Children may need additional experiences or extended practice with the new component, that is, dribbling and traveling. Simply note in your lesson plan book how far the class progressed, and begin the next lesson with a review and practice for mastery before moving to any new material.*

Lesson 2

Focus: Dribbling

Subfocus: Spatial awareness, speed, partner relationships

Objectives: By the end of this lesson the children will have learned to:
1. dribble with changes in speed.
2. maintain the dribble while starting and stopping travel.

              CUE: Push ahead (Push the ball slightly ahead of you as you travel and dribble)

              REVIEW CUES: Eyes over the ball/heads up
                                       Ball to the side

**Materials/
Equipment:** Playground balls (one per child)
                   Music for dribble and travel/stop

**Organization/
Management:** Selection of partners
                   Established protocol for response to signal

Introduction:
You have learned to dribble in self-space and are beginning to travel and dribble with control. Today we will add changes in speed to our travel as we dribble. Being able to increase or decrease speed as we travel can be the key to getting ahead of the opponent or evading the defense in game situations.

Content Development:
1.0   Our work will always begin with dribbling in self-space for control. After you select the playground ball you will use, find a space and begin to dribble with your preferred hand. Watch the clock, and time yourself for one minute.

Watching the clock will remind you to keep heads up.

 Teacher Checklist
Teacher observation of critical cues during the two- to three-minute warm-up, practice portion of the lesson:

Pads, pads, push, push
Height of ball
Bent knees

The checklist grid (Figure 18, p. 97) provides ample space for several checks of a skill, not just one assessment on a single day.

T   Repeat with your nonpreferred hand. How many of you improved your score from our last practice of dribbling?

T   Begin dribbling with your preferred hand. After five bounces, switch to the other hand; continue dribbling. Switch after each five bounces until the drum signal is given.

Don't stop the dribble, just switch hands; do this by pushing the ball at an angle to the side rather than straight down (model). This action moves the ball from one side/front of your body to the other for the switch of hands.

T   Remember the front/back stance we practiced. Show me the correct front/back stance for your dribbling in self-space. Continue your dribbling in self-space, switching between preferred and nonpreferred hands after each five dribbles.

Not only do you switch hands for the dribble, you must also switch the front/back stance to always have the opposite foot in front.

T   Practice the front/back stance switch with a jump.

T   Practice the front/back stance switch by walking: five, step left; five, step right.

2.0   Travel and dribble maintaining control and avoiding others.

Continue your travel and dribble practice, always looking for the open spaces.

Teacher Observation:

As the children dribble and travel throughout general space, observe their skills for specifics:

    Is the ball kept at waist height or below for the dribble?

    Do the children keep eyes forward rather than looking down at the ball when traveling?

    Is the ball to the side?

As I observed your dribble while traveling, I am pleased to see _____ (from cues above); or, I noticed some of you are still having difficulty with _____. Let's work on that for a few minutes.

I am very pleased with your progress on dribbling. We are beginning to gain control as we travel. Let's add one additional cue that will make the travel and dribble even better. Push the ball slightly ahead of you as you travel.

Remember, push ahead.

T   Travel and dribble throughout general space, concentrating on pushing the ball slightly ahead of you as you travel.

T   We must not forget the other hand! As you travel, dribble with the nonpreferred hand.

Don't get in a hurry; this one may be slower for a while.

3.0   Travel and dribble at the speed you think is best for maintaining control of the ball.

T   Travel and dribble, changing speeds as you go. Sometimes travel quickly, other times slowly. In a game situation you can often outwit an opponent with this change in speed.

Keep the ball within your reach as you change from fast to slow or slow to fast speed.

T   Travel at the maximum speed you can control with no collisions and no loss of the ball.

The height of the ball is still the same. What was it? Waist high.

T   Begin your dribble, and travel at the speed you like best. On signal, increase or decrease your speed. Each drumbeat will be a switch in speed—increase or decrease.

As you change speeds, remember to keep your eyes over the ball at all times.

4.0   Travel throughout general space, dribbling with control. Vary your speed, increasing and decreasing as you travel. When the music stops, stand in self-space and continue the dribble. The task is to maintain the dribble while starting and stopping. The combination of starting and stopping while dribbling is one way to fake the opponent in a game.

Remember, the angle of the ball changes as you switch from travel to stationary dribbling. When you are stationary, the ball can bounce directly downward; when you travel, you need an angle on the ball.

Keep the ball slightly to your side while stationary so you will be prepared to travel quickly. I am pleased to see you remember the front/back stance.

Repeat several times.

T   This time begin your travel-dribble in general space, looking for open spaces as you go. When you see an open space, dribble quickly to that space; stop. Dribble five times in that self-space as you visually find a new open space; travel quickly to that open space. The sequence is: travel-dribble to open space, stationary dribble 1-2-3-4-5, travel-dribble to open space, stationary dribble.

You may travel and dribble as fast or as slowly as you choose. However, control is the name of the game.

"Circle Switch"
We will use the three circles on the basketball court for our next dribbling task. Find a self-space inside one of the three circles. If your circle is overcrowded and another circle has only one or two dribblers, you may want to find a new self-space before we begin. Begin dribbling in self-space inside your circle. On signal, travel quickly with control of ball and body to your next chosen circle; it may or may not be the one nearest to you. When you are in that circle, find a self-space and continue dribbling in that self-space. On signal, travel again. That activity is very much like the one when you practiced starting and stopping your travel with the music but not stopping the dribble.

Remember, heads up to watch for other dribblers.

You may need to change directions and/or check your speed for control (Figure 19).

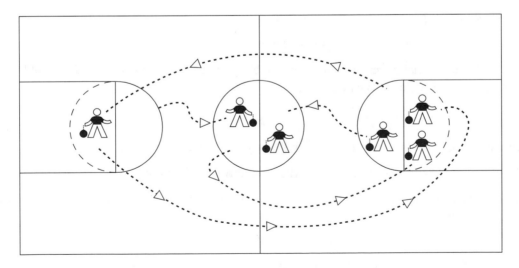

Figure 19   Circle Switch

131

"Corner Switch"

This one is like Circle Switch except that we are using the four corners of the blacktop area outside [or inside]. (*Designate boundaries for the corner spaces with sufficient room for one-fourth of the class to establish self-space for dribbling.*) Select a self-space in one of the four corners of the blacktop (gymnasium). Begin dribbling in that space. On signal, travel quickly to your next chosen "corner"; you have three from which to choose. When you arrive in that new space, stop traveling and continue to dribble in that self-space. On signal, travel again (Figure 20).

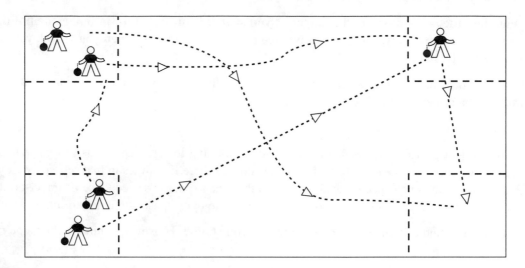

Figure 20   Corner Switch

C   Quickly choose a partner and sit one behind the other. The partner in front, partner "A," will begin to dribble and travel; partner "B" will follow, dribbling and traveling. Partner "A," travel at a speed that your partner can match and still maintain control of the dribble. Partner "B," try to stay within four feet of the lead partner at all times. If the lead partner stops, stop within four feet and continue to dribble until travel resumes.

Remember to keep your head up; it is critical now.

Focus your eyes on the back waist of the leader.

T   Reverse positions; partner "B" is now the leader.

T   Repeat the task with both partners again being leaders.

If you and your partner never lost control of the ball, never "lost" each other, and did not bump another person, raise your hands together.

Closure:

What new things did we add to our dribbling skill today?

Why is being able to change speed important when you travel and dribble?

Why is it important to keep the ball to the side rather than in front of you when dribbling in relation to others?

Reflection:

Can the children stop traveling and keep the ball within reach?

Can they travel, then stop, maintaining the dribble? Are they beginning to maintain control when traveling and dribbling?

Can they identify the factors leading to their loss of control when traveling?

As was true of Lesson 1, this lesson also contains enough information for more than a single lesson. Caution must be taken not to rush through a series of tasks just because they are written in a lesson plan. Teacher observation of skill and progression to the next task versus reteaching is critical if children are to master the skill.

Lesson 3

Focus: Dribbling

Subfocus: Spatial awareness, directions

Objective: At the end of this lesson the children will have learned to:
change directions while dribbling and traveling.

            CUE: Check your speed (Check your speed and bend your knees for good balance as
you change directions)

            REVIEW CUES: Eyes over the ball/heads up
Push ahead

**Materials/
Equipment:**   Drum
Playground balls (one per child)

**Organization/
Management:** Partner selection
Established protocol for response to signal

Introduction:

Thus far in our theme of dribbling, we have concentrated on dribbling in self-space and dribbling while
traveling. We have practiced dribbling with the right as well as the left hand. We have learned to change
the speed of our travel as we dribble. In all of our traveling tasks, we have moved in a forward direction. Today we will begin to change directions as we dribble and travel. Do you ever need to change
directions as you dribble in game situations?

Content Development:

1.0   On your own, complete the following (post on poster board or chalkboard):

- sixty seconds dribble with right hand—heads up!
- sixty seconds dribble with left hand—watch the clock or count to sixty
- five right hand, five left hand, continue to count of sixty
- Self-evaluation: knees bent
  - fingerpads
  - waist height

 Teacher Checklist
Evaluation of critical elements:
    Pads, pads, push, push
    Bent knees
    Eyes looking over the ball, not looking down at the ball

T   Even professional athletes begin each practice with the basics. How many times do you think
Michael Jordan has dribbled with each hand? Travel and dribble throughout general space, avoid-

134

ing contact with others. You may choose to start and stop or to increase and decrease speed as you travel.

 As you are resting for a moment, let's review the critical cues for dribbling and traveling—the cues that will bring control. Who can tell me what they are?

Eyes forward, looking over the ball/heads up to avoid collisions
Ball to the side
Ball at waist height

T   Which of the three do you most need to concentrate on? As you continue your dribbling and traveling, concentrate on the cue most important for you.

Teacher Observation:

Do the children keep eyes forward rather than looking down at the ball as they travel?

Is the ball kept low—at waist height or slightly below?

Is the ball to the side as they travel?

Can they travel for two minutes without bumping into others or losing control of the playground ball?

2.0   Dribble throughout general space, changing directions as you go: forward, backward, to the right, to the left. Travel at a speed that gives you control of the ball.

T   Continue to travel and change directions, always looking for the open space.

T   Dribble throughout general space. Each time you hear the signal, change the direction of your travel.

Remember to keep the ball slightly in front of you and to the side as you dribble.

Repeat the task with teacher signals for change of direction.

"Check" your speed and bend your knees for good balance when you change directions.

T   Dribble throughout general space with a controlled dribble. Each time you meet another person, change your direction quickly; continue your dribble.

T   Dribble with the "outside" hand when you travel. When you travel to the left, dribble with your right hand; when you travel to the right, dribble with your left hand.

T   Travel sideways with sliding steps. Remember when we did locomotors, I introduced the sliding used in dance (both feet momentarily being in the air). The sliding for today is the one used in sports—quickly moving your feet to the side with small steps (model). Hold the ball in your hands, and let's all slide to the right, to the left. Now travel to the sides and dribble.

C   Sit beside a partner. Decide who will be partner "A" and who will be partner "B." Partner "A," the first leader, will dribble while traveling forward, backward, to the left, and to the right. Partner "B" will attempt to maintain the side-by-side relationship at all times, changing directions as partner "A" changes. You will never travel more than five or six feet in any direction.

Remember to keep the ball slightly in front of you and to the side.

T   Travel to the right, dribble with left hand; travel to left, dribble with right hand. Repeat the task with partner "B" as the leader.

Repeat several times with change of leaders.

T   When you are comfortable with your skill in dribbling and changing directions, vary your speed. Sometimes travel quickly, sometimes slowly. This presents a greater challenge for the partner who is not the leader.

It is sometimes helpful to lower the height of the dribble slightly when traveling backward.

"Mirror the Teacher"
Scatter throughout general space with at least five feet between you and other persons. Stand so you are facing me. This activity is called "Mirror the Teacher" (*Children Moving,* Chapter 28). It is very similar to the side-by-side activity you did earlier with a partner. Your task is to change directions, start, and stop to match my changes in directions and speed.

Remember, you are to mirror my dribbling—when I travel forward, you will travel backward. I will use my free hand to indicate the way you are to travel.

Don't forget, a slide-step for travel to the sides; it is the most efficient way to cover a short distance.

"Frozen"
Travel in general space, dribbling as you go. If you lose control of the ball or bump another person, freeze in your self-space and hold the ball above your head. You are "unfrozen" when a person dribbling touches you on the shoulder. Your goal is to dribble without becoming frozen.

Don't forget to be good Samaritans as well as good dribblers.

"Dribble Tag"
I will now designate two persons as "taggers." Everyone, including the taggers, will be dribbling as before. There are now two ways to become frozen, either by losing control of the ball or by being tagged. Helpers can unfreeze you as before by touching you. Remember to hold the ball above your head if you need to be unfrozen.

> *Stop the activity after two to three minutes; rest for one minute and repeat with new taggers. Repeat "Dribble Tag" throughout the work on dribbling until all the children have had a chance to be taggers.*

How many of you were never frozen, either by losing control or by being tagged? I noticed several of you were excellent helpers, dribbling to get in position to unfreeze others while avoiding being tagged.

> *The listing of several application activities provides choice according to age of children, as well as alternates for revisitation or reteaching the lesson. Like most skill development lessons, dribbling will not be mastered in a single thirty-minute class.*

Closure:

What was the focus of our dribbling lesson today?

Why do you need to be able to dribble and travel in different directions?

How do you know which hand to use when dribbling to the right; to the left?

Reflection:

Can the children dribble and change the direction of their travel?

Do they change directions of travel without stopping dribbling?

Do they check their speed and lower the hips when changing directions?

Do they keep the ball at waist height or below throughout the dribbling?

Lesson 4

Focus: Dribbling

Subfocus: Pathways

Objectives: At the end of this lesson the children will have learned to:
1. dribble while traveling in curved or zigzag pathways.
2. keep the body between the ball and obstacles/opponents when dribbling.

CUE: Body between (Keep your body between the ball and the opponents as you dribble)

REVIEW CUES: Heads up/eyes over the ball
Push ahead

**Materials/
Equipment:**   Drum
Marker cones, tennis ball cans, or empty two-liter bottles
Hoops (half the number of students in class)

**Organization/
Management:**   Established protocol for response to signal
Division of general space into series of alleys five to six feet wide using shoe polish or plastic tape

Introduction:
Today we introduce the element of dribbling in different pathways. In a game situation, you will usually have opponents to avoid when you are dribbling. You can no longer travel only in straight pathways; you must be able to dribble in curved and zigzag pathways to avoid the obstacles. Our obstacles today will be stationary. Will that be true in game situations?

Content Development:
1.0   Okay, Michael Jordan, time for your review: Self-space dribble with preferred hand sixty times as you "eyeball" another person.

Self-space dribble with nonpreferred hand sixty seconds as you watch the clock.

T   Alternate hands: five left, five right, until you hit sixty.

Observe for individual children who still need assistance with: keeping knees bent, pushing with fingerpads, keeping ball at waist height or below.

T   Travel throughout general space, dribbling as you go. Practice starting and stopping as you travel; continue dribbling until you hear the drum. (Time for sixty seconds.)

T   This time as you travel, practice changing speeds—sometimes travel very quickly, sometimes slowly, but always with control. (Time for sixty seconds.)

T   Without traveling too far from home space, practice changing directions as you travel and dribble. (Time for sixty seconds.)

Teacher Observation:

Do the children keep eyes forward, looking over the ball rather than downward?

Do they dribble with the ball to the side, slightly in front as they travel?

Are they balanced (knees bent) when they change directions and when they pause in their travel?

2.0   Travel in different pathways as you dribble—curved, zigzag, and straight. Imagine there are stationary obstacles or opponents in your path.

Heads up! Look for the open spaces!

T   Let's practice the pathways one at a time. As you dribble and travel this time, you may travel only in straight pathways. When you meet another person or come to the outside boundary, stop and dribble in self-space. On signal (fifteen seconds), you may turn and select a new straight pathway.

I see the push with fingerpads. **Don't forget to bend your knees and to have a forward/backward stance when dribbling in self-space.**

T   Travel only in curved pathways this time—sometimes travel in large curved pathways, sometimes smaller, sometimes in a circle.

Remember to keep the ball to your side as you travel.

T   If you are fairly comfortable dribbling with either hand as we have practiced, switch hands as you travel the curved pathways.

A moderate speed will be best if you are switching hands.

The dribble should always be on the outside of the curve. If you curve to the left, dribble with the right. This keeps the ball to the side and always keeps your body between the ball and your opponents in a game situation.

T   Travel in a zigzag pathway with sharp changes in direction as you go.

Sometimes your zigzags looks more like curves; keep the angle very sharp. You may want to dribble slightly lower for good control as you zig and zag.

T   If you are really good at dribbling with either hand, try changing hands as you zigzag; you are moving much faster, so the switch is more difficult.

T   Create a pattern of straight, curved, and zigzag pathways as you travel. Know the order in which you will do them before we begin. If someone gets in your way, stop and dribble in self-space until they move, then continue your pattern.

3.0   (Set up marker cones [cans or plastic bottles] throughout general space. Vary the distance between the cones so there is no pattern.) Scattered throughout general space are marker cones that will serve as the obstacles for our dribbling. Travel in general space at a speed that is comfortable for you, dribbling with your preferred hand. Try to travel-dribble, without bumping a cone or another person or losing control of the ball.

T   Now try the task with your nonpreferred hand.

Remember when you worked on switching hands while dribbling? Now is the time when it really becomes important. Keep your body between the obstacle and the ball as you dribble. If you pass a cone on your left, keep the ball on your right side; if you pass a cone on your right, dribble with your left hand on your left side.

CUE: Body between (keep your body between the ball and the opponents as you dribble)

T   Travel as close to the cones as you can without touching them as you dribble.

T   Try some changes in direction. Don't always travel in a forward direction as you avoid the cones.

Remember, a slide-step is best for moving to the side a short distance.

> *Hoops scattered on the floor create a different challenge that is enjoyed very much by the children.*

"Human Obstacles"
(Divide the children into groups with no more than four or five persons per group. Each group will use one alley.) You will need only one playground ball for your group. One person will be the dribbler; he or she will stand at the end of the alley. The other persons in the group will find a self-space within the alley; arrange yourselves in a zigzag pattern. You will be the stationary obstacles around which the dribbler must travel. "Dribbler," your task is to travel-dribble the length of the alley, maintaining control of the ball at all times. "Obstacles," place your feet shoulder-width apart and your hands on your hips. You are stationary obstacles.

We have talked about keeping your body between the obstacle and the ball; that is now very important.

Dribbler, after you travel the alley down and back, switch places with someone in the alley. Continue until everyone has had an opportunity to be the dribbler.

No collisions with the stationary obstacles.

"Windmills"
Obstacles in the alleys, position yourselves in a basic defensive basketball position with arms extended outward. Extend the arms with one upward and one slightly downward—windmill fashion. Dribbler, travel and dribble past the person on the upward windmill side. Each time you face a new human obstacle, your decision regarding which side to dribble is determined by the position of the arms; always pass on the side of the upward arm (Figure 21). Obstacles, position arms before the dribbler begins his or her turn.

In a basketball game, the defense changes arm positions frequently; later we will practice with the human obstacles free to move arms.

Closure:

Our study of the skill of dribbling is becoming more complex. What new concept did we add today? Name the three pathways.

Why is it important to be able to dribble and travel in curved and zigzag as well as straight pathways?

When a basketball player is moving quickly toward the basket with no opponents between her and the basket, what pathway will she choose for the dribble? What pathway if the defense is between the player and the basket?

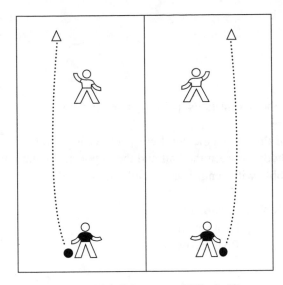

Figure 21   Diagram of Windmills

Reflection:

Can the children travel and dribble in each of the three pathways in general space?

Can they travel in curved and zigzag pathways to avoid collisions with stationary obstacles?

Lesson 5

Focus: Dribbling

Subfocus: Spatial awareness, directions, pathways, relationships

Objectives: At the end of this lesson the children will have learned to:
1. keep the body between the ball and the opponent or stationary obstacle.
2. travel-dribble with control of the ball and the body.

> **REVIEW CUES:** Ball to side
>   Push ahead
>   Body between

**Materials/
Equipment:**   Drum
Multicolored marker cones
Playground balls (one per child)
Hoops (half the number of children in class)

**Organization/
Management:** Established protocol for response to signal

Introduction:

Thus far in our study of dribbling, you have learned to dribble in self-space and when traveling. You have practiced changing directions, varying speed, dribbling in different pathways, and around stationary obstacles. From the beginning of our work in dribbling, you practiced dribbling with the preferred and the nonpreferred hand; we discussed the importance of being skilled with each.

In our last lesson you traveled around stationary obstacles and practiced switching hands for the dribble so the ball would be on the "outside" and your body would always be between the ball and the opponent/obstacles. That component will be very important today. You will be dribbling around an obstacle that is trying to gain possession of the ball—an opponent.

Content Development:

1.0   Begin your practice by deciding which review skill you wish to focus on first: changing directions, speed, pathways, or starting and stopping.

Teacher Observation:

Critical cues when traveling:
     Waist height
     Ball slightly to the side and in front of the body
     No collisions with others/no loss of the ball—control

T   Repeat your practice with the nonpreferred hand if you did not make any switches earlier.

C   Remember the game we did called "100 points"? We are going to repeat it today as a self-test for practice. Each of you has 100 points. On signal, you will begin dribbling and traveling. If you lose control of the ball, subtract 10 points; if you have a collision with another person, subtract 25.

(Play the game for two or three minutes.) How many of you improved your score from the last time we played?

C Let's repeat the activity. This time concentrate on changing directions and/or pathways.

Don't forget to change hands as you dribble from side to side.

2.0 (Place hoops and marker cones throughout general space, varying spacing and placement, so there is no set distance or pattern.) When we last worked on dribbling and traveling, you moved in different pathways to avoid the cones as stationary obstacles. As you travel and dribble today, concentrate on always having the playground ball on the "outside" as you dribble around the cone or hoop.

T Switch hands as you approach the cone or hoop.

Remember to adjust your speed for control.

C Count the number of cones and hoops you pass as you dribble. Give yourself credit only if you remember to switch the ball to the "outside," keeping your body between the obstacle and the playground ball you are dribbling.

Some of you will need to "check" your speed as you approach the cone or hoop, pause, and switch the dribble to the other hand; others will be able to switch hands with no change in speed. Either strategy is fine.

"Color Cones"
(Place multicolored cones throughout general space; position the children outside the perimeter of the work area.) This activity is designed to challenge your skills of dribbling and traveling, as well as dribbling in self-space. The multicolored cones are positioned in a color pattern. I will say a color sequence, for example, red, blue, purple. On signal, begin your travel-dribble throughout general space: dribble to the color cone that was first in the sequence (red); stop, touch the cone with one hand and dribble five times in self-space. Then travel-dribble to the next color in the sequence (blue) and repeat the self-space dribble. When you have completed the sequence, dribble as you travel back to your starting space.

Do you think you can do a four-part sequence? Listen to the colors.

This is a favorite and an excellent assessment of children's dribbling and traveling skills.

"Alley Obstacle"
Select a partner who can travel-dribble as well as you or slightly better. Decide who will be the first dribbler and who will be the "obstacle"; this time the obstacle/opponent will be trying to gain possession of the ball! The opponent is positioned anywhere in the alley, stationary position with feet planted. The dribbler is trying to travel-dribble the length of the alley maintaining possession of the ball. Neither person should bump, push, or reach in; that would be a foul in a game situation. If the defensive person gains possession of the ball, return it to the dribbler. After a minute or so, I will give the signal to change positions. It will probably take a couple of tries for each of you to feel comfortable with the defensive and offensive roles.

Dribbler, remember you must stay in the alley. Defense, remember you can only touch the ball, not the person.

Always keep your body between the opponent and the ball you are dribbling.

"Defense in the Hoops"
(*Scatter hoops in a space approximately one half the gymnasium or blacktop area. The smaller the space, the higher the skill component.*) Quickly sit beside your partner; decide who will be partner "A" and who will be partner "B." If you are an "A," stand inside one of the hoops. As an "obstacle," your task is the same as before—to gain possession of the ball. However, you may gain possession of any playground ball that comes near you, not just your partner's! If you are a "B," select a playground ball and stand on the sideline facing the opponents. Your challenge is to dribble to the other sideline without losing control/possession of the ball. You must stay within the side boundaries as you travel-dribble.

You must dribble—no running with the ball.

Remember, keep your body between you and the nearest opponent.

Dribblers, see how many times you can travel through the obstacles without losing the ball. Opponents, if you gain possession of the ball, raise it above your head to signal the "steal," then give it back to the dribbler so he or she can continue. After two minutes I will signal, and dribblers and obstacles will change places.

Dribbling in relation to a moving defense is a high-level skill. Don't move to this level until (and only if) the children are ready.

"One on One"
Stand approximately three feet from a partner, facing each other. Each of you has a playground ball; each will be dribbling. Your task is to gain possession of the playground ball your partner is dribbling while maintaining possession of your own playground ball.

Remember, there is contact with the ball only, not the person.

The strategy is whether to be the offense, aggressively trying to gain possession, or to be the defense, waiting for the person to approach you.

Keep your body between the opponent and the ball.

If you gain possession of the partner's playground ball, do one double bounce (ball in each hand) and return the ball to your partner for a new try.

Knocking the ball away is NOT gaining possession.

"Outwit the Defense"
(*Arrange cones in a zigzag pattern on one half of the play area.*) Quickly select five persons to be in your group; each group will need one playground ball. The first person in your group will dribble in a zigzag pathway around the marker cones. When you have passed the cones, dribble in a straight pathway to the end boundary. I say "straight" because you must avoid the opponent—me. I will attempt to gain possession of the ball or tap it away after you travel-dribble around the cones. When you reach the end boundary, dribble quickly down the sidelines back to your group so another person can have a turn (Figure 22).

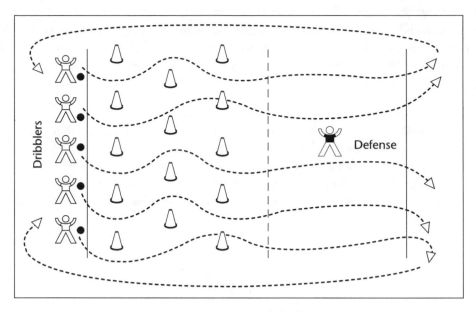

Figure 22   Outwit the Defense

Remember, there is only one defensive person—me. There are several of you dribbling at the same time. Vary your speed, change your directions and pathways. Ready? Begin.

Now I will select two persons to assist me as defensive players. Do you think you can outwit all three?

Closure:

Reflect for a moment. How do your dribbling skills now compare with how they were when we first began to work on dribbling? Which skills are still difficult for you? Which have you mastered?

Throughout this theme, what was our focus? Right, dribbling. Let's list on the flipchart all the concepts we added as we studied the theme of dribbling: self-space, general space, speed, directions, pathways, partner relationships, plus the components of offense and defense. What was your favorite activity? Why did you like it best?

Reflection:

Which objectives did the majority of the children meet?

Which skills do I need to reteach; which do I need to emphasize when we revisit dribbling?

Do I need to make changes in the progression?

Revisitation Activities
"Prediction" (dribbling combined with shooting baskets)
(Divide the children into five or six equal groups, no more than four or five children per group; position groups at one end of the gymnasium or blacktop facing the basketball goal). This activity combines our travel-dribble with shooting at the basket—basketball. You will be working as a total group—all points added together. I am going to predict how many points (two per basket) I think you as a class can make in two minutes. On signal, the first person in your group will dribble the distance to the goal and attempt a basket. After your shot at the basket, move quickly to the outside perimeter and travel-dribble, returning to your group. The next person will then begin his or her turn.

"Harlem Globetrotters" (dribbling combined with throwing and catching)
With a partner, in small groups, or working alone, make up a routine that will combine throwing, catching, and dribbling. Your decisions will include: floor pattern, skills or tricks to be performed, directions of travel, and partner/group relationships (for example, side-by-side, mirroring, together versus follow-the-leader). Don't forget the dribbling tricks you have learned as we have practiced each day. Practice your routines with the music, then you will get to show them to the class. (Select music such as "Sweet Georgia Brown." Figure 23 shows one student's routine.)

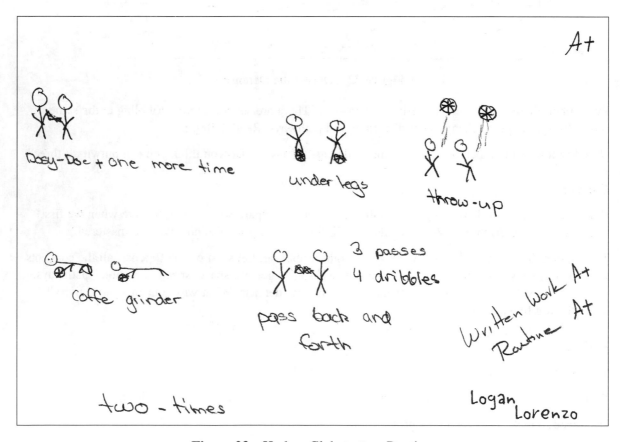

Figure 23   Harlem Globetrotters Routine

☑ Dribbling Evaluation

Focus: Dribbling

Objective: At the end of this lesson the children will have learned to:
complete a self-evaluation of their dribbling skills.

Materials/
Equipment: Playground balls (one per child)
Established protocol for paper, pencils (pick up, put away)

We have just completed our concentrated work on the skill of dribbling. If you look at our spiral (posted on the wall chart), you will notice we have progressed from a review of dribbling in self-space to the level of dribbling while avoiding stationary obstacles (or while someone is trying to take the ball away, or dribbling against a defense—depending on the progression of the theme).

Today you will do a self-evaluation of your dribbling skills. Look at the first task on your sheet, "dribbling in self-space." We did this skill several times. Remember our goal throughout the study was to attain 80 percent accuracy or above. If you did not lose control or move from your self-space more than two times when you did this skill, you will check the first column, "I am good at this skill." If you have more than two mistakes, check the second column. If you would like me to see the skill, place a check in the last column; a check in this third column can mean the skill is very good or you need some help. Either way, I will be sure to watch the skill.

> *Self-evaluations are excellent for children. Less teacher time is consumed with this type of evaluation compared to the teacher evaluating each child on each skill. Trust the children; they are very honest about their skills. This checklist, with a cover letter explaining the theme, becomes the report card to parents for this theme. (Guide the children through each skill evaluation, reviewing the task and the activity. Some classes will need to do the activity or skill for two to three minutes as a review before "testing.")*

Here are three examples of self-evaluations for dribbling (Figures 24–26). The evaluation you use depends on the critical elements taught, the cognitive level of the students, and their level of skill development/mastery. An evaluation should never be an embarrassment to children. It should help us as teachers to assess the skill level of the class and individual children's mastery of the elements. Coupled with journal entries, self-evaluations can provide valuable information on children's feelings about themselves and their skills.

Name _____ Homeroom _____

Dribbling Self-Evaluation

	I am good at this skill	I need to practice this skill	I would like my teacher to see this skill
Dribbling in self-space			
Dribbling while traveling			
Dribbling while starting and stopping			
Dribbling while changing directions			
Dribbling around obstacles			
Dribbling while someone is trying to gain possession			

Teacher comments:

Figure 24 Dribbling Self-Evaluation

Name _____ Homeroom _____

Self-Evaluation of Dribbling Skills 2

Dribbling in self-space	100% accuracy	80%	below 80%
Right hand			
Left hand			
Alternates			
Eyes focused forward			

Dribbling around the gym

No collisions with others			
No loss of control			

Dribbling in and around other people

No collisions with others			
No loss of control			

Pretend that a new student (Murgatroid) has just entered our school. What things does Murgatroid need to know to be good at dribbling?

Figure 25 Dribbling Skills Self-Evaluation

Dribbling Skills Test

Name ————————————— Homeroom —————————————

Test for Understanding:

1. The critical cues for dribbling are ————, ————, ————, ————.
2. The critical cue for dribbling and traveling is ————————————————

Self-Evaluation of Dribbling Skill:

	I still need to practice this skill	I'm pretty good at this skill	I'm very good at this skill
1. Dribbling in self-space with preferred hand			
2. Dribbling in self-space with other hand			
3. Switches of hand and feet			
4. Dribbling and traveling			

My favorite dribbling activity is:

I like this activity best because:

Figure 26 Dribbling Skills Test

Throwing and Catching

Lesson 1

Focus:	Catching
Subfocus:	Spatial awareness
Objective:	At the end of this lesson the children will have learned to: toss and catch balls while in self-space.

> **CUES:** Watch the ball (Watch the ball until it touches your hands)
>
> Reach (Reach for the ball; don't wait for it to come to you)

Materials/ Equipment:	Drum
	8-1/2-inch plastic balls (ten to twelve)
	Nerf balls (ten to twelve)
	8-1/2-inch playground balls (one per child)
	Hoops to hold balls (four to five)
Organization/ Management:	Children scattered in general space with sufficient space for self-toss/catch
	Established protocol for response to signal (proper placement of catching balls during teacher directions)

Introduction:

Today we begin a study of throwing and catching, with the emphasis on catching. You have practiced the isolated skills of throwing and catching earlier in physical education classes. Now we will test your accuracy of catching and will add the challenge of traveling. Most games and sports are combinations of throwing and catching in traveling situations. Who can name a game or sport that uses this combination? (Basketball, football, softball—discuss how throwing and catching are used in each.)

Content Development:

1.0   Before we get into the challenge of traveling, we must review the basic skills of throwing and catching. Scattered around the boundaries of our work space are hoops (boxes, crates) containing plastic balls, nerf balls, and playground balls. After you select the ball you are going to use, find a self-space where you will not interfere with others and practice tossing the ball upward and catching it.

Teacher Observation:

Are the children's eyes focused on the ball?

Do they catch with their hands or trap against their bodies?

Does the ball travel upward or at an angle away from the body?

T   As I observed your tossing and catching, I noticed some of you were having difficulty tossing the ball straight; sometimes the ball was going back over your head or so far in front you had to take a step to catch it. Remember, release the ball at shoulder height for a straight toss upward. Practice your toss and catch again as I observe.

T   Toss the ball higher than your head and catch it before it bounces without moving from your self-space.

The toss is looking better. If you begin to have trouble, remember, release at shoulder height, **arm motion upward.**

T   Now we are ready to concentrate on catching. Toss the ball higher than your head and catch it at midlevel. This is best for accuracy.

Keep your eyes on the ball until you feel it in your hands.

C   See if you can toss and catch without taking a step from your self-space.

After you toss the ball, "reach" for it rather than waiting for it to come to you. Extend your arms upward.

T   Toss the ball higher this time, still concentrating on reaching for the catch.

Remember, a straight toss is critical to staying in your self-space.

T   Practice tossing to different heights until you discover the best height for consistency on the catch.

If you are missing the catch or moving from your self-space to catch, the toss may be too high.

T   Repeat your practice with each type of ball: nerf, plastic, and playground.

C   When you discover the best ball for you and the best height for accuracy, see if you can toss and catch ten times with no mistakes.

 Partner Observation
Select a partner to watch your catching in self-space. The partner will watch for a straight toss upward and to see if you extended your arms to reach for the ball. Toss five times so the partner can give a "thumbs up" or "thumbs down" for each try; if you give a "thumbs down," tell your partner what needs to be corrected.

C   I will time you for one minute. See if you can toss and catch without moving from your self-space. If you as a class are perfect, not a single ball will touch the ground. Ready? Begin.

How many were perfect with no mistakes? How many were almost perfect—80 percent or above? Let's try again.

Closure:

What was the focus of our lesson for today?

What two cues were important for all your catching?

Reflection:

Do the children toss the ball upward in a straight path rather than at an angle forward or backward?

Do they visually track the ball into their hands?

Do they reach upward for the ball rather than trapping it against the body?

For older children who need the basic work on catching but who easily lose interest in practicing the skill, try these "just-for-fun" tasks at the end of a lesson.

T   Stand in self-space; place the ball between your ankles. Jump in the air to toss the ball upward; catch it with both hands.

T   Lie on the grass (or mat) with the ball in both hands. Toss the ball upward, execute a log roll and catch the ball before it bounces.

   Hint: Toss the ball slightly in the direction you are going to roll.

T   Stand in self-space with the ball between your ankles. Lean over and place both hands on the ground; execute a mule kick to toss the ball over your head. Catch the ball after one bounce.

   Catch the ball before it bounces.

The tasks can be presented individually or they can be set up as three stations at the edge of the work area. The tasks can be written on butcher paper with sufficient room left for children to sign their names as they master the skill.

Lesson 2

Focus: Catching

Subfocus: Spatial awareness, levels, stretching/curling

Objectives: At the end of this lesson the children will have learned to:
1. catch a ball at high level.
2. catch a ball at low level.

CUES: Thumbs together (Thumbs together for a catch at high level)
Pinks together (Little fingers together for a catch at low level)
Reach and pull (Extend your arms to reach for the ball, then pull it into your body)

REVIEW CUES: Watch the ball
Reach

**Materials/
Equipment:**   Drum
Nerf, plastic, playground balls (as for Lesson 1)
Hoops (boxes, crates) to hold balls

**Organization/
Management:**   Children scattered in general space with sufficient space for self-toss/catch
Established protocol for response to signal

Introduction:

In our last lesson you worked on tossing and catching with accuracy as defined within your self-space. This is fine as a beginning, but in dynamic game situations, you will need to catch the ball not only at that middle level but also at high and low levels. Who can tell the group a specific sports/games situation where you will need to catch a ball at high level? Low level?

Content Development:

1.0   Select the ball you are going to use today, and practice the self-space toss and catch you learned in our last lesson on catching.

Teacher Observation:

Do the children reach for the ball, catching with hands only rather than trapping it against the body?

Are they watching the ball until it touches the hands?

Is the toss going directly upward, above the head, rather than forward or backward at an angle?

Do I need to reteach certain cues?

Which individuals need assistance with this basic toss/catch?

2.0 Now let's concentrate on the level at which you will catch. Do you remember the three levels you learned earlier? Tell the person closest to you the three levels. They are _____, _____, and _____. Toss the ball five to ten feet above your head, and catch it at high level. We worked last time on reaching for the ball rather than waiting for it to come to us; now you need to really stretch your arms upward for the catch. (Allow several minutes of practice on extending/stretching the arms upward.)

T   I am seeing excellent extension of arms for the catch at high level. The second part for our focus is the hands. When you catch at high level, you need to put your thumbs together. Continue your practice now with two things to remember: extend your arms, thumbs together.

     CUE: Thumbs together/thumbs in

T   The next part is really hard. In a game situation, you will rarely catch at high level with your feet on the floor; you will usually be jumping in the air for the catch. This time as you practice, pretend you are catching a ball coming over the heads of the defense—not only will your arms be stretched upward, but your feet will be completely off the floor.

     Land softly by bending your knees as you contact the floor; remember, quiet landings.

     As I observe your practice, some of you are jumping too soon, landing before the catch; others are jumping too late, the ball is coming down on you. Knowing when to jump is an important part of catching at high level. This timing will come as you continue to practice. (*Allow several minutes of practice for children to master the timing for the jump.*)

C   Let's take a self-test of our catching at high level early so we will have a comparison after much practice. The next ten tosses will be your test. Give yourself a point if you remember to extend your arms upward, a point for thumbs in, and an extra point if you catch with both feet off the floor.

Many children will bend their knees to get their feet off the floor without increasing height or will catch with their hands extended outward at chest height rather than above the head. Verbal cues to individuals are helpful.

T   What shape does your body make when extended with your hands above your head and your feet off the floor? Right, a narrow shape. Practice the catch again; visualize yourself as extended high and narrow when you catch. Really s - t - r - e - t - c - h.

T   Can you handle one more piece of learning for the real catch? After you catch the ball, pull it close to your body. The basketball player who gets the rebound or the football player who intercepts the high-level pass knows the importance of this pulling in.

     CUE: Reach and pull

T   Now you have four things to remember when you catch at high level: arms extended, thumbs together, jump for the catch, pull the ball in after the contact. See if you can incorporate all four things as you catch at high level.

Partner Observation

Select a partner to watch your catching at high level. Partner "A" will toss and catch at high level ten times. Partner "B" will observe for the two criteria: feet off the floor and arms extended above the head. Partners will give you "thumbs up," one point if you meet both criteria. An extra point will be given if you remember to pull the ball in to your body after the catch. Switch after ten trials.

The height of the toss is important for a good catch; remember, five to ten feet above your head.

3.0   Toss the ball high in the air, and catch it at the last moment before it touches the ground. This is catching at low level.

Bend your knees so you are close to the ground when you catch.

Don't forget to watch the ball until it touches your hands.

T   Now, what must happen to your hands? Do you still want your thumbs together/thumbs in? No, now you need your little fingers together. Continue your practice of catching at low level, catching with fingers together.

CUE: Pinkies together/thumbs apart

Remember to pull the ball into the body for the completion of the catch just as when catching at high level.

C   I will time you for thirty seconds. Toss, then catch at low level. Try to complete the thirty seconds with no mistakes. Ready? Begin.

4.0   Stand ten to twelve feet from the wall. Throw the ball to the wall so it rebounds directly back to you. Catch it at medium level after one bounce.

Watch the ball until it touches your hands.

The "reach and pull" is the same: Reach for the ball, then pull the ball into the body for completion of the catch.

T   Throw the ball to the wall so it will rebound at a high level. Catch the ball as it rebounds from the wall while it is still high in the air.

Remember, feet off the floor, reach for the ball.

Stretch arms upward, not forward for the catch.

T   As I observe you catching, some of you are throwing the ball too hard; it is going back over your head. Practice your throwing for a few minutes concentrating on using just enough force to bring the ball back to you.

C   Practice until you can catch the ball five times without a mistake.

T   That looks much better. Now return to your practice of catching at high level after the throw to the wall.

S - t - r - e - t - c - h.

Feet off the floor.

What is needed for completion of the catch? Right, pull in the ball.

T   Now toss the ball gently to the wall, and catch it at low level after the rebound.

156

Adjust your force for a low-level rebound from the wall.

> *Provide individual or class cues as needed, based on observation.*

  Reach forward for the catch; don't wait for it to come to you.

  Pull it in; you may actually curl around the ball as you complete the catch.

T Take a giant step forward so your distance from the wall is less; now try your catches at low level.

C Use the next ten tosses for an evaluation. How many can you catch at low level?

 Self-Evaluation
We have only two to three minutes of class time left for practice. You may choose to catch at high level in self-space, low level in self-space, high or low level against the wall, or just toss and catch for accuracy in self-space. Compare your accuracy, the number caught in ten tries, to your earlier practice scores. Ready? Begin.

Closure:

What is the focus of our lesson today?

What two criteria are needed for best catching at high level?

Show me the hand position for catching at high level. At low level. What is the cue?

Why should you always pull in the ball for completion of the catch?

Why do you need to be able to catch at all three levels?

Alternate Closure:

Whew! You learned a lot today. Let's review some of the critical cues of our catching at different levels. When I say the word, give me the matching cue for high level catches:

arms	extended, reach
hands	thumbs together, thumbs in
feet	off the floor
completion of catch	pull to the body

for low level catches:

arms	extended, reach
hands	pinks together, thumbs apart
completion of catch	pull to the body

I believe you are ready for your written test. Readiness for the skills evaluation may take a bit longer.

Reflection:

Do the children extend arms high above the head for the catch at high level?

Do they catch with hands in proper position at high and low levels?

Do they reach for the ball rather than waiting for it to come to them?

Do they pull the ball into the body after initial contact at both high and low levels?

Lesson 3

Focus: Catching

Subfocus: Spatial awareness, stretching action

Objectives: At the end of this lesson the children will have learned to:
1. stretch arms forward and to the sides to catch the ball at different places around the body.
2. catch a ball with one hand.

                 REVIEW CUES: Reach and pull
                                  Watch the ball

**Materials/
Equipment:** Drum
Different types and sizes of balls: playground, plastic, nerf,
    tennis balls, 3-1/2-inch playground balls, rubber softballs, beanbags
Hoops (boxes, crates) to hold balls

**Organization/
Management:** Children scattered throughout general space with sufficient space to work safely
Established protocol for response to signal

Introduction:

In our last lesson we added the concept of catching at different levels to your study of throwing and catching. Today we will review the skills of accuracy in self-space and catching at high and low levels. Then we will add the challenge of catching the ball at different places around the body and catching with one hand. In a game situation the ball will not always come directly to you; neither will you always be able to make a safe two-hand catch.

    The first thing that will be different today is the type of balls used for catching. In our previous lessons you practiced with 8-1/2-inch playground, plastic, and nerf balls. When you came in the gym today, you noticed different types and sizes of balls. During your two to three minutes of warm-up, you may want to explore tossing and catching with different types of balls. Remember to return the ball to the hoop (box, crate) when you switch balls; this prevents someone possibly stepping on a ball.

Teacher Observation:

    Do the children reach for the ball rather than waiting for it to come to them?

    Do they focus their eyes on the ball until contact is made?

    Are they beginning to pull the ball to the body to complete the catch?

Content Development:

1.0   Select the type of ball you used last time. In self-space, practice tossing and catching the ball for accuracy (practice), then thirty seconds for self-testing of skill. Catch without moving from self-space or letting the ball bounce. Ready? Begin. How many improved your scores?

T   Toss and catch at high level ten times. Compare self-scores.

Reach for the ball.

Jump in the air for a really high catch.

T   Toss and catch at low level ten times. Compare self-score.

Don't forget, pull in the ball to complete the catch.

 Teacher Checklist
Observation of critical elements:
    Arms extended for catch
    Thumbs in (high), thumbs out (low)
    Reach and pull

T   (*Repeat the tasks with different types of balls.*) I will not be observing you for evaluation with the different types and sizes; that would not be fair on your first day with those balls.

You may need to toss some of the smaller balls with one hand, but for now catch with two hands.

C   Choose the type of ball that you think is best for your throwing and catching. Test yourself with ten catches at each level—mid, high, low. Now switch for the ball that you think is probably the most difficult for you. Test yourself again with ten catches at each level.

2.0   Select the ball you are most comfortable with. You may change to a different type at any time throughout the lesson. You have practiced catching at different heights; now you are going to practice catching the ball or beanbag at different places around your body. Explore tossing the ball or beanbag higher than your head and catching it at different places such as in front, to the sides, and behind you. In how many different places can you catch?

T   Sometimes you may need to twist, curl, or stretch to catch without moving from your self-space. Explore twisting, curling, and stretching as you toss and catch.

Remember to pull the ball toward your body to complete the catch. This not only protects the ball but will also help absorb the force when balls are thrown really hard.

T   Toss the ball in front of you so you must stretch to catch.

T   Toss the ball forward to the point you are almost off balance.

Remember to keep one foot firmly planted in self-space; pretend your foot is glued to that spot.

T   As I observe you tossing and stretching forward to catch, I notice some of you are having difficulty with the toss. Let's work on that for a moment. You have been concentrating on tossing the ball upward above your head for the self-space catch; now you need to toss the ball forward so it will be in front of you for the catch. Continue the practice of your forward toss—forward and upward.

T   Practice tossing the ball forward just beyond your reach so you must really stretch for the catch.

T   Toss the ball so you must stretch to your right to catch.

3.0   Purposely toss the ball "just beyond your extended reach." What happens when you try to catch? You will reach with one hand. This is a skill needed for many game situations. Toss the ball "beyond reach" to your right and catch with your right hand only.

Keep your left foot planted in self-space, as if on a softball base.

T   Toss to the left and catch with your left hand only . . . s-t-r-e-t-c-h.

Beanbags may be easier when first practicing these skills.

Don't forget, all catches should be pulled into the body for completion of the action.

4.0   Just as the balls will not all come to the same position for the catch, neither will they all arrive at the same height. Vary the height at which you catch so that sometimes you stretch in front high, sometimes in front low. Catch with two hands; catch with one hand only.

Always, reach for the ball—extend those arms.

Stretch high to the right, low to the left.

T   Have you used all the different types of balls and the beanbags? Try each type.

T   When combining catching at different positions and heights, you may sometimes need to twist or curl to catch. Toss several and twist or curl to catch.

T   Which of all the tasks you have practiced today is your favorite? Select the ball or beanbag you need for the task. Then think which task was the biggest challenge for you. Do you need a different ball for this one? Show both tasks to a friend. He or she may applaud your favorite and offer suggestions to assist you in mastering the difficult one. I will circulate among you to see them.

C   Have a friend watch you catch in self-space at medium level, high level, and low level. You will receive one point for each of the following:

Watching the ball
Reaching/extending arms for the catch
Pulling the ball to the body

Five bonus points can be earned for each catch you do that shows your friend that you can stretch to catch at different places around your body, for example, in front, to the left, to the right.

Closure:

What was the focus of our lesson today?

Why do you think we began class by repeating the self-space toss and catch from our earlier work?

What new skills did we add today?

Why is it important to be able to catch the ball in different positions around the body?

Why do you need to be able to catch with one hand?

Reflection:

Do the children reach for the ball when catching above the head, in front, and to the sides?

Do they pull the ball close to the body after they catch?

Can the children toss the ball so they have to stretch from a "fixed base" to catch it?

Is the class ready to throw and catch while traveling? Do certain elements of the skill need reteaching or more practice?

Lesson 4

Focus: Throwing and catching

Subfocus: Spatial awareness, traveling, levels

Objective: At the end of this lesson the children will have learned to:
catch a ball while moving in general space.

> **REVIEW CUES:** Open spaces (Look for the open spaces before you throw)
> Heads up (Keep your head up while traveling to avoid collisions
> with others)
> Reach and pull (Extend your arms for the catch, then pull the ball
> to the body before you continue your travel)

**Materials/
Equipment:**   Drum
Same as previous lesson (different types and sizes of balls)

**Organization/
Management:**   Spatial awareness while moving is critical to safety in this lesson

Introduction:

Today we introduce the skill you've been waiting for—throwing and catching while traveling. Very few games are played with no movement!

Content Development:

1.0   We have covered a tremendous number of critical cues in our practice of tossing and catching to self. Warm up today by practicing these skills (*post tasks on wall charts at several locations*):

Toss and catch for accuracy in self-space
Catch at high level and at low level
Catch at different positions around your body
Catch while stretched to the front, to the left, and to the right
Catch with one hand

T   Practice with each type and size of ball.

Use this practice time for class and individual observation, providing assistance to individual children as needed.

Teacher Observation:

> Do the children reach for the ball with arms extended?
>
> Do they pull the ball to the body after contact? Can they toss vertically or at an angle as needed for the catch?
>
> Do they extend arms in the direction needed (front, side, upward)?

A positive response to these questions for the majority of the class indicates the class is ready to progress to toss/catch and travel. Do not add traveling until the children have control of bodies and balls catching in self-space.

2.0 Toss the ball so you must travel to catch it. This is similar to the story of the hare playing tennis. You begin at point A, throw the ball, then run to point B to catch the ball before it bounces. (*Skills will regress to precontrol level when first practicing; monitor for safety. Allow three to four minutes for exploration.*)

 Be sure you have sufficient space to travel and not collide with anyone else.

T Adjust the distance of your throw so you need to travel only a short distance. Continue to toss and travel and catch at this shorter distance.

Watch the ball until it touches your hands.

T When you can throw and catch five times with no mistakes, increase the distance of your throw.

Remember "open spaces." They are critical now! Look for an open space before you begin the throw.

T Not bad. You are catching as you travel. However, many of us are using the cradle catch—ball against the body. Continue your practice, reaching for the ball when you catch rather than letting it drop into your arms.

C For the next two minutes continue to practice your "throw and go." I will observe for accuracy catching and extending arms to reach for the ball. Ready? Begin.

T As you increase the distance of your throws and travels, I am getting a bit concerned about spatial awareness and potential collisions. As you continue your practice, stop after each catch, look for an open space, then throw again.

3.0 Stand approximately ten to twelve feet from the wall. Throw the ball to the wall so it will not rebound directly back to where you are standing. You will have to move to catch the ball.

Watch the ball until it is secure in your hands.

T Throw the ball so you will have to move forward for the catch.

Remember, extend your arms for the catch.

T Throw the ball so it will rebound to the right or to the left. Now you must move to the side plus extend arms to the side.

Don't forget to pull the ball into your body after the catch.

C See if you can throw and catch against the wall ten times. Remember, you must move from self-space for the throw to count.

4.0   Now return to your "throw and go" in general space. Let's add levels to our practice. Throw, travel, and catch the ball at high level.

> Tell your neighbor the two criteria for high level: arms extended above your head, feet off the floor. Where are your thumbs? Together!

T   Don't throw the ball very far when you first begin practicing this skill. Concentrate on catching at high level. (*Continue to practice the "throw and go" at high level, concentrating on a single cue for each practice segment, for example, "This time I will observe for arms extended upward."*)

> When you first worked on jumping and landing, we talked about the importance of quiet landings—bending the knees to absorb the force. That is very important with the skill of traveling and catching at high level.

T   Throw, travel, and catch at low level.

> Catch the ball with weight balanced over your feet, not with your knees on the ground (a favorite way to catch).

T   Advanced: If you should lose your balance, tuck the ball close to your body, then curl and do a side roll (if taught outdoors on a grassy field). This is a favorite of skilled receivers in football; you will also see it at times in softball and baseball games.

T   We have only a few minutes of class time left. Practice your "throw and go" either at medium level for accuracy, at high level, or at low level. You may choose to practice in general space or against the wall.

> **Remember, open spaces!**

> Reach and pull.

This lesson is crucial for determining the direction of the theme. If your observation and the answers to the reflection questions are negative, do not continue with increasingly complex tasks of traveling. Reteach and provide more practice, teaching more difficult tasks at a later time when the class is ready.

Closure:

What new skill did we add today?

Did you enjoy traveling as you throw and catch?

What was the most difficult part of traveling and catching for you?

Can you tell me a game or sport that uses catching at high level on the move? Low level?

Why is the arm extension so important for this skill?

Reflection:

Can the children practice "throw and go" safely, that is, with no collisions?

Can the children catch the ball while moving in general space?

Do they extend their arms for the catch?

Can they catch at high and low levels, or do they need more practice on the basic "throw and go"?

Lesson 5

Focus: Throwing and catching

Subfocus: Partner relationships, body shapes

Objectives: At the end of this lesson the children will have learned to:
1. catch a ball thrown by a partner.
2. extend arms toward the ball thrown by a partner (to front, upward, to the sides).

                 REVIEW CUE: Reach and pull

**Materials/
Equipment:**   Drum
Variety of types and sizes of balls: plastic, nerf, rubber softballs,
3-1/2-inch playground, 8-1/2-inch playground, tennis balls

**Organization/
Management:**   Partners face each other across a distance of ten feet

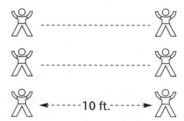

Introduction:

Thus far in our work on throwing and catching, we have concentrated on catching—tossing the ball to self and catching in self-space and while traveling. You have concentrated on accuracy at medium, high, and low levels. Today we are going to add a partner.

    Quickly sit beside a partner with whom you can work well. You will not need the partner for the first few review tasks, but selecting one now will save time during the lesson.

Content Development:

1.0   Let's begin our work today with a review of our basic catching skill. Select the ball you are going to use for your self-space practice. Toss and catch for accuracy while I observe for extended arms reaching for a ball and pulling it into the body to complete the catch.

Teacher Observation:

     Do the children reach for the ball with arms extended?

     Do they pull the ball to the body after contact?

T   You have been practicing your catch at high level, concentrating on arms extended above your head and feet off the floor. Today, let's focus for a few minutes on the body shape needed for a good catch at high level. What is it? Right, a narrow shape. Stretch upward for the catch. Ready? Begin.

   Remember to time your jump to catch the ball before it drops too low.

T   We have talked about pulling the ball into the body for completion of the catch. Exaggerate that movement by curling your body around the ball, like basketball players do. Continue your practice with a narrow/stretched shape for catching and a curled shape for completion of the catch.

T   Toss and catch at low level, just moments before the ball would touch the floor.

   Reach your arms toward the ball, then pull it in, curling your body over the ball.

C   When you are ready, test yourself on each skill with ten trials. Mentally record your score.

T   Take a minute to practice your toss and catch with travel. You may choose to throw in general space or against the wall.

   Remember to look for open spaces before you throw.

C   Test yourself with ten throws. Are you getting better at this one?

2.0   Stand facing your partner at a distance of ten to twelve feet. (You will need only one ball for each set of partners.) Throw the ball so your partner can successfully catch. The best level for this catching is medium, or chest high.

   Reach forward for the ball, catching with hands only.

   Throw with enough force for the ball to travel to your partner, but not so hard that he or she cannot catch it. Aim for your partner's hands, chest high.

T   When you and your partner can successfully throw and catch ten times, each of you take a giant step backward. Begin again to throw and catch.

   The key to the catch is after the throw; be very accurate.

C   Each time you are successful at catching ten throws, increase your distance with a giant step backward. Continue until you discover the maximum distance that permits you to keep your accuracy.

   When you make a mistake (failing to catch or moving from self-space), reduce your distance with a giant step closer together. Begin again to throw and catch.

C   Select the maximum distance that you think will still permit accuracy of 80 percent or above. At that distance, aim for twenty-five successful throws and catches. Judge your distance by the number of "giant steps" between you and your partner.

3.0   Return to the original distance of ten to twelve feet between partners. Throw the ball three to four feet above your partner's head so he or she must catch at high level, with feet off the floor, hands above head.

   Thrower: The throw is crucial to receiving at high level. Remember, aim three to four feet above your partner's head. Two types of throws work well for this: use an overhand throwing action for a direct pathway to the high level, or use a two-hand arching (rainbow) throw that begins to descend as it reaches your partner.

   Receiver: Time your jump so you are in the air when the ball is above your head.

Remember, stretch upward with a narrow shape, reach for the ball, then pull it into the body to complete the catch.

This is the interception in basketball and football, the high catch in baseball, the rebound in basketball. **Reach and pull.**

C   Partner "A" will be the receiver. Partner "B" will throw ten times to high level. Partner "A" will attempt to catch ten times at high level; mentally record your score. Partner "B" then becomes the receiver; repeat ten throws.

4.0   Partner "A," assume a catcher's position—low level, weight balanced over feet. Partner "B" will now throw so partner "A" can catch without moving from that position. Partner "B," stand ten to twelve feet from partner "A." After ten trials, switch thrower and receiver positions.

Use an underhand throwing action. The true focus of this task is on the person throwing the ball.

T   Now try an overhand throwing action.

T   Catcher, place your hands where you want the ball to come. Partner with the throw, test your accuracy by throwing so that the catcher does not have to move hands to receive the catch.

Catcher, you may place your hands in front, to the left, or to the right.

Thrower, adjust the force of the throw so your partner will be successful.

Catcher, remember to absorb the force of the throw by pulling the ball toward the body after contact with the hands.

"Strike Out"
If you can throw three times so your partner does not have to move hands to catch the ball, give yourself credit for a strike. However, remember that four balls (catcher moves hands to receive) equal a walk.

5.0   (Sufficient space for safety is crucial for this task.) Let's combine throwing for accuracy with extensions to the side for the receiver. Partner "A," stand in self-space as if positioned on the base in a softball or baseball game. Partner "B," throw the ball to your partner, purposely throwing to the side so the receiver must stretch to catch the ball.

Receiver, keep one foot secure in self-space as if on the "base," and extend your arms to the side to catch the ball.

Thrower, when first practicing this skill, tell the receiver which side you are going to throw to.

Remember the one-hand catch you practiced earlier. Use that one-hand catch to extend even farther to the side to catch the ball.

Don't forget to reach and pull. Pulling in is even more important when catching with one hand.

C   Around the edge of our work area are five stations for additional practice of the skills you worked on today. You and your partner will get a chance to practice throwing and catching for accuracy at medium level, high level, and low level at each of the stations:

Station 1: nerf balls
Station 2: rubber softballs
Station 3: tennis balls
Station 4: 8-1/2-inch playground balls
Station 5: variety of odd sizes and types of balls

Your task is this: Choose a station. Practice for two to three minutes with your partner, throwing and catching at medium level. Then do a self-test of ten trials. Repeat for high level and low level. You may then choose to move to another station or to stay there for additional practice.

If you are having difficulty with the tasks today, you may wish to practice at Station 4 until you are confident with those skills.

Remember the maximum distance for accuracy you found earlier with your partner. You may need to decrease that distance for different types of balls.

Some classes may need a chart at each station with tasks listed. Some classes may need to be divided into groups and rotated on signal until they are ready for independent rotation.

Closure:

During the first part of our lesson today, we talked about the body shape needed for receiving a pass at high level. What was that shape?

After pulling a ball in for the completion of the catch, what shape should the body make?

Show me the direction of your arm extension when receiving a pass at medium level from a partner. At high level.

Describe a game situation when catching at high level is used. Low level.

Reflection:

Do the children extend their arms for the catch when a partner is added?

Do they "pull in" the ball and then curl around it?

Do the children throw with enough accuracy for the receivers to practice catching?

Do they need a lesson on throwing for accuracy at different levels?

Lesson 6

Focus: Throwing and catching

Subfocus: Spatial awareness, partner relationships, traveling

Objectives: At the end of this lesson the children will have learned to:
1. catch a ball thrown by a partner while traveling.
2. catch a ball while others are trying to intercept the pass.

CUES: Heads up (Keep your head up to avoid collisions with others when traveling and throwing or catching)

Extend (Extend your arms for the catch to give you the added "inch" and to avoid interception by the defense)

**Materials/
Equipment:** Drum
Same as previous lesson (different types and sizes of balls)
Hoops (one for each two students)

**Organization/
Management:** Established protocol for selection of partners
Hoops scattered in general space for "Receivers and Interceptors"

Introduction:

In our study of throwing and catching, you have practiced tossing and catching in self-space and while traveling; you have worked with a partner for accuracy of throwing and catching. Today we combine throwing and catching with partners and traveling. Our work is getting closer to the dynamic game situation.

Content Development:

1.0 Practice and review catching skills in self-space or at a wall:

Toss and catch for accuracy
Catch at high level
Catch at low level
Extend to the sides for the catch

Practice and review throwing and catching skills with a partner

Toss and catch for accuracy
Catch at high level
Catch at low level
Catch with extensions to the sides

 Teacher Checklist
Observation of critical cues:
Extensions
Reach and pull

168

T   Practice and review individual "throw and go" in general space, concentrating on the accuracy of your catches.

Remember to look for the open spaces before you begin to move.

T   Select a partner with traveling and catching skills similar to your skills. On signal, both of you will begin to move in general space, throwing and catching.

Remember, the midlevel catch is best for accuracy; aim your throw at chest level for your partner's catches.

Adjust the speed of your travel to your catching abilities; don't move so fast you will not be able to catch.

C   I will time you for one minute. See if you and your partner can throw and catch while moving with few mistakes.

If you caught every pass, you might not be challenging yourself enough. Increase the distance of your throw or the speed of your travel.

Remember, heads up!

2.0   One other type of receiving we have not yet practiced is used often in games. It involves a twisted body shape when receiving the pass—catching over the shoulder. Stand beside your partner, both facing the same direction. (*For safety, have all children move in the same direction across the field or gymnasium.*) Partner "A," holding the ball, gives a verbal signal for partner "B" to travel. Partner "B" runs away from the beginning point. When the runner is about ten to twelve feet away, partner "A" calls "now" and throws the ball. Partner "B," the receiver, twists the upper trunk to catch the ball over the shoulder. After five trials, switch receiver and thrower. This throw and catch permits you to catch and continue moving.

Receiver, turn only your upper trunk; keep your feet in the direction of the run. Look over your shoulder to track the throw.

Thrower, tell the receiver which shoulder you will throw over (right or left) before travel begins. Throw the ball as directly as possible to the target—your partner's hands.

Just for fun, you may want to make up a new "signal" for your partner to twist.

 What body shape and action is used for this skill? You have learned three body shapes for receiving. Watch the sports section of the newspaper this week for a picture of receivers catching the ball with a twisted, narrow, or curled shape, or receivers catching at high and low levels. We will make a display of the different shapes and levels.

"Receivers and Interceptors"
Select a partner whose throwing and catching skills are about the same as your skills; sit beside that partner. Scattered throughout general space are hoops. Partner "A," stand inside a hoop; all the "A" persons are a team. You are going to be throwing and catching the ball. You must keep both feet inside the hoop, but you can jump upward to catch at high level and extend your arms to the sides for catching.

"B" partners, you are the interceptors. You will be traveling! You are trying to intercept the ball as the other team throws to teammates in hoops. You cannot touch an opponent or enter their hoops. If you do intercept a pass, give the ball to the person inside the hoop nearest you (Figure 27).

I will time you for two minutes, then the interceptors and the receivers will switch places. Ready? Begin.

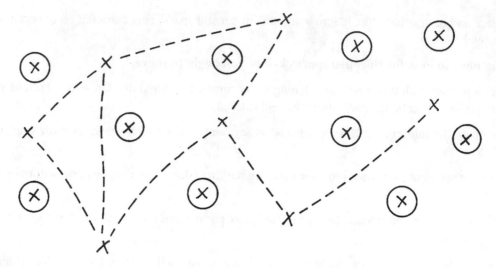

Figure 27   Receivers and Interceptors

Throwers, remember, you can throw the ball to high, medium, or low levels. Your objective is to complete the two minutes of throwing and catching with no interceptions. Look for "open persons."

Interceptors, try to catch the ball in flight, not just deflect it. You receive a point only if you catch the ball.

T   Let's try the game with two balls.

T   Let's try with different types of balls.

Closure:

What happens to skill levels when we add partners plus travel?

What happens to your skills when you play in a gamelike situation?

Why do you think skills decrease?

Reflection:

What skills do I need to reteach?

Is this class ready for a higher level of throwing and catching?

⊞ Throwing and Catching Evaluation

Focus: Throwing and catching

Subfocus: Levels, traveling, partner relationships

Objective: At the end of this lesson the children will have learned to:
evaluate their catching skills relative to accuracy and levels.

**Materials/
Equipment:**   Sizes and types of balls used throughout previous lessons
Paper, pencils
Established protocol for picking up and putting away materials

We began our study of throwing and catching by practicing tossing and catching in self-space for accuracy. You learned to catch at different levels and in various locations around your body. You were introduced to the skill of throwing and catching while traveling, a challenge for the best of us. With partners, you practiced throwing and catching at varying distances and high and low levels. We applied the skills of throwing and catching in a variety of gamelike situations.

Today you will do a self-evaluation of your throwing and catching skills, then an evaluation of throwing and catching with a partner.

Early in the theme you practiced tossing and catching without moving from self-space. That is the first task on the evaluation sheet. I will time you for sixty seconds. If you do not move from self-space or the ball does not touch the floor, place a check in the 100-percent category. If you make only one mistake, write 90 percent in the second column; two mistakes mean a check in the 80-percent column. If you make more than two mistakes, check the last column on the right, below 80 percent. You will have one to two minutes of practice before we test each skill. Ready? Begin your practice. (*Repeat for each skill to be tested.*)

Here are three examples of evaluations for throwing and catching with a partner. The evaluation you use will depend on students' level of skill or mastery. The first example (Figure 28, p. 172) is the most basic.

The second assessment example (Figure 29, p. 173) adds high and low level catches with a partner. This test is usually reserved for upper elementary students.

The third assessment example (Figure 30, p. 174) is a partner check for distance and accuracy, with choices for types of balls and distances. Children enjoy this evaluation as a challenge activity after the lesson on partner relationships.

Lesson 7 and the final project are for those classes that were successful combining throwing, catching, and traveling. They may be used when the theme is revisited.

Name ———————————————— Homeroom ————————————————

Partner ———————————————— Date ————————————————

Self and Partner Evaluation of Throwing and Catching Skills

Category I: Self-space	100% accuracy	80%	below 80%
Toss and catch for accuracy (one minute)			
High level catch — feet off the floor — arms extended			
Low level catch			

Category II: Distance zones with partner

Throw and catch with partner distance zone 1			
Throw and catch with partner zone 2 or 3 (circle chosen)			

Category III: OPTIONAL—JUST FOR FUN

Throw and go		

What is your best skill?

What is your favorite skill?

WHAT IS THE CUE FOR A PROPER CATCH?

Figure 28 Throwing and Catching Evaluation Form

Name ——————————————————— Homeroom ———————————————

Partner ————————————————— Date —————————————————

Self and Partner Evaluation of Throwing and Catching Skills

Category I: Self-space	100% accuracy	80%	below 80%
Toss and catch for accuracy (one minute)			
High level catch feet off the floor arms extended			
Low level catch			

Category II: Partner skills			
Throw and catch with partner zone 1, zone 2			
High level catch score for receiver			
Low level catch score for thrower			

Comments about Throwing and Catching Skills

What do you feel best about?

What would you like me to watch?

Figure 29   Throwing and Catching Evaluation with High and Low Catches

Name _____ Homeroom _____

Partner _____ Date _____

Partner Evaluation of Throwing and Catching Skills

Type of Ball	Distance	Score/10
	Zone 1 10–12 feet	
	Zone 2 15 feet	

The best type of ball for accuracy with my partner was:

The best level for accuracy in catching is: high, medium, low (circle one).

The catcher in a baseball game receives the ball at what level?

       high, medium, low (circle one)

A pass intercepted in a football game is usually at what level?

       high, medium, low (circle one)

A new student named Murgatroid has just arrived at our school. What would you tell Murgie about catching so he will be successful?

On the back of this page draw a picture of yourself catching a ball. (Grade 3)

Figure 30 Partner Evaluation for Distance and Accuracy

Lesson 7

Focus: Throwing and catching

Subfocus: Spatial awareness, traveling, pathways

Objective: At the end of this lesson the children will have learned to:
travel in straight, curved, and zigzag pathways while throwing and catching.

> **CUES:** Heads up (Keep your head up to avoid collisions as you throw or catch and travel)
>
> Reach and pull (Extend your arms for the catch, then complete the catch by pulling the ball to your body)

**Materials/
Equipment:**   Different types and sizes of balls

**Organization/
Management:**   Partners, side-by-side 

Introduction:

Earlier in our theme of throwing and catching, we introduced the skill of throwing and catching while traveling. You practiced "throw and go" alone and with a partner. You quickly discovered that the combination of traveling and catching takes extended practice.

When you were practicing traveling and catching, you concentrated on catching with little thought to the way you traveled or the pathway created as you moved. Today we will begin to focus on the pathway of the travel.

Content Development:

1.0   Select the ball you need for review of your skill of traveling and catching with the "throw and go" situation we did several lessons earlier. Be sure you have an open space, then begin your travel.

Start with a short distance and a not-so-fast speed.

T   When you feel confident with your skill, increase the distance of your throw.

Teacher Observation:

    Are the children traveling at a safe speed, avoiding collisions?

    Do they extend their arms for the catch, followed by pulling the ball to the body?

Don't forget to reach and pull.

T   Catch at different levels.

2.0   Stand beside your partner. Partner "A" is the thrower; partner "B" is the receiver. Partner "A," give the verbal signal "go"; partner "B," travel in a straight pathway from the starting point beside your partner. Stop, turn, receive the pass. Partner "A," travel quickly to the space beside your partner (model). Repeat, switching thrower and receiver.

For safety, we will all travel in the same direction across the playground.

T   Receive the pass at high level.

T   This time travel in a curved pathway before you receive the pass.

T   Practice traveling to the left and to the right.

Did you complete the pass by pulling in the ball?

T   Begin your travel in a straight pathway to your right, then quickly change and travel to your left creating a zigzag pathway. Turn to face your partner for the catch.

Don't make the pathways too complex; concentrate on being in position to receive the pass.

T   Travel the zigzag pathway, then catch at low level.

T   Pretend you are evading an opponent. Travel a combination of pathways, turn and receive the pass.

T   Change to a different type of ball and repeat the series of tasks.

"100 on the Go"
Select the ball you think is best for you and your partner when traveling, throwing, and catching. We are going to do a version of "100 points on the go." You and your partner will be working together as a team; you will have a collective score. On signal, begin traveling in general space, throwing and catching with your partner. You may use any pathways you wish; you may catch at the levels you choose.

You have 100 points as a team. Your objective is to complete the activity with your 100 points. If the ball touches the ground, subtract 10 points. If you have a collision with someone, subtract 25 points. Let's have a practice before we begin. Ready? Travel. (*Allow two to three minutes of activity.*) Stop and rest.

How many kept a perfect score? An almost perfect score? A not-so-perfect score?

(*Repeat the activity.*) How many improved your score? Did you make any adjustments to better your activity score, or were you just lucky? What adjustments did you make?

Closure:

What was the focus of our lesson today?

Name the three pathways.

Compare your accuracy while traveling, throwing, and catching alone versus with a partner. What makes the difference?

Reflection:

Can the children consciously travel different pathways while throwing and catching?

Does the receiver reach for the ball and pull it to the body?

Are they throwing with accuracy to the receiver, or do we need lessons with a focus on throwing to stationary and moving targets?

Throwing and Catching, Final Project

Focus: Throwing and catching

Objectives: At the end of this lesson the children will have learned to:
               1. design a strategy of throwing and catching while traveling.
               2. complete the throwing/catching sequence of the strategy.

Today we will begin a project that combines all the skills we have studied in our theme of throwing and catching. You will be throwing, catching, and traveling with a partner. You will be making decisions concerning pathways, levels, and body shapes. You will design a strategy, or play, to move the ball the length of the playing field.

Quickly select a partner. Sit together so you can see the chalkboard (flipchart). We will design a play together before you create one. What is our objective? Right, to move the ball the length of the field. You will do that by combining traveling and passing. (Diagram on the board as you discuss.)

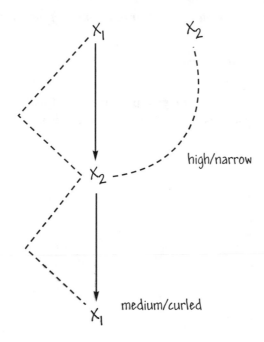

Stand beside your partner.

    X-1 has the ball
    X-2 travels in a chosen pathway
        X-1 throws the ball
        What level, body shape for the receiver?
            X-1 runs a pathway
            X-2 throws the ball
            What level, body shape for the receiver?

Continue the combination of pathways and passes until you have moved the length of the field. I have provided paper and pencil for each set of partners. On the paper, diagram your strategy of pathways and passes. The following codes will help you:

X-1 = Susan
X-2 = Mary
_ _ _ _ = pathway
_____ = pass

Be sure to indicate the level of the catch and the body shape for receiving. I will circulate to assist you.

As you design your strategy, practice the pathways of travel and levels of catches. Some of you will work best by practicing as you go; others will find it best to complete the written work, then practice.

When your design is complete, practice with your partner until you run the play three times with no mistakes.

When you are ready I will observe your strategy. As I observe, I will look for the following:

Straight, curved, and zigzag pathways
Levels of catching
Accuracy of catches
Body shapes to match levels of receiving

These points of observation become the criteria for assessment of the strategy:

Accuracy of catches
Completion of strategy as diagrammed

C   If you would like to do so, after I observe your play in action, I will assign a defense so you can really see how good your strategy is. (Figure 31 shows one pair's strategy.)

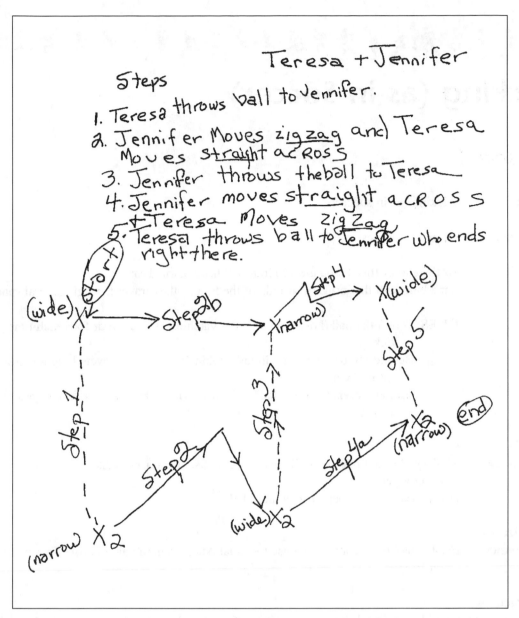

Teresa + Jennifer

Steps

1. Teresa throws ball to Jennifer.
2. Jennifer Moves zig zag and Teresa Moves straight across
3. Jennifer throws the ball to Teresa
4. Jennifer moves straight across + Teresa Moves Zig Zag
5. Teresa throws ball to Jennifer who ends right there.

Figure 31   Example of a Child-Designed Strategy for Throwing and Catching

179

Kicking (as in Soccer)

Lesson 1

Focus: Kicking (as in soccer)

Subfocus: Spatial awareness

Objective: At the end of this lesson the children will have learned to:
tap a ball with the inside or outside of the foot as they travel through general space.

                    CUES: Watch the ball (Focus on the ball, watching it touch your foot each time you kick)

                               Behind the ball (Contact directly behind the ball for travel along the ground, not in the air)

                               Tap, tap (Gently tap the ball so it stays within three to four feet of you at all times)

**Materials/
Equipment:**   Slightly deflated playground balls, soccer balls, and plastic balls
      (one per child)
Hoops scattered on perimeter to hold balls

**Organization/
Management:** Established protocol for response to signal (stand behind ball with one foot resting on ball)

Introduction:
Earlier in the year you learned to dribble playground balls and basketballs. In a later study, you will be introduced to the tap-dribble of a hockey stick and puck. Today we begin another type of dribble, the tap-dribble of a soccer ball.

    In this theme you will learn the correct technique for a soccer dribble, the skill of trapping, dribbling to avoid opponents, and kicking to a target. At a more advanced level, we will introduce the skill of punting as used by the goalie in the game of soccer.

Content Development:
1.0   Select a ball from a hoop. Find a self-space three to four feet from others and stand in ready position—one foot resting on the ball. On signal, begin traveling throughout general space, kicking the ball gently with the inside of your foot. Alternate kicks between your right and your left foot. This is a soccer dribble.

Turn your toes outward like duck feet as you dribble the ball along the ground.

The key is a gentle tap; this will keep the ball within "reach"—three to four feet in front of you.

T   Continue your tap-dribble, concentrating on keeping the ball within a short distance of you at all times.

Watch the ball until it touches your foot each time you kick.

2.0   Can you tap-dribble with the outside of your foot? Continue your practice of the soccer dribble, kicking with the outside as well as the inside of your feet.

Now your toes turn slightly inward for the tap-dribble.

Continue children's practice of the tap-dribble for several minutes, providing class and individual cues as needed.

C   Using the inside and outside, right and left foot, see if you can tap-dribble the ball without bumping into another person or going outside our large boundaries for one minute. Ready? Begin.

The key is a controlled tap, not a kick for distance.

Teacher Observation:

   Do the children gently tap the ball rather than kicking for distance?

   Is the ball traveling on the ground rather than in the air?

   If the answer to these questions is negative, continue the focus on the above tasks; if the answer is positive, proceed with new tasks.

T   Tap-dribble the ball as you travel in general space. Gradually increase your speed, but keep the ball within "reach" at all times.

You almost need two sets of eyes now: be aware of others, yet focus on the ball during the contact.

Remember "open spaces"; you need a clear path for the tap-dribble.

T   Continue your tap-dribble as you travel throughout general space. When you approach another person, tap the ball with the outside of your foot to pass to the side of them, then continue your dribbling.

Remember, a gentle tap.

C   Let's review for a minute the skills you have learned today: dribbling with alternate feet with the inside and the outside of each foot, and avoiding collisions of ball or body with others as you travel. This time as you travel, think of all those skills; move throughout general space dribbling as you go. Focus on one particular skill from today and execute it to perfection until you hear the signal to stop.

T   As I observed you tap-dribble, I saw you focusing on dribbling with either foot and keeping the ball within "reach." I did not see many of you dribbling with the outside of your foot. This time focus on tapping the ball with the outside of your foot to "pass" someone each time you meet another person or when you hear the drumbeat.

T   Choose the skill that you need to practice most: dribbling with the inside of the foot, alternating feet, dribbling with the outside of the foot. Practice that skill for the next few minutes. I will circulate to help you as needed.

Closure:

What new theme did we begin today?

This kicking skill is used in what sport?

Why is it important to keep the ball within "reach" as you travel?

What does "within reach" mean?

Reflection:

Can the children tap-dribble as they travel in general space?

Can they tap-dribble with either foot?

Do they demonstrate both ball and body control as they travel?

Children's Movement Vocabulary

A physical educator was introducing the tap-dribble of soccer by relating it to the sport of soccer. Trevor was frantically waving his arms, seeking teacher acknowledgment. When recognized, Trevor proceeded to explain the game of soccer. "I know all about soccer. This is what you need to play the game:

> a large backyard
> a ball about the size of a basketball
> a Dad to watch you play
> and a dog to chase the ball after you kick."

Welcome to children's soccer!

Lesson 2

Focus: Kicking (as in soccer)

Subfocus: Spatial awareness

Objective: At the end of this lesson the children will have learned to:
stop the ball with the foot, as in trapping.

               CUES: Watch the ball (Watch the ball as you tap and as you trap)
                        Trap (Trap the ball by placing your foot on top, slightly behind the ball)

**Materials/
Equipment:**   Slightly deflated playground balls, soccer balls, and plastic balls (one per child)
Hoops around perimeter to hold balls

**Organization/
Management:**   Established protocol for response to signal

Introduction:

During our last lesson you practiced dribbling the soccer ball as you traveled in general space. You did the tap-dribble with the inside of your foot, alternating right and left feet. You practiced tapping with the outside of your foot as if passing another person. In reality you practiced only half of the needed skill; being able to "stop" the ball properly is the second half of dribbling in soccer. Trapping goes with dribbling like catching goes with throwing. The focus of our lesson today will be on stopping the soccer ball—trapping.

In game situations you will need to trap the ball to "check" your speed, to change directions, to avoid collisions, and to receive passes. It is a very important part of soccer.

Content Development:

1.0   Begin your work today by traveling throughout general space, dribbling as you go. Alternate right and left feet as you tap-dribble. Don't forget to use the outside of your foot as well as the inside.

Teacher Observation:

     Do the children keep the ball within "reach" as they tap-dribble?

     Do they avoid collisions with others?

The tap-dribble looks good. You are remembering from the first lesson to watch the ball yet be aware of others.

 Teacher Checklist
Use this time for observation of critical elements of the tap-dribble from the first lesson:
    Gentle tap, keeping ball within "reach"
    Contact behind ball for travel along ground

2.0   Travel through general space tap-dribbling the ball as you go. When you wish to slow the forward motion of the ball, place your foot on top of the ball, slightly behind the ball. Slowing the travel or stopping the ball is called "trapping" in soccer. Continue your travel through general space with the soccer dribble, trapping the ball and then continuing your travel.

T   Use the trap as a momentary pause in your travel. Your foot will not actually rest on the ball but will touch on top as a way to slow the speed. Touch to slow, then travel.

Remember, place your foot slightly back of center, not on top of the ball.

T   Tap-dribble the ball in general space. Each time you hear the drum, quickly trap the ball, coming to a complete stop. (*Continue dribbling and trapping for two to three minutes to allow children practice time and to permit observation of skills.*)

Don't forget, your foot is slightly behind the ball. What will happen if you place your foot directly on top of the ball?

Balance over your support leg so you will be ready to move again quickly.

T   Tap-dribble the ball at a moderate speed, moving among others in general space. When you hear the drum, trap the ball within three seconds. I will give you a verbal count so you can check yourself.

T   Practice your three-second trapping with your left and your right foot. A skilled soccer player is equally good with either foot!

T   Increase the speed of your travel. Can you still stop the ball within three seconds of the signal?

Remember, keep the ball within "reach" for easier and quicker trapping on signal.

C   Let's test your trapping skills. Begin your tap-dribble through general space. On signal, trap the ball within three seconds. Your goal is to be completely stopped by the count of 1-2-3. How did you do?

T   Travel throughout general space. Each time you meet another person, trap the ball, pause for a moment, then continue your travel.

A quick, accurate trap is now critical to avoid a collision. **Remember, foot at an angle behind or in front of the ball, never on top.**

T   Pretend you are in a game situation. Dribble throughout general space, increase and decrease the speed, tap the ball with the inside and then the outside of your feet. Trap the ball frequently for practice.

T   Continue your practice and add a change of directions. Each time after you trap the ball, change the direction of your travel.

Remember, two sets of eyes: watch the ball; be aware of others.

"Individual Soccer"
I will time you for two minutes during which you will dribble in general space avoiding others and keeping the ball three to four feet from you. Each time you hear the drum, quickly trap the ball with one foot. Ready? Begin.

How many of you had no collisions? How many of you used both your right and your left foot? Good, that was our practice!

Give yourself 100 points. If you complete the next two minutes with no collisions and without losing the ball, you will keep your 100 points. A collision or a lost ball subtracts 10 points. Ready? Begin.

Increase the speed of your travel as you tap-dribble through general space. Just for fun, let's repeat the "Individual Soccer" and compare our scores with travel at moderate speed and faster speed. Do you think there will be a difference? (Repeat 100 points activity.)

Let's focus on our trapping. Give yourself 100 points. Begin traveling and dribbling. Each time you hear the drum, quickly trap the ball. I will count three seconds for you. If you have a collision or fail to trap the ball within three seconds, subtract 10 points. Ready? Begin.

You can quickly lose points this way; control is the key.

How many kept all 100 points? How many kept at least 80 points, no more than two mistakes?

That is our goal for any skill theme—80 percent or better.

Closure:

What skill did we add to our study today?

Why is it important to be able to stop the ball at will?

Tell the person beside you what stopping the ball with your foot is called.

Reflection:

Are the children now able to kick the ball so it travels along the ground, not in the air?

Do they use both the right foot and the left foot for the tap-dribble?

Are they beginning to use both the inside and the outside of the feet for the tap-dribble?

Can they stop the ball by trapping it with one foot?

Can they stop the ball on signal?

Do they trap with the foot at an angle on the ball, not directly on top?

Although soccer is rapidly becoming one of the most popular youth sports in the United States, with millions of youngsters ages seven to eleven involved, we must remember that not all children are involved in youth sports programs; not all have been taught the basic skills. As with all skills, do not move too quickly based on observations of a few highly skilled children in the class.

Lesson 3

Focus: Kicking (as in soccer)

Subfocus: Directions, pathways

Objectives: At the end of this lesson the children will have learned to:
1. tap-dribble the ball, changing directions to the right and to the left.
2. tap-dribble the ball in different pathways.

A Note About Cues: Although several cues are listed below, it is important to focus on only one cue at a time. When the children have mastered that cue, then focus on the next one.

CUES: Gentle taps
Inside/outside (Use the inside of your foot and the outside of your foot to tap the soccer ball left and right)
Heads up (Keep your head up to avoid collisions)
Hips over feet (Keep your body centered over your feet for good balance as you change directions)

This lesson plan is written with a combination of pathways and directions, as the two are so closely connected in the theme of kicking for soccer skills. Depending on the skill of the children and the length of class periods, the lesson plan may need to be broken down into two separate lessons, one with a focus on directions, another with a focus on pathways.

**Materials/
Equipment:** Slightly deflated playground balls, soccer balls, plastic balls
Marker cones (the more cones, the more difficult the task)

**Organization/
Management:** Established protocol for response to signal

Introduction:
In our earlier lessons on dribbling, you learned to tap-dribble with alternate feet, to "pass" with the outside of the foot, and to trap the ball for a momentary pause or for a complete stop. Today you will dribble the ball in different pathways and avoid stationary "opponents" (marker cones). These tasks will combine dribbling and trapping.

For your warm-up, select the ball you need and tap-dribble in general space. Practice alternating feet, tapping with the outside of your foot, and trapping the ball. Vary the speed of your travel as you are dribbling.

Content Development:

1.0   Tap-dribble in general space, concentrating on alternating contacts between your right and your left foot.

Remember to keep the ball within three or four feet of you.

T   Look for the "open spaces" as you tap-dribble. Try to travel to every open space in our work area before the signal is given to stop.

T   Pretend you need to go to the left or right of someone; tap the ball with the outside of your foot, then continue your tap-dribble.

T   Practice trapping by chanting to yourself, "Tap, tap, tap; tap, tap, tap; tap, tap, tap, *trap*." Continue the pattern as you practice the soccer dribble in general space.

Don't forget to practice with your left and your right foot.

 Teacher Checklist
Observation of critical cues:
    Successful trap with foot on top, slightly behind the ball
    Tap-dribble with ball within three to four feet

2.0   Tap-dribble the ball in general space. Each time you meet someone, quickly tap the ball with the outside of your right foot to avoid a collision; continue your dribble.

T   Repeat with a pass to the left.

T   This time when you meet someone, trap the ball and execute a one-quarter turn away from them; continue your dribble.

This trap is a pause to check your speed in order to change directions; it is done very quickly so you can continue your travel.

Maintain a balanced position over your support leg. You are traveling quickly, trapping, and trying to turn.

T   Purposely, travel quickly toward another person. Just before you would be "too close," trap and turn. Continue your dribble, looking not for an open space but for another person to dribble toward.

Remember, there should be no collisions of soccer balls or bodies.

C   Let's test your dribbling and trapping skills. On signal, begin dribbling through general space, purposely tap-dribbling toward others, trapping, and continuing the dribble. Your challenge is to never lose the soccer ball or bump another person.

3.0   As you catch your breath, let's review the three pathways. What are they? Dribble the ball in a straight pathway across the field. If you meet another person, trap the ball, wait for them to pass, then continue. Remember, straight pathways only.

T   Now travel in large curved pathways. Use a moderate speed for a smooth curve.

T   Zigzag quickly across the field as you tap-dribble the soccer ball. This one is almost natural if you alternate tapping with right and left feet.

T   Mentally map the pathways you will use to dribble, using as much space as you can. Will you curve, zigzag, then go straight, or will you zigzag, go straight, then curve? What will your design be? On signal, begin to travel your soccer pathways.

Make the pathways very clear. I should be able to identify the pathway by watching your tap-dribble.

4.0   (*Scatter marker cones throughout general space in no particular arrangement.*) The marker cones will be your "opponents." Your goal is to tap-dribble through general space without bumping into the cones with the soccer ball or your body. Ready? Begin.

Now you must watch for the cones, plus twenty-five other people and twenty-five soccer balls.

T   Purposely dodge the cones to the right then to the left, tapping with the outside of your foot as you pass the cone.

Remember, the ball should always be within "reach."

T   Now practice your trap and turn. Each time you approach a cone, trap the ball, turn, then continue your dribble.

T   For the last few minutes, combine the dodging skills you have learned to avoid bumping the cones or colliding with others. You may "pass" to the right or to the left with the inside or the outside of your feet. You may trap and turn. You may use different pathways. Focus quickly on continuing the dribble after you pass each cone.

"Keeping It Perfect: Zero, Zero"
Let's challenge your dribbling and trapping skills with the activity "Keeping It Perfect: Zero, Zero."
The object of the game is to still have a perfect score after two minutes of activity. On signal, begin to tap-dribble in general space at the speed you choose. When you hear the drum, trap the ball within the three-second count. (Taken from *Children Moving,* Chapter 26.)

You earn negative points if you:

Don't trap the ball within three seconds.
Bump into another person or the ball they are dribbling.
Bump into a marker cone.
Lose control of the ball you are dribbling.

(Two minutes of dribbling in general space. Two minutes of trap and turn. Two minutes of zigzag and curved pathways around cones.)

At the end of each two minutes, we will stop for a moment of rest to calculate scores. Remember, a perfect score is zero.

Closure:

Today we added pathways and stationary obstacles to our study of dribbling. Why do you need to be able to dribble in different pathways?

What ways did you learn to avoid the marker cones, your "opponents"?

What do you think would be the difference if the opponents were moving persons?

Reflection:

Can the children change directions without losing control of the balls they are dribbling?

Can they keep the soccer balls within "reach" when dribbling in different pathways?

Are they in control rather than being led by the ball? Can they trap at will? Can they move the ball where they want it to go?

Lesson 4

Focus: Kicking (as in soccer)

Subfocus: Force

Objective: At the end of this lesson the children will have learned to:
kick the ball along the ground with sufficient force and accuracy to send it ten to
    twelve feet to a target—goal or person.

                CUES: Behind the ball (Make contact directly behind the ball for travel along the
                      ground)
                  Under the ball (Make contact slightly under the ball for travel through the air)
                  Gentle taps/hard kicks (Gently tap the ball for the dribble; kick hard for the
                      goal)

**Materials/
Equipment:**   Slightly deflated playground balls, soccer balls
Marker cones, milk jugs

**Organization/
Management:**   Milk jugs scattered in general space as obstacles
Marker cones for goals (five to six feet apart) around outside boundaries
Established protocol for selection of partners

Introduction:
Today we add a key component to the game of soccer—kicking to a partner and kicking for the goal.
Thus far you have practiced the tap-dribble, keeping the ball within "reach" for control and easy trap-
ping. Today the ball will travel a greater distance; more force will be needed behind the kicking action.

    Before we begin our work with partners, practice the tap-dribble as you travel through general
space. Vary the speed of your travel—sometimes moderate, sometimes very fast, but always with control. Practice trapping with a pause, a stop, and a change in direction. As you practice, I will observe for
one thing only—control.

Teacher Observation:

    Does the ball travel along the ground?

    Do the children use both the left and the right feet for the tap-dribble?

    Can they trap with either foot?

Content Development:
1.0   Select a partner with whom you can work well. Position yourselves in open space ten to twelve
feet from each other. Practice kicking the ball with the inside of your foot to your partner. Receiving
partner, trap the ball and kick it back across the field.

The only difference between the tap-dribble and sending the ball to your partner is the amount of force;
you are still making contact with the inside of your foot.

T   As I observed your warm-up kicking, I noticed some of you are having difficulty sending the ball along the ground to your partner. Remember, contact should be directly behind the ball so it will travel along the ground. Continue to practice kicking to your partner, concentrating on the contact.

Watch the ball until your foot makes contact.

T   Practice kicking with your right foot and with your left. In game situations you will need to be skilled at passing with either foot.

Remember, contact is with the inside of your foot.

T   You and your partner will now begin moving in general space at a slow to moderate speed. After you tap-dribble three to four times, pass the ball to your partner.

You will need to "check" your speed slightly prior to the kick; do this with a slight trap of the ball.

Receiving partner, remember to trap the ball before you begin dribbling.

T   Continue your dribbling in general space at a distance of ten to twelve feet from your partner. When you hear the drum, pass the ball to your partner by kicking it along the ground.

T   Can you pass with the outside of your foot as well as the inside? Try this skill as you continue your practice of dribbling and passing.

T   Now for the really fun part. Kick the ball slightly ahead of your partner so he or she will not be waiting for the kick but will actually be receiving "on the move." This is another use of "open spaces," the space ahead of your partner; it is a skill that is very important in a game situation.

As you become more skilled and more familiar with a partner, you will adjust the force of the kick to their speed of travel. For now, kick the ball to the open space four to five feet ahead of them as they are moving.

Receivers, adjust the speed of your travel to receive the pass "on the move."

2.0   (*Place sets of marker cones five to six feet apart around the outside boundaries.*) That is one type of kicking you will need for soccer—kicking along the ground to pass to a partner. The other type is kicking for a goal, scoring a point. This type of kick can travel along the ground or through the air. Select the kicking ball you will use, and position yourself approximately ten to twelve feet from a set of marker cones around the work area. From a stationary position, practice kicking the ball along the ground to score a point between the cones. Your partner will retrieve the ball for you; after three kicks, trade places with your partner.

Watch the ball until your foot makes contact.

Remember, contact behind the ball for travel along the ground.

Retrieving partner, do not attempt to block the kick; only retrieve the ball.

T   When you are comfortable with your stationary kicking, dribble a short distance and then kick for the goal, still focusing on the ball traveling along the ground.

Remember, balance your weight on the support foot.

Follow through in the direction of the goal; don't stop the swing of the kicking leg.

T   Travel in general space, dribbling the soccer ball as you go. On signal, quickly dribble within ten to twelve feet of the cones, then kick for a goal.

Watch the ball until contact is made.

(*After two minutes, have kicking and retrieving partners switch places.*)

T   In a soccer game the ball can travel along the ground or in the air to the goal. You may choose to kick the ball either way for the next few minutes of practice.

Remember, behind the ball for travel along the ground, under the ball for travel through the air.

T   (*Scatter milk jugs throughout general space; marker cones around the outside boundaries will still be the targets.*) Travel in general space combining the skills of dribbling, trapping, and avoiding obstacles. On signal, travel to an open space and kick the ball between two cones—kicking for a goal. Quickly retrieve the ball from your partner and continue dribbling, listening for the next signal to kick for a goal.

T   Partners serving as goalies: just for fun, practice blocking—catch the ball or deflect it, preventing a goal from being scored. If you catch the ball, give it to your partner who is the kicker. After two minutes we will switch positions. (*If taught indoors, and if space permits, everyone can be dribbling and kicking for the goal as there is no need for a goalie.*)

Remember, contact behind the ball for travel along the ground; contact under the ball for travel through the air.

T   Approach the goal from an angle, either right or left of the goal, and kick with the inside of your foot.

T   Travel and kick for the goal on your own; I will not give a signal.

Although you "check" your speed for control before you kick, don't come to a complete stop. Make the dribble and kick for the goal a continuous action.

T   We have only a few minutes of class time left today. You may choose to practice kicking any of the following ways:

Kicking along the ground, passing to a partner
Kicking for the goal from a stationary position
Dribbling toward the goal and then kicking
Dribbling around the obstacles and then kicking for the goal

Closure:

What important skill did we add to our study today?

Review for me the difference between kicking along the ground and in the air. Where is contact made for each?

Reflection:

Can the children kick the ball along the ground to a stationary partner?

Can they kick the ball slightly ahead of the partner when both are moving?

Can they kick the ball with accuracy to a goal approximately six feet wide?

Are they beginning to combine dribbling around obstacles and kicking for a goal?

Lesson 5

Focus: Kicking (as in soccer)

Subfocus: Spatial awareness, partner relationships

Objective: At the end of this lesson the children will have learned to:
tap-dribble and kick for a goal while an opponent attempts to gain possession
    of the ball.

CUE: Control

**Materials/
Equipment:**   Slightly deflated playground balls, soccer balls
Marker cones, milk jugs

**Organization/
Management:**   Milk jugs scattered in general space as obstacles
Marker cones for goals around perimeter of work area
Established protocol for selection of partners

Introduction:
In our theme of kicking, you have practiced the tap-dribble with the inside and the outside of your feet. You have learned to change directions and pathways as well as to make quick turns to avoid obstacles and imaginary opponents. Today you will have an opportunity to try those skills against a real opponent in one-on-one soccer.

For your warm-up, select a ball and practice your tap-dribble in and out, around the jugs. Zigzag, trap and turn, and pass to the sides as you move with skill and control. (*Allow two to three minutes of practice; observe and provide individual assistance as needed.*)

Teacher Observation:

Do the children travel and dribble with control of both kicking the ball and their bodies?

Can they pass to the right and to the left of the obstacles?

Can they travel in straight, curved, and zigzag pathways?

Are they beginning to travel and dribble without constantly looking down at the ball?

Do they trap the ball as needed to "check" speed and gain control?

Content Development:
1.0   Travel in general space with different pathways as you zigzag and curve among the obstacles. Try to maintain a constant speed with no collisions.

Spatial awareness is critical. You must have an eye on the ball you are dribbling, the obstacles in general space, and others who are also traveling.

T   Purposely approach the jugs, check your speed, and execute a one-quarter turn to avoid them.

Remember, keep weight balanced over feet as you trap and turn.

T   Purposely approach the jugs, then tap the ball to the side to pass the obstacle.

Pass to your left with the inside of your right foot or the outside of your left foot. Pass to your right with the inside of your left foot or the outside of your right foot.

T   Travel as quickly as you can, dribbling with control. I am going to signal frequently by hitting the drum. When I do so, trap the ball immediately.

Balance over your support leg.

T   Increase your speed.

The key is control.

2.0   Select a partner whose tap-dribble skills are very similar to yours. Find an open area where you can practice your skills. Cooperatively decide the boundaries of the area. Partner "A," travel and dribble the ball in this area. Partner "B," attempt to gain possession of the ball with your feet. You may trap the ball or tap (not kick) it away. Contact the ball, not the person.

During the first minute, partner "A" is the dribbler; partner "B" is trying to gain possession. Partner "B," if you do gain control of the ball, give it back to partner "A" for more dribbling. At the end of one minute, we will switch offensive and defensive positions.

T   Offense, use all the skills you have learned to dodge the opponent: change speed and directions, pass around him or her, trap and turn. Can you keep possession of the ball within your boundaries for one full minute? Ready? Begin.

C   For application of the kicking skills you have practiced thus far, you and your partner may choose one of these three tasks:

1. Continue your one-on-one soccer practice of dribbling and maintaining possession of the ball with the partner trying to take away the ball.
2. Set up two marker cones within your area to serve as a goal. Partner "A" will tap-dribble until within ten to twelve feet of the goal and then kick for the goal. Partner "B" will attempt to gain possession of the ball. After each kick for the goal, switch positions.
3. Design a game using the tap-dribble and kick for the goal you have been practicing. With your partner, decide the boundaries, scoring, and rules of the game.

Closure:

What new component did we add to our kicking skills today? Compare your skills for avoiding stationary obstacles to skills for avoiding a moving opponent.

Which skills did you use when trying to keep possession of the ball and avoid the opponent?

Reflection:

Can the children dribble with control when another person is attempting to gain possession of the ball?

Do they keep the ball within "reach" when the opponent is nearby?

Can they tap-dribble and travel toward the goal when the opponent is moving?

▨ Kicking Evaluation

Focus: Kicking

Subfocus: Spatial awareness, time, pathways, directions, force

Objective: At the end of this lesson the children will have learned to:
evaluate their progress in mastering the basic skills of kicking as used in soccer.

**Materials/
Equipment:**   Evaluation sheets (see Figure 32), pencils

**Organization/
Management:** Established protocol for picking up, putting away materials

We have just completed a study of kicking as it is used in soccer. You began with a tap-dribble to move the ball in general space, keeping it within three to four feet of you. You practiced dribbling the ball with either foot and with both the inside and the outside of each foot. You learned the skill of tapping with either foot and dribbling in different pathways. You dribbled to avoid stationary obstacles and moving opponents. You also practiced kicking for a goal.

These are not the only kicking skills of individual and partner soccer, but they are major skills. Even the most advanced players must have mastery of these basic skills. Today you will evaluate yourself in relation to these skills. Each test item will be rated on a scale of 1 to 10 with a score of 10 being the best. You will give yourself a score on each of the skills listed.

> *I have found it best to do the evaluation with the children; that is, read each item, reminding them when we did it in class. This seems to tune them in to the item and refresh their memory of how they did on the task.*

Name _____ Homeroom _____

Soccer Skills (Kicking)

|---|
 1   2   3   4   5   6   7   8   9   10

1–3	I still need to practice this skill
4–6	I am pretty good at this skill
7–8	I am very good at this skill
9–10	This is my best skill
*	This is my favorite skill

Skill	Score
1. Tap-dribble in general space, alternating feet.	
2. Tap-dribble with the outside of each foot.	
3. Tap-dribble while moving very fast.	
4. Avoid collisions with others while dribbling.	
5. Trapping the ball with one foot.	
6. Dribbling without bumping marker cones.	
7. Dribbling when partner is trying to gain control of the ball.	
8. Kicking for the goal.	

Figure 32 Evaluation Form for Kicking (as in soccer)

Jumping and Landing

Lesson 1

Focus: Jumping and landing

Subfocus: Spatial awareness

Objectives: At the end of this lesson the children will have learned to:
1. prepare correctly for jumping by bending knees and swinging arms.
2. land correctly with bent knees, ankles, and hips.

        CUES: Swing and spring (Swing your arms and bend your knees in preparation for the jump)
        Squash (Bend knees to absorb the force to land softly and quietly)

**Materials/
Equipment:**   Ropes (one per child) or tape (chalk) on floor or blacktop

**Organization/
Management:**   Established protocol for response to signal
    Ropes positioned throughout general space with sufficient space for jumping and landing safely.

Introduction:
The focus of our lesson today is jumping and landing. We did basic jumping for distance and jumping for height in other lessons. You used jumping and landing in throwing and catching to receive at a high level. You practice(d) it in our weight transfer study as a means of transferring onto, off of, and over small equipment and off of large apparatus. The basketball player needs it to capture the rebound; football players use it to intercept and receive passes. Soccer players need the skill to head a ball in the midst of opponents.

    Gymnasts use the skill of jumping and landing in vaulting, as a preparatory takeoff for aerial stunts, and for transfers onto and off large apparatus. It is an essential tool for the ballet dancer and a means of expression for the modern dancer. (*This part of the introduction can also be conducted as a question and answer session, with children discussing how jumping is used in games, gymnastics, and dance.*) And those are only a few of the sports that have jumping as a vital component. You probably know many more. Jumping and landing is an important skill for you to master. It will appear throughout our work in physical education.

Content Development:
1.0   (*Scatter individual ropes throughout the work area—ropes extended.*) Stand behind a rope. Assume a ready position; bend your knees and swing your arms in preparation for the jump. Jump forward over the rope, landing softly on the other side. You may choose to jump for height or distance as I observe for proper takeoffs and soft landings.

T   Remember our cue: swing and spring, swing and spring . . . jump! (*If you observe students having difficulty with basic jumping and landing, review the introduction to jumping in Part I, Introduction to Skills.*)

Push with your toes for a really powerful jump.

T   Continue your practice, concentrating on jumping for height over your rope: swing and spring, swing and spring. Jump.

Which direction do your arms swing for a jump for height? Upward.

T   Now let's concentrate on soft landings. Squash! Bend your knees, ankles, and hips to absorb the force and land quietly.

T   Jump for height as if outreaching an opponent for the rebound in basketball.

T   Jump for height as if intercepting the touchdown pass in football.

C   Jump for height four times; attempt a higher jump each time as if breaking the height for the *Guinness Book of Records*.

Push with your toes for power.

Squash for a soft landing.

1.1   Now focus on jumping for distance. The takeoff is still from two feet; the landing is still on two feet.

Swing your arms forward.

Squash for a soft landing.

C   Jump for distance three times; attempt a longer jump each time.

2.0   All our jumps thus far have been with two-foot takeoffs and two-foot landings. Several of you have wanted to take a running start and take off with one foot. Let's all try that kind of jump. Move backward several feet from your rope. Approach the rope with several small running steps. Using a one-foot takeoff, jump over the rope, landing on two feet.

Spatial awareness is very important with everyone running and jumping. Do you have a clear pathway and landing area?

Bend your knees and crouch low for this landing.

T   Use small running steps to approach and a one-foot takeoff to jump for height.

The jumping action is now continuous; don't stop the run and then jump.

Really stretch upward.

T   Practice jumping over your rope, taking off on one foot and landing on two with a full squash—a yielding landing.

Use your running approach for a one-foot takeoff.

Swing arms upward after the takeoff.

2.1   Using small running steps to approach your rope, jump over your rope with a one-foot takeoff and a one-foot landing on the opposite foot. Do you remember what this type of jump is called? A leap.

Raise your arms to the sides to assist you in gaining height plus distance.

T   The dancer's leap and that of the professional basketball player is light and soft, as if suspended in midair. Think those thoughts as you continue your leap.

Don't forget to absorb the force as you land. That is critical when landing on only one foot.

T   Leap across your rope as if you just received the lead part in the New York City Ballet.

T   Leap across your rope as if crossing the widest puddle you have ever seen.

C   Practice jumping over your rope for height and distance. Use the different types of jumps to determine which type is better for height and which for distance:

> Two-foot takeoff, two-foot landing
> One-foot takeoff, two-foot landing
> One-foot takeoff, opposite foot landing

(Discuss which jumps are better for height, which for distance, and why.)

Closure:

What was the focus of our lesson today?

Why is jumping important in games? In dance? In gymnastics?

Which type(s) of jump require a running approach?

Why is bending the ankles, knees, and hips so important for landing from the jump? Yes, it is quiet, but what is the real reason for the squash?

Reflection:

Do the children bend their knees and swing their arms in preparation for jumping from two feet?

Do they bend to absorb force upon landing regardless of the type of jump?

Do they swing their arms upward or outward depending on the choice of height or distance?

Lesson 2

Focus: Jumping and landing

Subfocus: Shapes, spatial awareness

Objective: At the end of this lesson the children will have learned to:
make shapes in midair when jumping and landing.

CUES: Heads up (Keep your head and shoulders up for good balance)
Full squash (Absorb the force by bending your knees as if sinking into the
floor)

**Materials/
Equipment:**   Individual ropes (one per child)
Wall chart for rope configuration

**Organization/
Management:**   See Figure 33 for "Jumps and Shapes" rope configuration
Established protocol for selection of partners

Introduction:
Jumping and landing consists of three phases: takeoff, flight, and landing. In our last lesson you practiced the correct takeoff and landing. Today we will focus on "flight"—what happens while you are airborne. The "flight" phase of jumping and landing is important in gymnastics and dance; it is an advanced skill in games and sports.

Content Development:
1.0   Because you will need maximum in-the-air time, our jumps today will be jumps for height, not distance. Select your space behind a rope or tape line, and practice jumping for height with two-foot takeoffs and two-foot landings. I will observe to see if you have remembered our cues for both.

Teacher Observation:

Do the children bend their knees and swing their arms in preparation for the jump?

Do they swing their arms upward?

Do they bend ankles, knees, and hips upon landing to absorb force?

Do I need to reteach, or is this class ready to move forward?

Which students need individual assistance?

2.0   I am extremely pleased with your bending of knees and swinging of arms for the jump and with your quiet, soft landings. Let's move on to the portion of the jump that takes place while you are in the air. Jump over your rope, staying in "flight" long enough to make a shape.

It's not as easy as it sounds. Really get height on your jump by a swing of your arms and the push of your toes.

T   Jump over your rope, forming a wide shape in the air. Extend your arms and legs away from the body for a truly w-i-d-e shape.

Keep your head and shoulders up for a balanced landing.

Full squash to absorb force when landing. This is called a yielding landing; your landing comes to a complete stop.

T   Explore different wide shapes while in flight over your rope. Can you make four different wide shapes?

C   Select your favorite wide shape. Practice until you can repeat it exactly the same three times.

Remember, full squash; balanced landing.

3.0   Jump over your rope, making a narrow shape while in the air.

This is the same shape you needed when you practiced catching a ball at high level—stretch your entire body for a full extension.

Remember, you are jumping for height, not distance.

Yielding landings—sink into the floor.

4.0   The next two shapes are a little more difficult. We will introduce them today and practice them throughout the year. See if you can make a rounded shape by tucking all body parts close to your middle and curling your spine forward.

Keep your head up throughout this jumping action.

Recovery for a good landing is crucial here. **Land in a balanced position on your feet.**

T   Twist your body into new shapes while in the air.

Push upward and lift your arms for sufficient height.

T   Explore different twisted shapes while in midair.

 Partner Observation
Throughout all our work on jumping, landing in a balanced position with knees bent to absorb the force is crucial. After a couple of practice jumps for height, let your partner observe the jump and the landing, with a focus on the landing. You will do three jumps; after each your partner will give you a thumbs up if:

  1. you landed in a balanced position, with no extraneous forward motion or falling down.
  2. you bent your knees for a full squash.

"Matching Jumps and Shapes"
Select a partner with whom you would choose to work on a sequence. You may arrange your ropes in any of the configurations shown on the wall chart (Figure 33).

Put together a series of matching jumps and shapes in flight with your partner. Your shapes will need to be the same; the type of jump and the timing of the jumps will also need to be the same.

Begin facing your partner with sufficient space for safe landings. Select a shape to make in flight; practice that body shape before you add the jumping action so your shapes will be identical. Then try to match the jump, the shape, and the landing.

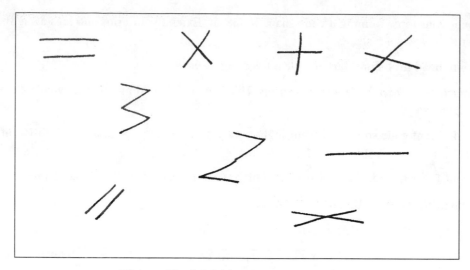

Figure 33 Matching Jumps and Shapes

After you are comfortable with one shape and one jump, add the second, and so forth. Continue until you have a series of three or four jumps. Match your swing and spring action. Match your balanced position when you land with bent knees, ankles, and hips.

Remember, you have practiced both two-foot and one-foot takeoffs and landings.

If you wish, you can add locomotor movements to your sequence.

I will watch your sequence at any point in time:

    if you need assistance.
    if you need a check for progress.
    when you think it is complete and ready for evaluation by another group.

Closure:

What new concept did we add to our skill today?

Name the four shapes that were revisited today.

Why are round and twisted shapes in flight more difficult than narrow and wide?

Reflection:

Can the children stay in the air long enough to create a body shape in flight?

Do they still land in a balanced position after making a shape in midair?

Lesson 3

Focus: Jumping and landing

Subfocus: Symmetrical/nonsymmetrical, spatial awareness

Objective: At the end of this lesson the children will have learned to:
make symmetrical and nonsymmetrical shapes in midair when jumping and landing.

               CUES: Heads up (Keep your head and shoulders up for good balance)
                         Full squash (Absorb the force by bending your knees as if sinking into the floor)

**Materials/
Equipment:**   Individual ropes (one per child)
Four-by-six-inch note cards with recorded sequences
Four-by-six-inch blank cards, pencils for children's recordings

**Organization/
Management:** Sufficient space for jumping and landing safely

---

This lesson on symmetrical and nonsymmetrical shapes in flight is an alternate to body shapes in flight. It can follow Lesson 2 as a revisitation to jumping and landing later in the year or can be used for the study of shapes at a higher grade level.

Introduction:
(Refer to Lesson 2.)

Teacher Observation:

      Refer to Lesson 2.

Content Development:

1.0   We have studied the four basic body shapes: wide, narrow, round, and twisted. You have practiced them in stationary balances and in relation to jumping and landing. Today you will learn two new names for shapes—symmetrical and nonsymmetrical.

A symmetrical shape is one in which both sides look exactly alike. Standing in your self-space, make a wide shape with both sides of your body the same. If I folded you in half vertically, the sides would match; this is symmetrical.

    Jump over your rope, creating a symmetrical shape in midair.

    Push with your toes and swing your arms for power and midair "hang time."

    Full squash for a soft landing.

T   Create four different symmetrical shapes in flight.

T   Symmetrical shapes are easiest to create with stretching or curling actions. See if you can create symmetrical shapes in flight with each of these actions.

C   Select the two symmetrical shapes that are your best. Practice until you can repeat each one three times with perfection. Ask a friend to watch your jump-land action to see if the shape is truly symmetrical.

2.0   The other new name for a shape is nonsymmetrical. What do you think that word means? Correct, the two sides are not alike. Jump over your rope making a nonsymmetrical shape in midair.

A balanced landing is critical for this one. You are slightly off-balance in a nonsymmetrical shape. Bring both feet under you, head and shoulders erect for a balanced landing.

T   Create four different nonsymmetrical shapes while jumping over your rope.

C   Choose your best nonsymmetrical and symmetrical shapes—one for each. Ask a friend to watch your jumping and landing with these two shapes in flight. The friend will give a "thumbs up" if the shapes are correct, a double "thumbs up" if the landing is balanced with a full squash. The challenge is this: Can you repeat the jump-land action with these shapes three times with no changes in shapes or landings? (Informal peer assessment.)

T   When we started our lesson today, all our takeoffs and landings were two feet to two feet. Try the different jumping patterns you have practiced as you create the shapes in flight.

Remember, a full squash for a balanced landing.

T   Combine the basic shapes with symmetrical and nonsymmetrical elements in the following ways:

> wide, symmetrical
> curled, symmetrical
> narrow, nonsymmetrical
> wide, nonsymmetrical
> curled, nonsymmetrical
> twisted, nonsymmetrical

(On four-by-six-inch cards, record sequences that include the following: takeoff—one foot, two feet; landing—one foot, two feet; body shape—wide, narrow, curled, twisted, symmetrical, nonsymmetrical. An example would be:

> *takeoff: two feet*
> *flight: wide shape*
> *landing: two feet)*

C   On the table are cards with jumping and landing sequences recorded. Select a card and create a sequence of takeoff, flight, and landing. Practice the sequence until you can do it three times to your satisfaction, then show it to a friend. Trade cards with the friend and create a new sequence with the directions on his or her card.

T   Create a sequence of your own combining takeoff and landing with shape in the air. Record your new sequence on a blank card on the table. They may be selected as challenges for another class.

 The above sequence work can easily be adapted for assessment with the addition of criteria.

204

Closure:

What two new words did we learn today?

What is the difference between symmetrical and nonsymmetrical?

Do you find one more difficult than the other to create while in flight?

Reflection:

Can the children jump with sufficient height to create the shapes while in midair?

Do they land in a balanced position?

Do they absorb force by bending knees, ankles, and hips upon landing?

Lesson 4

Focus: Jumping and landing

Subfocus: Spatial awareness, shapes, turning/twisting actions

Objectives: At the end of this lesson the children will have learned to:
1. execute a quarter turn in midair while jumping and landing.
2. land in a balanced position when jumping from low apparatus.

CUES: Heads up (Keep your head and shoulders up for good balance)

Full squash (Absorb the force by bending your knees as if sinking into the floor)

Materials/ Equipment: Individual ropes (one per child)
Low-height balance beams, benches, tables

Organization/ Management: See Figure 34 for equipment setup

Introduction:

Today our lesson will focus on a part of jumping and landing that is often used in gymnastics—jumping in relation to equipment and jumping with turns in midair. Jumping in relation to equipment includes jumping onto apparatus (mounts), jumping over equipment (vaulting), and jumping off apparatus (dismounts). That is our focus for today: jumping off apparatus with a yielding landing—a full squash for a balanced, complete stop.

Prior to jumping off apparatus, which involves the added factor of height, let's review what you have learned about jumping and landing. Practice jumping for height over your rope or tape line on the floor while I observe your preparation for jumping and your landings.

Teacher Observation:

Do the children swing their arms and bend their knees in preparation for the jump?

Do their arms swing upward when jumping for height?

Do the children land with knees, ankles, and hips bent to absorb the force of the landing?

Do they land in a balanced position, weight equally distributed over feet?

Remember, teacher observation during the two to three minutes of practice at the beginning of class is the time for observation of the total class, checklist of critical cues, and notes for individual assistance.

Content Development:

1.0   I am extremely pleased with your jumping and landing thus far. I observed the "swing and spring" we discussed the first day of our work and the swinging of your arms in the direction needed—upward. I also noted the bending of knees upon landing; this will be extremely important when you jump off gymnastics apparatus.

T   Practice your jumps over your rope again, concentrating on landing "like a gymnast." When gymnasts compete, they must land in a balanced position and hold that balanced position. This time, when you land from your jump, bend your knees, ankles, and hips to absorb force, but also try to land with your weight equally distributed over your feet, so you will stay in that position.

It will help to have your feet shoulder-width apart when you land.

T   Continue to practice your jumps concentrating on feet slightly apart, head and shoulders up for good balance.

Eyes forward, don't look down.

T   Remember the cartoon from "Calvin and Hobbes" where Calvin always raises his arms in the gymnastics pose and says "Ta Da!" no matter what happens (model). Although this is a funny cartoon, there is a reason for the extension of the arms upward—the regaining of balance. Use your arms to help you maintain balance when you land from your jump.

2.0   Jump over your rope, executing a one-quarter turn while in the air. Land in a balanced position with your trunk centered over your feet, center of gravity low.

This landing requires a full squash. What is that called?

Focus on the landing and quarter turn, not on the distance of the jump.

C   Practice your quarter turn until you can do three of them to perfection. Perfection will mean (1) swinging your arms and bending your knees in preparation, (2) bending your knees and ankles when landing, and (3) landing balanced with feet not moving after. When you think you have the turn perfected, ask a friend to watch. (Informal partner assessment.)

T   When your quarter turn is perfected, try a half turn while in midair, landing to face the direction from which you started.

Swing your arms upward and around as you twist your trunk to help you turn while in the air.

Don't forget to land balanced.

Ta Da!

T   Practice your quarter and half turns both clockwise and counterclockwise.

3.0   Positioned in general space are two low benches, two low tables, and a low balance beam. Select the station at which you will choose to work first; if there are more than six people at that station, make a different choice. From a standing position on the bench (beam, table), use a two-foot takeoff to jump high in the air. Land on two feet in front of the bench (beam, table).

Remember, you are jumping for height, not distance.

Swing and spring the same as when jumping over the rope on the floor.

Head and shoulders up! Full squash!

T   Continue to practice jumping off the piece of apparatus, concentrating on the height of the jump and a yielding landing.

T   Now let's concentrate on the most difficult part of this jump—landing in a balanced position. As a gymnast you will want your feet to remain stationary upon contact with the floor or mat. See if you can jump off the bench (beam, table) and land with your feet shoulder-width apart and stationary.

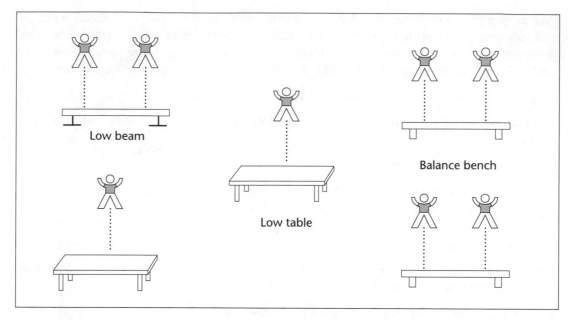

Low beam

Low table

Balance bench

Figure 34   Jumping and Landing off Low Equipment

Hold that position by swinging your arms either downward after the landing or down and up. Ta Da!

Bending knees and keeping your head up are now very important.

C   Practice until you can complete three "perfection" jumps. Your criteria will be:

> Swing and spring
> Arms upward for height
> Balanced landing with full squash

When you think you have perfected the jump, have a partner watch and give you a "thumbs up" for success or a "thumbs down" for continued practice. If you receive a "thumbs down," be sure your partner tells you what to correct. (Informal peer assessment.)

T   Rotate until you have practiced at each station. The changes in height from beam to bench to table may make a difference for you.

T   When you have received a "thumbs up" for good jumps and good balance at a station, you may want to try jumping off the equipment with a quarter turn in midair.

The balanced landing is now more difficult due to the turn. Keep your feet parallel and slightly apart; head and shoulders up for balance.

Remember, your arms will swing upward and around as you twist slightly for the turn.

T   Try the quarter turns both clockwise and counterclockwise.

> *Don't rush this study for children. Mid-elementary classes usually spend one to two lessons just on proper takeoffs and balanced landings when jumping from low apparatus. Remember, the goal is mastery, not exploration.*

Closure:

What two things did we add to our study of jumping and landing today?

In addition to the arms swinging upward for the jump with a turn in midair, what else must the body do to initiate the turning action?

Why is it so important to bend the knees upon landing when jumping from the beam, bench, or table?

What are the keys to landing in a balanced position?

Reflection:

Can the children execute a quarter turn in midair and land in a balanced position?

Can they jump from the height of a low beam, bench, or table and land in a balanced position?

Do they bend knees, ankles, and hips upon landing?

Do they use arms in preparation for the jump, to attain height on the jump, and to regain balance upon landing?

> *Depending on the content theme to follow and the age of the students, I usually teach the theme of jumping and landing in one of the following combinations: lessons 1,2; 1,3; or 1,4. Basic shapes in flight or symmetrical and nonsymmetrical shapes can be added as a revisitation during the year or next year, as a more advanced lesson.*

Jumping and Landing Evaluation

Focus: Jumping and landing

The evaluation form example here (Figure 35) focuses on safety in landings as a prerequisite to more advanced combination work in gymnastics. It is based on previous work on balances and beginning rolling actions.

Name _____ Homeroom _____

Date _____

Jumping and Landing in Gymnastics

Name the two cues for a proper landing in gymnastics.

What is a yielding landing? Why is it needed when jumping off apparatus?

Partner evaluation: Excellent   Satisfactory   Still practicing

Jump and land

Quarter turn

Half turn

Worksheet: Choose either A or B to be graded by a partner

A. Jump, land, balance:

B. Jump, land, roll:

Criteria for evaluation: *Criteria established/discussed with children, for example:*

vertical jump off apparatus	full squash
balanced landing	full recovery—Ta Da
stationary balance	correct rolling action

Figure 35   Evaluation Form for Jumping and Landing

Balancing

Lesson 1

Focus: Balancing

Subfocus: Bases of support, spatial awareness

Objective: At the end of this lesson the children will have learned to:
maintain a balanced position on a chosen base of support for three seconds.

        CUES: Stillness (No wiggles, no wobbles—hold perfectly still for three seconds)
                  Tight muscles (Muscular tension is the key to holding the balance)

**Materials/
Equipment:**   Individual gymnastics mats, carpet squares for outdoors
Chalkboard or flipchart, paper, pencils

**Organization/
Management:**   Established protocol for moving mats, placement on floor, listening position

Introduction:
Today we begin the study of balance, one of the two main themes of gymnastics. Gymnastics consists of balancing and transferring weight. The combination of the stillness and movement makes interesting routines on the floor and on large apparatus.

When you were first introduced to the concept of balance, we discussed what the word means; we established the criteria for balance. Can anyone recall the two criteria? It's been a long time since that first lesson. Watch me as I stand on one foot, and tell me if I am "balanced" (model, standing in a front scale with arms waving, almost falling over). Was I balanced in that position? No, I was about to fall over. Watch again (model, with firm base of support, but arms moving). What about that one? I was not about to fall over, but was I balanced? No. Balance means I can hold the position perfectly still, and I am not about to fall over—not about to lose the balance.

The second criteria is being able to hold the position for several seconds; we will say three seconds for our work. Many of you could kick up into a handstand, but only a few of you can hold it for several seconds. It is not a mastered skill unless it is under control, held perfectly still for several seconds.

Ask your neighbor what our two criteria are for balance in gymnastics. If you hear holding perfectly still and three seconds, your neighbor has answered correctly.

Content Development:
1.0   Show me a balance that you think you can hold perfectly still for three seconds.

    Remember, a wide base is most stable.

211

T   When I observed your balances, I noticed some of you were stretched out on the mat as if you were resting; others were standing on two feet. Challenge yourself with a true gymnastics balance, a position that is not a resting or normal pose for you.

As you challenge yourself with a gymnastics balance, you will find the balance is easier to hold stationary if you tighten the muscles in your stomach and those in the body parts not serving as bases of support.

CUE: Tight muscles

T   Sit in listening position on your mat. On signal, tighten the muscles in your arms and legs.

The trick is to tighten the muscles without changing the appearance of the body parts. I should not see your arms and legs move, but I could feel the tightness of the muscles if I touched your arm or leg.

Tighten your abdominal muscles. Don't forget to breathe.

Good, I sense your understanding of this important cue for balancing in gymnastics.

T   Try your balance again, concentrating on tightening the muscles. Remember, I will not see the balance change, but you will feel the muscular tension as you hold the balance.

C   Let's pretend I am taking a photo of the balances. What happens if you move when a photo is being taken? Hold perfectly still for three seconds. Ready? Balance.

You are (third) graders; we will do everything in threes. Choose three balances that you think you can hold perfectly still. Practice each one, counting to yourself: one thousand one, one thousand two, one thousand three. After you practice, we will take the "photo shoot" as a test of our stillness in balances.

2.0   Repeat a balance you just did. (*Select a student whose balance is stationary for the model.*) John, what is Matthew's base of support? What body parts are touching the mat? (*Repeat with another student whose base of support is different.*)

T   Balance with a base of support different from the base you used for your first balance, holding the balance perfectly still for a count of three seconds.

Remember, tighten the muscles.

T   Balance with still a different base of support.

Remember, hold perfectly still for the "photo."

T   Let's see how many different body parts we have used as bases of support. (*Select several students with different bases to demonstrate their balances; ask a neighbor to name the body parts used as bases. Write the list on the chalkboard or flipchart.*) Thus far, we have seen balances on combinations of feet, hands, head, knees, and elbows. Did anyone have a balance that used other body parts as bases of support? (*Watch the additional balances and continue to list on the board.*) Good, now we have added stomach, shoulders, back, and one hip. Our list now looks like this:

head	hands
knees	elbows
stomach	back
hip	feet
shoulders	

T   I know one base of support we have not listed. Sit in listening position on your mat. What is your base of support when seated? Rock back and lift your feet slightly off the mat. What is your base of support now? Right, the base of your spine. Hold this balance stationary as we count for three seconds.

Tighten your abdominal muscles to hold this one.

T   Balance on the base of your spine with one leg extended forward.

Tighten your abdominal and leg muscles for good balance. (*Add base of spine to the listing on the chart.*)

T   Look at the list of bases of support on the flipchart (chalkboard). Using the body parts in different combinations, see how many balances you can create.

Remember to widen your base if needed.

T   Challenge yourself by reducing the width of your base of support so the base is very narrow.

Now tightening your muscles will be even more important.

T   Challenge yourself by making some of your balances inverted.

Tighten the muscles of your stomach and free body parts to assist in holding inverted balances.

T   I will name the bases of support from our listing. Create a balance with these body parts as the base. Be creative; make your balance different from all others in the room. Show me a balance on feet and hands.

Remember the criteria: stillness for three seconds.

Show me a balance on knees and elbows.

Hold until I snap the photo.

Show me a balance on shoulders plus _____.

Show me a balance on head plus _____ plus _____.

(*Continue with different combinations of body parts as bases of support. Focus on stillness and maintaining the position for three seconds with each new balance.*)

C   Select your three favorite balances from all you tried today. Practice each one again to be sure you can hold it absolutely still for three seconds. When you are confident, ask the person next to you to watch your balances. They will watch for the following: stillness, ability to hold position for three seconds, and muscular tension. Your partner will give you a "thumbs up" or a "thumbs down" depending on the stability of your balances.

 Select your three favorite balances from all you have tried today; be sure each one has a different base of support. Practice each one until you can hold it absolutely still for a three-second count. Get a piece of paper and a pencil from the assignment table. Draw each of your balances; label the base of support. After you complete the drawing, show each balance to the person on the mat nearest you. They will give you a __✓+__ if the balance meets the two criteria, a __≈__ if you still need to practice the balance, a __✓−__ if you cannot hold the balance.

Closure:

What theme did we begin to study today?

What are the two criteria for a good gymnastics balance?

What are the cues you learned for holding the balance stationary?

Reflection:

Can the children hold a gymnastics balance stationary for three seconds—no wiggles, no wobbles, no loss of balance?

Can they balance on different bases of support?

All too often, lessons in gymnastics are simply an introduction to the skills for children, an exploration rather than mastery. Muscular tension, alignment of body parts over a base of support, and counterbalance are critical for development of good gymnastics balances and weight transfers. Many of these lessons will require more than one class period for mastery. Do not rush; wait until you observe that the children have mastered the skills before moving on. Gymnastics is no different from games skills in this respect.

Children's Movement Vocabulary

"Fete"—Your base of support when standing.

Lesson 2

Focus: Balancing

Subfocus: Bases of support, spatial awareness

Objectives: At the end of this lesson the children will have learned to:
1. balance in an inverted position.
2. link balances together in a sequence.

> **CUE:** Smooth transitions (Move slowly from one balance to the next one for smooth transitions)

> **REVIEW CUES:** Stillness
> Tight muscles

**Materials/
Equipment:**   Individual gymnastics mats, carpet squares for outdoors
Chalkboard or flipchart, paper, pencils

**Organization/
Management:**   Established protocol for moving mats, placement on floor, listening position

Introduction:

Earlier in our study of balance you practiced balancing on different bases of support. We identified two criteria that every balance should have. Who can tell me those two things? Correct, stillness for three seconds. Let's begin our work today by practicing our balances on different bases of support. You may have been practicing some that were challenging for you, perhaps inverted or with narrow bases of support. Try some favorites, some challenging, and some new ones as you practice.

+--+
| Teacher Observation: |
| |
| Can the children hold their balances for three seconds? |
| |
| Do they tighten their stomach muscles and free body parts? |
| |
| Which children need individual assistance? |
+--+

Content Development:

1.0   Balance on your favorite bases of support. Hold that position as I observe for stillness and tight muscles.

T   Select another base of support, and hold that balance.

      Be creative. Your balance should be different from those near you, even if the base is the same.

T   Each time you hear the drumbeat, change your bases of support and hold the new balance. When you have exhausted your repertoire, sit in your listening position.

      Hold each balance very still; don't rush thinking of the next one.

      I can actually see the tightening of the muscles—excellent!

2.0 Let's focus on inverted balances for a few minutes. Inverted is a large word that means what? Upside down. Creating an inverted balance simply means your head will be lower than some other body parts; that does not mean you have to do an Olympic handstand or a headstand. Show me an inverted, upside down balance.

You may need a wider base of support when trying to hold an inverted balance.

T   Balance on your shoulders, head, and upper arms with your legs extended; this is an inverted balance.

If your legs are extended upward so they are over your hips, the balance will be easier to hold stationary. This is called *alignment,* and it is very important in gymnastics.

T   Balance on your head, two hands, and one leg with the other leg extended upward.

Stretch this leg for a full extension; I should be able to see the muscular tension in the extension.

T   Create inverted balances on these bases of support:

Head, one foot, one hand
Head and knees
Hands, one knee

When your head is involved as a base of support, it is important to distribute your weight equally among all the body parts that are bases.

T   Create three new inverted balances, holding each very still for a count of three seconds.

> *If children begin to experiment with frogstands and headstands as inverted balances, it is then time to teach them the proper mechanics for assuming and maintaining these positions. (Refer to* Children Moving, *Chapter 23.)*

3.0 You have balanced on different bases of support and have explored some inverted balances. From all the balances you have practiced, select your three favorites. Practice one time to be sure each has a different base of support and that you can hold each stationary for a count of three seconds. Show me your first balance—hold for the photo, 1, 2, 3, click. Now show me your second balance—1, 2, 3, click. Now your third.

T   Thus far, we have done all the balances separately, with no thought of linking them together. Let's focus on changing from one balance to another—the transition. Repeat the three balances you just did, experimenting with the order in which you do them; it may be 1, 2, 3, or 2, 3, 1, or some other combination.

Link your balances together in a smooth, flowing action.

Make the transitions between the stationary balances purposeful movements, as in a sequence.

T   Assume your first balance—hold very still, 1, 2, 3. On signal, very slowly, very smoothly move into your second balance—hold for the photo—1, 2, 3. Now smoothly into your final balance—1, 2, 3, rest.

Are you pleased with your balances and with the order in which you performed them? If not, use the next few minutes to make changes. If you are satisfied with your balances and with the sequence, ask a friend to watch and give you an evaluation of bases, stillness, and smooth transitions. If you would like, I will observe your balances after you show them to a friend. Remember, after someone is a friend to you, be a friend to them; watch their balances.

C   Select your favorite balances, each with a different base of support. Practice both the balances and the movements between each. On signal, we will "videotape" the sequence. Now we will pretend we are filming the balances plus actions between each, not just taking still photos of the balances. Ready? Begin.

 Videotape
After the pretend videotaping of sequences, and when the children are ready, videotape each sequence. The videotape can then serve for self-assessment and teacher assessment, followed by a joint discussion/evaluation.

Closure:

What does the word *inversion* mean?

If your base of support is narrow and you are having difficulty holding the balance stationary, what can you do to the base for more stability?

What is it called when you combine balances and movements between the balances?

Reflection:

Can the children balance in an inverted position?

Are they beginning to balance on more narrow bases of support?

Are the body parts held firm with muscles tight?

Can the children combine balances and transitions into simple sequences?

Teaching alignment of body parts over base of support and extending body parts from the base for counterbalance are very important components in the study of balance. The best time for introducing them, however, is as teachable moments. You will observe a child who needs to extend and tighten muscles for counterbalance; you will observe a child who needs proper alignment of body parts over the base for good balance. At that point, I suspend the planned lesson and proceed to teach the component that arises as extremely important. Both components are best taught when the need arises rather than forced into a separate lesson.

Lesson 3

Focus: Balancing

Subfocus: Basic shapes, spatial awareness

Objective: At the end of this lesson the children will have learned to:
hold gymnastics balances in wide, narrow, curled, and twisted shapes.

               REVIEW CUES: Tight muscles
                                     Stillness

**Materials/
Equipment:**   Individual gymnastics mats, carpet squares for outdoors
Chalkboard or flipchart

**Organization/
Management:** Established protocol for moving mats, placement on floor, listening position

Introduction:

In our earlier lesson we reviewed balancing on different bases of support. We established the criteria for a good balance as absolute stillness for three seconds. During your warm-up today, practice those balances you have been working on for some time but have not yet mastered. I will move around the room to provide individual assistance.

Teacher Observation:

       Is muscular tension present in the children's balances?

       Are they beginning to be stable in inverted balances?

       Do they challenge themselves with increasingly difficult balances?

This independent warm-up time provides an excellent opportunity for individual challenge to the more highly skilled and one-on-one assistance to those less skilled.

Content Development:

1.0   Today we add to our study of balance the four basic body shapes. Who can tell me what they are? Correct—wide, narrow, round, and twisted. In your self-space, explore balancing in the different shapes.

     Stillness for three seconds is still the rule!

T   Show me a gymnastics balance with a very wide shape.

     What body parts make a wide shape? Arms and legs. Extend arms and legs not involved as bases of support for a very wide shape. Stretch your fingers; point your toes.

T   Now make a wide shape balance on a different base of support.

Tighten the muscles to hold very still.

1.1   Balance with a narrow body shape.

The same body parts that create a wide shape create a narrow shape—arms and legs close together this time.

T   Choose an additional narrow shape balance with a different base of support.

C   See if you can create two wide and two narrow balances, each with a different base of support.

1.2   Explore rounded shapes for gymnastics balances.

A round shape comes from curling the spine. This one is sometimes difficult to create differently from others in the class; be creative.

T   From your listening position in self-space, slowly curl your spine forward into a round shape; tuck all free body parts close together for a tight, round shape.

T   Slowly curl your spine to one side as you create a different round shape.

      Carefully curl your spine backward, resulting in an arch of the back, also a curled shape.

1.3   On a favorite base of support, twist body parts to create a twisted shape.

      Remember, twisted is not the same as crossed; rotate the body parts—arms, legs, trunk, neck.

2.0   Assume a balanced position on your chosen base of support. Keeping that base, extend, curl, and twist free body parts into different shapes.

      Remember, place arms and legs apart or close together for wide and narrow; spine curled to round; rotation for twisted.

Tighten the muscles to hold the balance.

T   After you meet that challenge, balance on a new base of support and create the shapes with free body parts.

Remember to align body parts over the base.

T   You are fourth graders (apply appropriate grade), so the magic number for you will be four. Create four balances, each with a different base of support. After you establish each base, move free body parts into wide, narrow, round, and twisted shapes. This means you will actually create $4 \times 4 = 16$ balances!

      As you move into each balance, hold the three-second count before changing.

T   From all the balances you have done today, choose your four favorites, one to represent each of the basic shapes—wide, narrow, round, twisted. On signal, show me each of the balances. Ready? Show me wide; hold, 1, 2, 3, rest. Show me narrow; 1, 2, 3, photo. (*Continue with round and twisted.*)

C   Challenge yourself by using a different base of support for each of the four balances.

At the assignment table you will find prepared papers divided into four parts with space for you to diagram your four balances that represent the shapes studied today. Use stick figures to draw your balance for each shape. Label the shape plus the base of support (grade four and above— no repeating a base). After you have drawn your balances, practice a couple of times for stillness, then ask a friend to evaluate for you. Check your paper against the list of directions on the board before you are evaluated:

Draw each balance
  Label the shape
  Label the base of support
  Practice for stillness, three seconds
  Ask a friend to watch

"Body Shape Statues"
Quickly choose three other persons with whom you wish to work. You will have a group of four. You are going to build a "Body Shape Statue." Each person in your group will create a balance demonstrating one of the basic shapes—wide, narrow, round, twisted. You are a statue, not four separate statues; you must be connected to one other person in the group.

Can you make the statue with each person in your group using a different base of support?

Can anyone in your group hold an inverted balance?

I will give you two to three minutes to practice, then we will look at the Body Shape Statues.

> *After the children have created stationary group balances, challenge them to change the "Body Shape Statue" into a "Movable Shape Monster" by moving as a unit in self- or general space. This usually ends in a collapse of giggles.*

Closure:

What did we add to our study of balance today?

Review for me: What are the four basic shapes?

What body parts create wide and narrow? Rounded?

What happens to create a twisted shape?

Reflection:

Can the children create balances in each of the basic body shapes?

Can they combine balances on different bases of support and body shapes?

Are they holding balances absolutely stationary for three seconds?

Do they challenge themselves with more difficult balances each day rather than just repeating easy ones?

Children's Movement Vocabulary
Knee pits: Your base of support when hanging from your knees on the apparatus.

220

Lesson 4

Focus: Balancing

Subfocus: Levels, spatial awareness, transitions

Objectives: At the end of this lesson the children will have learned to:
1. create balances at different levels—low, medium, high.
2. extend free body parts for balance and counterbalance.
3. align body parts over the base for stability.

CUES: Extensions (Extend free body parts for stability in your balance)
Alignment (Toes over knees, over hips, over shoulders to form a straight line)

REVIEW CUES: Tight muscles

**Materials/
Equipment:**   Individual gymnastics mats, carpet squares for outdoors
Aluminum foil torn in ten-inch to twelve-inch lengths, scissors

**Organization/
Management:**   Established protocol for moving mats, placement on floor,
listening position

Introduction:

Thus far in our study of balance in gymnastics, you have learned to balance on different bases of support and in wide, narrow, curled, and twisted shapes. Some of you have been challenging yourself each day with narrower bases of support and inverted balances; others have been refining those balances they were more comfortable with. During your warm-up time today, challenge yourself to try a narrower base, perhaps an inverted balance, or practice one you felt could have been mastered last time with "just a little more practice."

I will move about the room to assist as needed and to observe for three-second stillness. I may touch you as I walk past to see if you have the muscular tension needed for good balance in gymnastics. Did you know that if the muscular tension is really there, I could lift you or hold you upside down and your gymnastics "shape" would still be intact?

Teacher Observation:

Are the children in control as they try different new balances?

Are they beginning to balance on narrower bases of support?

Do they attempt simple inverted balances without placing pressure on the neck and head?

Content Development:

1.0   From all the balances you have done thus far, show me your favorite, the one you know you can hold perfectly still. What is your base of support? What body parts are free? Extend those body parts away from the base of support.

This extension of free body parts helps add stability to the balance.

T   Balance on the base of your spine. Extend legs and arms . . . s-t-r-e-t-c-h.

You may choose to extend legs and arms forward in a narrow shape, apart in a wide shape, or in a combination of legs together and arms apart.

T   Balance on your knees and elbows. Change the base to only one knee and one elbow. Extend the free leg and arm. The extension of opposites is called counterbalance. An extension beyond the base in one direction requires an extension in the opposite direction. (*Explore extensions beyond the base in one direction, resulting in a loss of balance.*)

T   Balance on your head, two hands, and one foot. Extend the opposite leg upward.

T   Explore balances on different bases of support, extending free body parts for balance.

This extension of free body parts adds not only stability but also class for the gymnast; no floppy wrists or nonpointed toes.

2.0   You have done balances on different bases of support and in different shapes. As I have observed those balances, some of them have been at low level, some at medium level, and some at high level. Let's focus on those levels for a few minutes. Balance on a base of support at low level that shows a wide shape.

Don't forget, a gymnastics balance is a balance that requires muscular tension. Challenge yourself.

T   Balance on a base of support at low level that shows a narrow shape.

Excellent extensions of arms and legs.

T   Explore different bases of support as well as curled and twisted shapes at low level.

Hold each one for a three-second count before you move to the next one.

3.0   Your balances at low level are very good. You are able to hold them stationary for three seconds; you are capable of using many different bases of support. Now let's focus on balances at the middle level. Create a balance and use free body parts for extensions away from the body at medium level.

T   Some of you appear to be drawing a blank for balances at this level. Show me a balance on two hands and one knee; extend your free leg upward.

T   Let's make it a bit more difficult. Balance on one hand and one knee with the free arm and the free leg extended to front and back.

If you have this narrow base of support, is it better for you to have opposite knee and hand as bases or the knee and hand on the same side? We just did this with knee and elbow. The extension for counterbalance is the same—opposites.

T   Continue to explore balances at medium level. Don't forget, use different bases of support and different shapes.

Tighten the muscles as the balances become more difficult.

T   An inverted balance is often the best way to combine balance at high level and body shapes. Balance on your shoulders and arms with legs extended upward. Create different body shapes with your legs:

    Extended, together—narrow
    Extended, apart—wide
    Curled toward the trunk—what level now?
    Twisted with the trunk

The secret to an inverted balance is the alignment of body parts over the base: toes over knees, over hips, to form a straight line.

CUE: Alignment

T   Assume another of the inverted balances you have been practicing. Create different body shapes while in this balance.

Remember, align free body parts over the base for stability.

As you practice inverted balances, if you are doing a balance that involves your head as a base of support and you begin to lose your balance, remember to simply tuck your head and roll safely out of the balance.

C   Think of all the balances you have created since we began this study—different bases of support, four different shapes, three different levels, some inverted. Select the four that are your favorites; add to that your most challenging, the one you have just mastered after much practice. Let's combine these five balances into a sequence. Use the next few minutes to practice them; select the order in which you will show them. I will be the "still photographer" as we view them. (*Allow practice time, then let the children demonstrate their balances, as a total group, or half, then the other half.*)

When a group is demonstrating balances for the class, they will need to do them twice. Ask the observers to watch the entire group the first time, then focus on one person the second time. The observers will need cues on what to look for: shapes, levels, bases of support, inverted balances.

C   Your still life photographs look great. You were able to hold the balances absolutely stationary for the three-second count. We observed many different combinations of body parts as bases of support. We noted different ways of forming each basic shape, even when bases were identical. Now let's concentrate on the movement between each of the balances—the transitions. Repeat your balances, making the movements out of and into the next balance part of your sequence.

CUE: Smooth transitions

I will allow you a few minutes to practice your sequence for the final viewing.

"The Gymnast"
(*Provide each child with a piece of aluminum foil and access to scissors. Not all will need scissors.*)
This piece of aluminum foil will become a gymnast today. We will work through the steps together (Figure 36):

1. Tear (or cut) the foil into the shape of a cross (model, plus show on chalkboard or flipchart).
2. Cut (or tear) the bottom length of the cross so it is two sections of the cross.
3. Gently squeeze each cross section into an "arm" for the gymnast.
4. Squeeze each long section into a "leg."
5. The top portion is formed into a rounded "head."

Mold the gymnast into the balance you wish to create—bases of support, shape, level, perhaps inverted. Your gymnast should be able to hold that shape when you place it on the floor in front of your mat.

Create with your body the balance your gymnast is holding so still.

Exchange with your neighbor; now try to copy that balance.

223

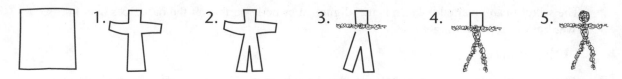

Figure 36   Diagram for Gymnast

Would you like to display your gymnasts for others to see? We will ask the librarian if we can display them for a few days, then you can take them home to demonstrate for Mom and Dad bases of support and shapes in gymnastics.

Closure:

What new component did we add to our study of balance today?

What are the three levels?

Why are extensions important in gymnastics?

How does alignment of body parts help us with inverted balances?

What level was the most difficult for you? Why?

What level is your favorite for gymnastics balances? Why?

Reflection:

Can the children combine balance on different bases of support and body shapes with levels?

Can they hold an inverted balance for three seconds?

Do they extend free body parts for balance and counterbalance?

Can they come out of a position safely, whether intended or due to loss of balance?

Are they ready for low apparatus?

224

Lesson 5 (Designed as a two-part lesson)

Focus: Balancing (on low apparatus)

Subfocus: Bases of support, levels

Objective: At the end of this lesson the children will have learned to:
balance on different bases of support on various pieces of low apparatus.

         REVIEW CUES: Tight muscles
                             Alignment
                             Extensions

**Materials/
Equipment:** See Figure 37 for apparatus setup

**Organization/
Management:** Established protocol for moving apparatus, and response to signal/listening position
Rules for working safely on apparatus

Introduction:
You have practiced balancing on different bases of support, at different levels, and in different shapes. Your work on the mats has been excellent; your balances are now held stationary for a three-second count. Today you will use all that information for balancing on various pieces of gymnastics apparatus—low apparatus. Balances that were easy on the floor will be more difficult with the added height of the apparatus.

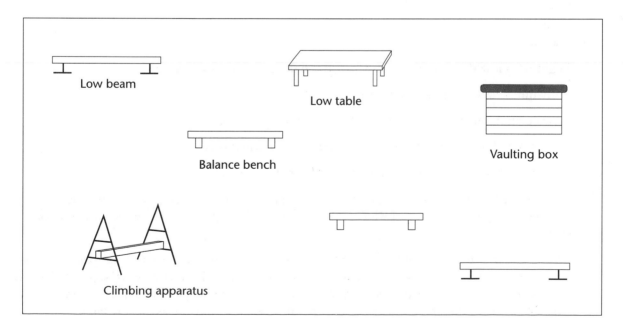

Figure 37 Low Apparatus for Balances

Content Development:

(Position apparatus throughout work area with sufficient space for working safely on the apparatus, getting on and off, and moving between stations. The number of children at each station is determined by the number of pieces of apparatus available. The following are well suited for this lesson: low balance beam, balance bench, low table, stackable vaulting box, climbing apparatus.)

1.0   Before you begin working on the apparatus, select a small mat for practice and review balancing on different bases. The selection of base is your choice. I will name the critical cue that I want you to concentrate on.

T   As you balance, focus on aligning body parts over the base of support for good balance. I should see absolute stillness as you hold your balances for three-second counts.

T   Now create a balance that demonstrates extensions of free body parts.

Remember to really stretch for a true extension.

Throughout all your balances, I should sense the muscular tightness as you hold them perfectly still.

Observe for cognitive understanding and skill mastery.

Your warm-up on the mats shows me you are ready for the apparatus. Those three cues—alignment, extensions, and muscular tightness—will be even more important when you balance on the apparatus.

2.0   Balance on the apparatus, using the following bases of support:

Knees and hands
Knee and two hands
Base of spine
Stomach
One foot

Begin with a wide base of support for good balance on the apparatus.

Remember to hold each balance for three seconds.

T   Balance on different combinations of body parts as bases of support.

Extend free body parts to counterbalance on an elevated surface.

Be sure your weight is centered over your base of support.

C   From all the balances you have practiced, select your best three for that piece of apparatus. Practice until you are confident with each, then ask another person at your station to watch for stillness.

T   *(Rotate the groups to each of the stations, repeating the task for each new piece of apparatus.)* As you move to a new station, you will again practice balances on different bases of support. You will be able to repeat some of the balances at each station; at others the piece of apparatus will dictate what balances are possible, for example, the narrow balance beam versus the low table.

Tighten the muscles to hold very still on the apparatus.

T   Have you tried an inverted balance on the apparatus? Choose apparatus with a wide surface for your inverted balances.

Remember, weight equally distributed on all bases.

3.0   Select the station at which you can do your best balances. For some of you that will be the low, narrow beam; for others it will be the higher, wider table. Return to that station to put together a sequence of balances on apparatus. Practice different bases of support until you have four balances that you can hold perfectly still.

Each balance should have a different base of support.

Change the level for at least one of your balances.

Add one inverted balance.

Remember our work on transitions; practice your balances in a different order to decide which is best.

 Student Project
On the assignment table are papers with a summary of the assignment on the front and a sketch of the apparatus on the back. Choose the paper to match the station at which you are working. After you have selected your balances and have practiced them to meet the criteria we discussed in our first balance lesson, draw your balances on the apparatus sketch. Let's list on the flipchart the steps in completing this project:

1. Choose paper to match chosen apparatus
2. Draw balances on sketch (stick figures)
3. Number the balances in order of your sequence
4. Memorize your sequence of balances
5. Let a friend at the same station watch for a "dress rehearsal"
6. I will watch when you are ready

Criteria for evaluation:
Balances drawn
Different bases of support for each balance
Balances numbered and performed to match order
Beginning and ending shape
Sequence memorized

Extra credit:
Creativity (a touch of me!)

Closure:

Today we began our balance work on apparatus. What is the difference between doing the balances on the mats and on the apparatus?

Which bases of support are the most stable on the apparatus?

Did you try an inverted balance on the apparatus? Was it different from the inverted balance on the mat?

Why did you choose the particular apparatus for your sequence?

Reflection:

Can the children balance on different bases of support on each piece of apparatus?

Are they comfortable trying balances on the apparatus?

Do they follow the rules for safety when working on the apparatus?

Are their balances held stationary with evidence of muscular tension and extensions for counterbalance?

I have found it very helpful to have the criteria for evaluation on a prepared slip for each student evaluation. The assessment is completed on the slip and stapled to the student's project paper to be placed in his or her portfolio.

Name:

FINAL GYMNASTICS SEQUENCE:

Beginning shape:

Balances:

    Stillness—3 seconds
    Bases of support

Ending shape:

- -

Creativity:

Level of difficulty:

Lesson 6 (Designed as a two-part lesson)

Focus: Balancing (on low apparatus)

Subfocus: Bases of support, body shapes, levels

This lesson should be taught following a review of Lessons 1 through 4, from the second year of the study of balance.

Objective: At the end of this lesson the children will have learned to:
balance with different bases of support and body shapes on various pieces
     of low apparatus.

             REVIEW CUES: Tight muscles
                            Alignment
                            Extensions

Materials/
Equipment: See Figure 37 in Lesson 5 for apparatus setup

Organization/
Management: Established protocol for moving apparatus, response to signal/listening position
                      Rules for working safely on apparatus

Introduction:
You have reviewed balancing on different bases of support, at different levels, and in different shapes. Your work on the mats has been excellent. Your balances are held stationary for a three-second count; you are creating balances at different levels. All of you are working on some type of inverted balances.

    Last year you balanced on different bases of support on the low apparatus. This year you will use all that information for balancing on the apparatus and add creating body shapes with your balances.

Content Development:
(Position apparatus throughout the work area with sufficient space for working safely on the apparatus, getting on and off, and moving between stations.)

1.0   Before you begin working on the apparatus, select a small mat for practice and review balancing on different bases. The selection of base is your choice; I will name the critical cue that I want you to concentrate on.

T   As you balance, focus on aligning body parts over the base of support for good balance. I should see absolute stillness as you hold your balances for three-second counts.

T   Now create balances that demonstrate extensions of free body parts.

    Remember to really stretch for a true extension.

    Throughout all your balances I should sense the muscular tightness as you hold them perfectly still.

2.0   Balance on the apparatus using different combinations of body parts as bases of support.

T   Last year we studied all the body parts that can serve safely as bases of support in gymnastics. They are listed on the chalkboard; see how many you can use as you practice your balances:

knees	elbows
feet	hands
head	base of spine
back	shoulders
stomach	hip

Have you thought of any new ones since last year?

Don't forget that a wide base is more stable.

T   Balance on a more narrow base on the apparatus.

CUES: Tight muscles, extensions, alignment

T   When you are at the stations where you are the most comfortable, practice at least two inverted balances. If you already have mastered one, then try a new one.

Be sure your weight is centered over your base of support.

T   When you are ready, balance on hands only on the apparatus.

Don't forget, hands only does not always mean a headstand or handstand.

T   Add levels to your balances.

3.0   As I observe your balances, I see stillness and the ability to hold a balance for three seconds. I note different bases of support and different combinations of body parts as bases. Let's focus on the shapes being made with the balances—wide, narrow, round, twisted. As you continue the rotation to the different pieces of apparatus, concentrate on creating a balance for each of the basic shapes.

Challenge yourself with each balance.

Let's review quickly. What body parts create wide and narrow—arms and legs. What body part is involved in the round shape—spine. What body parts are involved in the twisting action—arms, legs, trunk, head. Continue your practice with these reminders.

T   As you move to each station, select the four best balances of all you have created to show wide, narrow, round, and twisted.

Don't forget our first two criteria for good balance.

C   Select the station at which you can do your best balances. Remember, the station at which you can do your best is not always your favorite station. Return to that station to put together a sequence of body shape balances on apparatus. Practice your balances to be sure you can hold each perfectly still. Challenge yourself with the following:

Each balance will have a different base of support.
The sequence will include at least one change of levels.
One balance will be inverted.

Practice your balances but also your transitions.

When your sequence is completed, ask a friend to watch and mentally check the things that should be included.

Student Project

On the assignment table are papers with a summary of the assignment on the front and a sketch of the apparatus on the back. Choose the paper to match the station you have chosen for your sequence. After you have completed your sequence and have asked a friend to watch it, draw your balances on the apparatus sketch. When you are ready, I will watch your sequence.

Criteria for evaluation:
  Balances drawn
  Different bases of support for each balance
  Change of levels
  An inverted balance
  Balances numbered and performed to match order
  Beginning and ending shape
  Sequence memorized
  A balance on hands only
  Creativity (a touch of me!)

Depending on the weight transference themes studied this year and the work completed on jumping and landing, the approach to the apparatus and the dismount from the apparatus can be included in the assignment. (See Figure 38 for a sample assignment sheet.)

Closure:

Today we expanded our study of balance to include work on the low apparatus. What was the new component added to our study this year?

What is the difference between doing the balances on the mats and on the apparatus?

Which piece of apparatus was best for your inverted balances?

Which shape was easiest? Most difficult?

Reflection:

Can the children combine balance on different bases and body shapes on the apparatus?

Can they hold the balances very still for the three-second count?

Do they safely come out of the balances, accidental or intended?

Are they ready for large gymnastics apparatus?

Name _____ Homeroom _____

Apparatus _____ Date _____

Apparatus:

I.

      A. Approach to apparatus

      B. Mount onto apparatus

II.

      A. Balances (minimum of 4)

        Draw each balance, label base and shape

        Extra credit for inverted and/or hands only balance

      B. Transitions between balances

PLACE DRAWINGS ON BACK OF THIS PAPER

III.

      A. Dismount

        Jump from apparatus, proper landing

      B. Ending shape (Ta Da)

(Back of paper has predrawn apparatus, for example, balance beam, parallel bars, bench, climbing frame, triangle.)

Figure 38   Sample Assignment Sheet Including Mount and Dismount

Lesson 7 (Designed as a two-part lesson)

Focus: Balancing (on low apparatus)

Subfocus: Bases of support, shapes, levels, partner relationships

---

This lesson is to be taught following a review of Lessons 1 through 4, during the third year in the study of balance.

Objectives: At the end of this lesson the children will have learned to:
1. balance on different bases of support on a small surface (milk crate or box).
2. balance in wide, narrow, round, and twisted shapes on a small surface.

CUES: Tight muscles (Tighten the muscles for good balance)
Alignment (Body parts balanced over base)
Extensions (A counterbalance for each extension)

**Materials/
Equipment:**   Large gymnastics mats
Milk crates or packed boxes (one per child)
Carpet squares or small mats to place on crate (if desired)
Paper, pencil

**Organization/
Management:**   Established protocol for moving equipment, response to signal/listening position,
selection of partners
See Figure 39 for apparatus setup

Introduction:
You have practiced balancing on different bases of support and in the four body shapes. You balanced at low, medium, and high levels. You are beginning to master some inverted balances. Today we will apply those skills to milk crates and boxes, balancing on a small surface with your body off the floor.

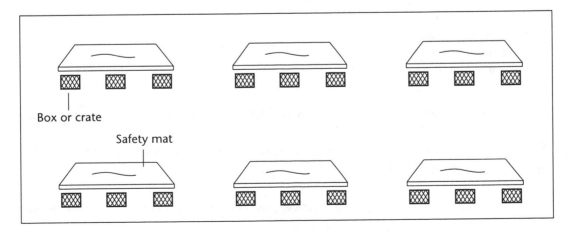

Figure 39   Balances on Crates and Boxes

233

You may choose to use a milk crate or a box stuffed with paper so it will not collapse. Be sure the box (crate) is snug against the large mat so it will not slip. You may wish to place a small mat or carpet square on top of the crate for a cushioned surface.

Content Development:

1.0   Explore balancing on different bases of support on your crate or box.

Teacher Observation:

Can the children balance with body completely on the crate?

Is their weight centered over the crate?

Can they perform the balances on the crate without extraneous motion of arms?

Do I need to reteach balancing on the crate or box with body parts on the crate and body parts on the floor (for example, two hands on crate, one foot on the floor; base of spine on crate, hands on floor behind crate)?

T   As you are working on the crate or box, you quickly learn that balances that were easy on the floor are more difficult because of the size and height of the box (crate). Practice balances that have a solid base of support:

Stomach
Base of spine
Knees and hands

Two cues we learned earlier are critical when balancing on crates (boxes), alignment and extensions:

Align body parts over the base for a stable balance.
If you have an extension of a free body part from the center, extend a body part in the opposite direction for counterbalance.

 If you are unsure of your balance, have a friend brace the crate by holding the bottom of the crate.

T   Balance on the crate with the following bases of support:

Knees and elbows
Two knees and two hands
Two hands and one knee
One foot
One hip

2.0   Create inverted balances on the crate (box) by having your head lower than other body parts.

 When you try inverted balances on the crate (box), always have a friend secure the crate (box) by holding it with both hands.

If your head is off the crate (box) when inverted, you need an extension in the opposite direction for counterbalance.

234

T   Balance on your shoulders, holding the crate (box) with both hands. Extend your legs (or one leg) upward.

Your weight must be equally distributed on the crate for this one.

T   Balance on one knee and two hands; extend the free leg upward.

3.0   When we balance on an elevated surface, the tendency is to keep our bodies at a low level close to the box or crate. Experiment with creating balances at medium and high levels.

Remember, weight centered over the box—balance and counterbalance.

Don't forget the muscular tension that maintains the balance.

Some children will be ready for inverted balances, such as frogstands and headstands, on the boxes and crates. Introduce these skills only for those individuals who are ready (intratask variation).

4.0   During earlier lessons you have practiced balancing on different bases of support, at different levels, and in inverted positions. Now let's concentrate on the shapes you are making in each of your balances on the crate (box). Balance on the crate, creating a very wide shape.

T   See how many different wide shapes you can make on the elevated surface.

I should almost see the muscular tightness as you hold the position.

T   What bases of support will help in creating narrow shapes? Try balancing on the base of your spine with legs and arms close together. Still extend your legs close together. S-t-r-e-t-c-h your legs for a full extension.

T   Balance on one hip with counterbalance extensions creating a narrow shape.

T   Some of you are ready to balance on shoulders and arms, creating narrow plus inverted shapes.

Tighten the stomach muscles.

T   Being creative with round shape balances is often very difficult. Try to create at least two balances that demonstrate a round shape:

    Knees and lower legs on crate
    Frogstand on crate
    Balance on back
    Balance on base of spine

Don't forget the shape is round.

T   Create balances with a twisted shape.

Move slowly into the twisted shape. The action itself moves you off balance; shift weight to remain over the center.

Children with good upper body and arm strength will be ready for the challenge of balancing on hands only: tip up, legs extended in front, legs extended to the sides, and handstands. These are, again, intratask variations—individual challenges.

C   Your balances with different bases of support, changes in levels, and body shapes look good. Now you are ready for the real challenge of today. Select four balances that are your best ones for demonstrating bases of support. Decide in what order they will be done, then do all four balances without touching the mat; that is, stay on the crate (box) until you complete all four.

Does that change the order in which you will do them?

The original criterion does not change: absolute stillness for three seconds!

T   Now that your balances are secure, concentrate on the transition between each balance. Make it smooth like a gymnastics sequence.

This challenge may be repeated with a focus on levels or shapes.

C   Select a partner whose skills of balancing on the crates (boxes) are similar to your skills. You and that partner are going to create a four-part sequence on the crates.

1. Your sequence must have four balances. You may choose to focus on bases of support or body shapes.
2. Use changes of levels and inverted balances to add to your sequence.
3. You and your partner may choose a side-by-side relationship or a mirror image facing each other.
4. You may choose to do all balances and transitions simultaneously or in copycat fashion.

Remember, this is a cooperative endeavor. Choose only those balances both of you can do successfully.

Make every movement a part of your sequence.

When you have completed your sequence, record it on paper:

    Illustrate each balance.
    Label the base of support or shape it represents.
    Indicate changes in levels; note inverted balances.

Practice together for accuracy and timing. Come to me when you are ready for me to see the finished product.

 Partner Project
The children's sequence drawings with an attached paragraph explaining the theme are an excellent communication to parents. Teacher comments and evaluation can be written on the recorded sequence or evaluation slip attached.

Closure:

What is different about balancing on the crates and boxes? Why is it more difficult?

What was the most important cue for you in maintaining balance on this elevated surface?

Reflection:

Can the children hold stationary balances on the crates (boxes)?

Do they appear comfortable on an elevated, smaller surface such as a crate or box?

Can the children hold stationary balances on the crates (boxes)?

Do they appear comfortable on an elevated, smaller surface such as a crate or box?

Revisit this theme next year, adding symmetrical and nonsymmetrical balances on crates.

Lesson 8 and Beyond

Focus: Balancing (on large apparatus)

Following a successful study of balance on the floor (mats) and balances on low apparatus, children are ready for an introduction to balance on large gymnastics apparatus. The progression of skills follows very closely that on the mats and low apparatus: balances on apparatus, bases of support, body shapes, transitions between balances, approaches to and mounts onto apparatus, and dismounts from apparatus. At a more advanced level of skill development, students also study transfers into and out of balances on apparatus, combinations of balances and transfers, as well as transfers onto and off of apparatus beyond jumping.

Specific pieces of gymnastics apparatus, for example, parallel bars or balance beam, may dictate the types of approaches and dismounts that can be safely performed by the children. Any specific safety factors or restrictions pertaining to a particular piece of apparatus should be noted.

I have found it very beneficial to post safety rules and student responsibility pertinent to each piece of large apparatus. They are reviewed frequently as a safety reminder for all classes. Figure 40 is an example of this type of poster.

Balance Beam

Safety check: Mats in place
                     Turn-bolts secure

Rules: When jumping off/dismounting the beam,
             land on feet only.

Figure 40   Safety Poster

Transferring Weight

Lesson 1

Focus: Transferring weight (across mats)

Subfocus: Spatial awareness, rolling

Objective: At the end of this lesson the children will have learned to:
travel across the mat using a forward rolling action.

A Note About Cues: *Several cues are listed below for the skill of rolling. Each is critical for safety and skill mastery. I focus on them individually and collectively.*

CUES: Hands down (Place your hands on the mat on the outside of your knees)
           Chin tucked (Tuck your chin onto your chest)
           Round back (Curl your spine like the letter "C")
           Bottoms up (Hike your bottom high in the air)
           Tip and push (Tip over, placing your shoulders, not your head, on the mat; push with your hands)

**Materials/
Equipment:**   Small mats (one per child)
Carpet squares for outdoors

**Organization/
Management:**   Established protocol for response to signal, listening position
Spacing of mats for safety

Introduction:

Earlier in our gymnastics study, you practiced balancing on different bases of support and in different shapes. We added the challenge of balancing in an inverted position. Throughout all that work, the emphasis was on body control (tight muscles, alignment) and holding the balance perfectly still for three seconds.

That work was fun; the new skills were challenging. But the emphasis was stillness. We talked about the action part of gymnastics; we even worked on smooth transitions between our balances. Today we begin a series of lessons that will focus on the actions of gymnastics—transferring weight to move into and out of balances, across mats, and onto, off of, and over apparatus.

Today our focus will be on traveling across mats by rolling, transferring weight from feet to rounded backs with a return to feet. We will begin with a review of the rolling action and the curled spine needed for the roll. On your mat, practice a tuck forward roll to move across the mat.

Teacher Observations:

Do the children curl spines, creating a round shape for rolling?

Do they maintain the round shape throughout the action?

Do they roll without bumping heads on the mat?

Do they return to a stand after the roll?

Content Development:

1.0   I am extremely pleased with your forward rolls and with your memory of the important cues. Your preparation for the rolling action showed me rounded backs and chins tucked. All that is super. However, some of you were having difficulty staying rounded.

T   Practice your rolls again, stay tucked throughout.

T   Try to stand up after you complete the forward roll across your mat.

The key is the push with your hands when you first begin.

Stretching your arms upward at the completion of the roll will help you stand.

Watch out for the bad habit—no crossed feet!

 When you think your forward roll is perfect—rounded back, tucked chin, return to feet—let a friend watch you do two rolls across the mat. The friend will give you one point for correct technique, an additional point for returning to a standing position after the roll.

2.0   If you are comfortable with your basic roll across the mat, practice beginning your roll from different positions—squatting, kneeling, standing. This creates transferring weight from different levels.

The cues you first learned are still important:

Tuck your chin to your chest.
Push with your hands so your head does not touch the mat and so you will return to a stand.
Keep your back curled in a round shape.

T   Purposely control the speed of the roll so you move as slowly as possible. This will be very important when you roll across large apparatus—balance beams, tables, vaulting boxes.

T   We have only a few minutes left in our class time today. You may choose to practice your basic rolling action combining two forward rolls across the mat, you may practice coming to a standing position after the roll, or you may continue to experiment rolling from different starting positions.

Closure:

Today we reviewed a skill from long ago. What was the basic skill of our lesson today?

Tell me the important cues I must have for rolling correctly across the mat.

Why would we want to begin rolls from different positions?

Reflection:

Can the children execute a tuck forward roll correctly?

Can they return to a standing position after the roll?

Can they roll from a variety of positions?

Children's Movement Vocabulary

Fizickel: Are we coming to fizickel education today?

Lesson 2

Focus: Transferring weight (across mats)

Subfocus: Spatial awareness

Objective: At the end of this lesson the children will have learned to:
transfer weight momentarily to hands.

A Note About Cues: Although several cues are listed below, focus on only one cue at a time. When children have mastered that cue, then focus on the next one.

CUES: Strong arms (Hold your arms really strong for good balance)
Tight muscles (Tighten the muscles in your stomach and arms to hold the balance)
Alignment (Feet over hips, over shoulders, over hands for good balance on hands)

REVIEW CUE: Quiet landings

The series of tasks presented in this lesson are separate yet connected units for mastery. They are not tasks that will be mastered in a few minutes; neither will all the tasks be presented within a single lesson. They are presented here as a group; teach them scattered throughout the year, by intratask variation within a lesson, and only when observation reveals mastery of previous tasks and sufficient arm-upper body strength for safety.

**Materials/
Equipment:**   Gymnastics mats, large and small
Carpet squares for outdoors
Crates and/or boxes

**Organization/
Management:**   Established protocol for response to signal, listening position
Spacing of mats for safety

Introduction:

In our last lesson of transferring weight, you practiced traveling across the mat by rolling, transferring weight from feet to rounded back. Today you will begin learning the skills of transferring weight to hands for travel across the mat. The expert gymnast is highly competent in both these areas.

If only we had the magic formula like Popeye, you could just eat spinach and have strong arm muscles for taking weight on your hands. It's not that easy; however, all your fitness work throughout the year will now pay off—strong arm muscles for weight on hands!

Content Development:

1.0   Stand behind your mat or carpet square. Place your hands shoulder-width apart on the mat and kick up so your weight is momentarily on your hands only.

Tighten muscles to make strong arms.

When you return to your feet, land softly.

T   Begin in a forward/backward stance, one foot in front of the other; use this starting position to kick one leg upward.

> *Allow several minutes of practice as children experiment with kicking one leg upward, keeping the other close to the floor. Being comfortable with this position and being able to return to the floor in a balanced position are critical to further work of weight on hands.*

Bring your feet back to the floor in the same place as when you started.

T   Practice taking your weight on your hands, beginning with a 1-alligator count. Increase the time your weight is on your hands to 2-alligator. If you wish, you can try for 3 alligators.

C   Set a goal for yourself: 1, 2, 3 alligators. Practice until you can achieve that goal three times.

Always keep strong arms.

Don't forget: quiet landings.

T   When you are comfortable taking your weight momentarily on your hands, kick slightly higher.

Remember the body alignment and muscular tension we talked about when we did our balances? Both will be important now. As you kick higher, you will feel your hips over your shoulders; tighten your stomach muscles to hold that alignment.

If you should feel yourself off balance, about to fall over, twist slightly to bring your feet down in a different place.

T   You may now choose to practice either the alligator count or a higher kick and straighter legs when inverted. I will move throughout general space for assistance and to watch when you wish me to do so.

Remember, quiet landings; I should not hear your feet as I move about the room.

2.0   Using the forward/backward stance, transfer your weight to both hands on the mat. While you are inverted, bring your legs together in the air, twist your body slightly, and purposely bring your feet to the mat or floor in a new place. (*Intratask variation for those children who are ready.*)

Bring your legs together quickly; snap them quickly to the floor.

T   When you are comfortable with a quarter-twist action, try a half turn, bringing your feet to the floor so you are facing the place you started.

Keep your arms strong.

Keep your feet together, snap quickly down.

C   Select the place where you are going to bring your feet to the mat—a slight twist, quarter turn, half turn. Say aloud, point to the spot, or touch the mat; practice your twisting action in the air until you can bring your feet down at that very spot.

T   While balanced on your hands, slowly walk on your hands, executing the half-turn. Bring your feet slowly to the floor.

Hips over shoulders for good alignment and balance.

3.0   Stand behind your mat or carpet square in a forward/backward stance. Transfer your weight from your feet to your hands to travel across your mat, as in a cartwheel.

The step action continues throughout the transfer: foot, foot, hand, hand, foot, foot.

T   Don't worry if your transfer does not look like the gymnast's cartwheel; focus on transferring from feet to hands to feet, starting at one end of your mat and ending at the opposite end of your mat. Practice this action for the next few minutes.

Observe, provide individual assistance as needed.

T   You have the action—foot to foot to hand to hand to foot to foot. Now begin to extend your legs toward the sky; really s-t-r-e-t-c-h your entire body.

Keep your legs in a wide "V" in the air.

One key to a successful cartwheel is to reach downward, not forward with your hands. This is a different use of alignment than we have discussed.

C   Practice taking weight on hands and traveling across your mat until you can complete the foot-foot, hand-hand, foot-foot action two times.

3.1   (Intratask variation) Stand behind your mat or carpet square with a forward/backward stance. Using this step action, transfer your weight to both hands with sufficient force so your legs travel over your hands to the other side of the mat. You will then be balanced in a "bridge" with your weight on hands and feet.

Bend your knees slightly as your feet come down to the mat or floor so your feet will be under you, not extended outward.

Practice a quiet, soft landing.

Strong arms—no collapse.

3.2   (Intratask variation) When you are really good at this transfer, you will be able to do a walkover. Keep your legs in the steplike stance as they travel airborne. As your feet touch the ground, push with your hands really hard so you move into a standing position.

Keep your feet in the steplike stance throughout.

P-u-s-h with your arms.

4.0   Gymnastics consists of work on the mats and work on the apparatus. For some of you it seems more like gymnastics when we use the equipment. For the last few minutes of our time today you may choose to continue work on the transfer you have been practicing, or you may begin to practice transferring weight from feet to hands on the crate. You will be surprised to find that many of the skills of transferring weight from feet to hands are easier with the crate or box.

 Be sure a friend holds the crate (box) steady.

Closure:

What component of transferring weight did we introduce today?

Transferring weight from feet to hands requires strong muscles in what body parts?

Why is arm and upper body strength important in gymnastics?

Reflection:

Can the children take their weight on hands momentarily?

Are they beginning to kick legs upward with enough height to have hips momentarily over their shoulders?

Are they beginning to tighten stomach and leg muscles to hold a firm position when inverted?

Are they able to twist slightly to come down safely when off balance?

Lesson 3

> *This lesson is designed with jumping and landing as a prerequisite; observation during the first few minutes will answer the question of revisitation or review of those skills.*

Focus: Transferring weight (onto)

Subfocus: Balancing, jumping and landing

Objective: At the end of this lesson the children will have learned to:
transfer weight onto low equipment (boxes and crates) with spring and step takeoffs.

> **CUES:** Squash (Bend your knees to absorb force when you land)
> Heads up (Keep your head and shoulders erect for good balance)

**Materials/
Equipment:**   Gymnastics mats, large or small
Carpet squares for outdoors
Crates or boxes

**Organization/
Management:**   Mats scattered in general space with sufficient space to approach and transfer onto crates safely

Introduction:
During our study of balance, you practiced different balances on the crates and on low equipment. We discussed the "getting on" but did not work on different types of approaches. You simply stepped up on the crate or climbed onto the vaulting box.

When you began to practice taking weight on your hands, we talked about feet in a forward/backward stance or parallel when transferring weight to travel across the mat. Today you will learn the two types of takeoffs used in gymnastics and when each is used. They are important as approaches to apparatus and as the lead-up actions to transfer weight to other body parts on the mats.

Practice jumping and landing on your mat, taking off on one foot and then on two feet, as I observe for safe landings.

> Teacher Observation:
>
> Do the children bend their knees and swing their arms in preparation for the jumping action?
>
> Do they bend knees, ankles, and hips to absorb the force of the landing?
>
> Do they land quietly?
>
> Do I need to reteach/review jumping and landing?

Content Development:
1.0   Stand approximately ten feet from your mat. Approach the mat with small running steps. Just before you reach the mat, use a two-foot takeoff to jump in the air and land in the center of the mat.

This approach is very similar to the spring takeoff on a diving board.

Practice soft, quiet landings.

T   Approach the mat with small running steps. Using the spring takeoff (two feet), jump high in the air, making a wide body shape while airborne. Land on two feet in a balanced position.

Remember, use a two-foot takeoff.

Keep your head and shoulders erect for good balance.

T   Practice the approach and the spring takeoff, making different shapes while airborne.

T   Return to your starting position, approximately ten feet from your mat. Approach with small running steps. Use a *step takeoff* (one foot) to go airborne. Land on two feet in the center of your mat.

Don't forget: a one-foot takeoff, a two-foot landing.

C   Practice several times until you can execute a step takeoff with a two-foot landing confidently.

T   Execute the approach four times: two times with a spring takeoff and two times with a step takeoff.

Landings will always be on two feet—soft and quiet.

2.0   Select the crate or box you are going to use today. Remember to place it against the edge of the mat so it will not slide forward. Approach your crate (box) from the ten-foot distance. Use a spring take-off to jump onto the crate. Land in a balanced position on the crate (box).

Bend your knees, ankles, and hips for a soft landing.

Keep your head and shoulders erect for good balance.

Focus your eyes straight ahead.

T   This time as you practice, decrease the speed of your travel to the box (crate); concentrate on the spring takeoff.

C   Practice until you think you have the proper spring takeoff. Ask a friend to watch your approach, takeoff, and landing on the crate. "Thumbs up" if correct.

T   Approach your crate and use the step takeoff to transfer onto the elevated surface.

CUES: Soft landings
            Heads up

C   Practice both approaches until you are confident each is correct, then ask a partner to watch. Tell the partner in advance which takeoff you will use—spring or step. The partner will then watch to see if the takeoff matches what you said. One point for doing the one you stated; an additional point for landing with bent knees, ankles, and hips. (Informal peer assessment.)

3.0   Remember the balances you did on the crates and boxes focusing on bases of support? They included feet and hands, knees, stomach, head and hands, hands alone, and many more creative ones. Practice your different balances using small, running steps as your approach and either a spring or step takeoff to transfer from the floor onto the crate or box.

Travel at a speed you can control; you are to stop on the box!

Before you begin the approach you must decide what body parts are going to be your bases of sup-

Use the spring takeoff when you need power or height; use the step takeoff for slower, more controlled transfers.

I'm still seeing some off-balance landings; some of you are almost tipping over the box rather than landing in a balanced position. This usually signals too much speed in the approach—slow down.

C   Practice putting several balances together while on the box or crate. Approach, takeoff with a balance landing, balance, balance.

As you practice, decide which balances are suitable as "firsts" to follow the transfer. Some, such as stomach, are better suited for the middle of the sequence.

 When you have a minisequence of approach, takeoff, balanced landing, balance, balance, I will watch for proper takeoff and landing.
   Create a minisequence with a step takeoff and one with a spring takeoff. Record this portion of your sequence and place it in your portfolio for safekeeping. When we add the portion of dismounting the crate and an ending shape, the sequences will be ready for videotaping.

Closure:

What did we add to our study of transferring weight today?

What are the two types of takeoffs? When is each used?

Reflection:

Can the children jump onto the crates (boxes), landing in a balanced position?

Do they bend knees, ankles, and hips when landing?

Do they keep head and shoulders erect?

Do I need to reteach jumping and landing onto an elevated surface?

Can the children label and correctly use a spring takeoff? A step takeoff?

Lesson 4

Lessons 3 and 4 of Transferring Weight may be combined with Lesson 1 of Balancing, increasing the complexity of sequences.

Focus: Transferring weight (off)

Subfocus: Jumping and landing, rolling

Objectives: At the end of this lesson the children will have learned to:
1. transfer weight off a low box or crate by jumping.

        CUES: Swing and spring (Bend your knees and swing your arms in preparation for the jump)
                Squash (Bend your knees to absorb force when you land)
                Heads up (Keep your head and shoulders erect for good balance)

        2. transfer weight off a low box or crate by rolling.

        CUES: Hands down (Place your hands on the mat)
                Chin tucked (Tuck your chin onto your chest)
                Round back (Curl your spine like the letter "C")
                Tip and push (Tip over, placing your shoulders, not your head, on the mat; push with your hands)

**Materials/
Equipment:**   Gymnastics mats, large and small
Carpet squares for outdoors
Crates or boxes

**Organization/
Management:**   Mats scattered in general space with sufficient space to approach and transfer onto and off of crates safely

Introduction:
During our last lesson on transferring weight, we introduced the two types of takeoffs needed in gymnastics. You practiced a spring takeoff on two feet for power and height; you practiced a step takeoff on alternate feet for slowness and control of certain actions. Today we will add the third part of the gymnastics sequence—the dismount from apparatus, getting off the equipment. Gymnastics sequences include all three components: mounts, balances with transitions, and dismounts.

Practice jumping off your crate or box and landing safely on the mat in front. You may choose to practice making shapes in the air, quarter and half turns while airborne, or just landing correctly from this height. I will observe for soft, quiet landings as I watch your jumps.

Teacher Observation:

Do the children bend knees, ankles, and hips to absorb force when landing?

Do they keep head and shoulders erect for good balance?

Do I need to reteach jumping and landing in relation to height?

Content Development:

1.0   Stand on the crate or box. Jump off, landing on your feet. After you land on the mat, complete one forward roll across the mat.

Use soft landings, balanced landings.

Be sure the back is rounded for the roll, head tucked.

T   As I observe this combination action, I notice some of you are not really completing the landing before you begin the rolling action. Continue your practice, concentrating just on the jumping and landing for a few minutes—good height on the jumps, arms swinging upward, balanced landings with feet shoulder-width apart. . . . Much better.

T   Now that the jumping and landing are under control, focus on the forward roll across the mat as you practice: jump, land/squash, roll.

Push with your hands to return to a stand after the roll.

Remember: chin tucked, back rounded like the letter "C." Sometimes we call this "C & C."

2.0   Balance on the crate or box on two hands and one knee. Extend the free leg backward as in a knee scale. Transfer off the crate by placing your hands on the mat and rolling off.

Roll slowly, with control.

T   Explore transfers off the crate from different balances. Experiment with transfers from different bases of support and at different levels.

Remember, you can transfer off the crate to the front, to the back, or to one side.

T   Practice transfers, other than jumping, at low level before attempting them at higher levels.

 If you were successful at transferring from feet to hands to travel across the mat, you may wish to try a feet-to-hands transfer off the crate. This transfer has two safety requirements: notify me, then ask a friend to steady the crate.

3.0   You have been introduced to some challenging, rather difficult tasks during the last few lessons. For the next few minutes of activity, choose the skill you wish to practice:

Spring and step takeoffs
Transfers onto bases other than feet
Transfers to hands only on crates
Transfers off by jumping—shapes and turns
Jumping and rolling
Transfers to hands on the mat

Use soft, balanced landings. Remember, "C & C."

I will assist you with areas of difficulty or watch your accomplishments. Remember, a person working next to you can do the same.

C   Last time we worked on balances on the crates (boxes) as well as approaches to the crates (boxes). You recorded your balances, the approach, and the mount on paper and placed it in your portfolio. Next lesson we will add the dismount of your choice to that work for a sequence on the crates. Between now and our next lesson, think of the work you have already completed and the new part to be added. What will be your dismount? Will you make any changes in your balances?

Closure:

What did we add to our study of weight transference today?

What is important to remember about transferring weight off the crates and boxes? About jumping? About rolling?

Reflection:

Do the children jumping off the crates land with bent knees, ankles, and hips on the mat?

Can they make shapes and execute turns while airborne and still land in a balanced position?

Can they combine jumping and landing with rolling, keeping rounded backs for the rolls?

Can they transfer off the crate in ways other than jumping?

Lesson 5

Focus: Transferring weight (into, out of balances)

Subfocus: Twisting, curling, stretching actions; rolling

Objective: At the end of this lesson the children will have learned to:
transfer weight into and out of balances by twisting, curling, and stretching.

CUE: Control (Absorb the force as you transfer out of and into a new balance)

**Materials/
Equipment:**   Small and large mats, carpet squares for outdoors

**Organization/
Management:**   Established protocol for response to signal, listening position

Introduction:
We have worked on balancing on different bases of support, combining a series of balances into a sequence, and linking the balances together with transitions. Our lesson today focuses on specific types of transitions, moving into and out of balances by stretching, curling, and twisting. To the experienced gymnast, every movement is a planned action; the transitions are a major part of the sequence.

Before we begin, let's review the actions of twisting, stretching, and curling; they will be the actions you will use to transfer from one balance to the next. Stand in self-space and stretch your arms to reach as far as possible. Stretch your trunk, feeling the tightness of your stomach and back muscles. Curl your spine until your back is round. Slowly uncurl, then curl again. Twist your trunk while keeping your feet firmly planted in self-space.

Teacher Observation:

> Do the children move the total body or body parts in the action named?

> Do they appear to understand the actions of stretching, curling, and twisting?

Content Development:
1.0   Stand at the edge of your mat. Balance on one foot, extending arms forward and the free leg backward for counterbalance. Stretch your arms forward until you are pulled off balance. When you feel yourself falling off balance, transfer your weight to your hands, tuck your head, curl your back, and roll across your mat.

Keep strong arms to support weight for the transfer; your head does not touch the mat.

Remember, chin tucked, back rounded—"C & C."

T   Repeat the balance, and transfer into the rolling action. This time roll into a new balance.

Remember, stillness for the balance before the roll.

2.0   Explore balancing on different bases of support, then stretch in one direction until you are off balance. As you move off balance, transfer your weight to a new base of support.

252

Absorb your weight as you transfer to avoid injury.

Move slowly to maintain control.

T (Intratask variation) Balance on your head and hands as in a headstand. Push with your hands, tuck your head, and roll out of the headstand.

Stretch your toes toward the sky; tighten your stomach muscles to hold the headstand.

T Repeat the headstand, and transfer into the rolling action. Roll into a new balance.

C Create three balances that you can stretch to move out of, moving into a new balance following each stretching action.

Remember, hold a three-second count for each balance.

Stretch until off balance each time.

3.0 Balance in a shoulder stand with your upper back, head, and arms serving as your base of support. Extend your legs toward the sky. Keeping your legs stretched, slowly twist your trunk and legs. Bring your legs to the mat above one shoulder; transfer into a new balance.

If you twist to your left side, bring your feet down over your left shoulder.

Before you begin twisting, tighten your stomach muscles to hold the balance.

T With your feet stationary, twist your body in different directions until being off balance brings about a transfer onto a new base of support.

Twist slowly.

T Explore balancing on different bases of support and twisting free body parts until your weight is transferred to a new base of support.

4.0 Think of all the many balances you created when we studied bases of support, body shapes, levels, and inversion. Balance in those positions. Use the actions of stretching, curling, and twisting to transfer out of the balance and into a new one.

Concentrate on smooth transitions.

C Choose your three favorite balances from today that show transferring weight into and out of the balance by stretching, curling, and twisting. Within this sequence of three, try to demonstrate weight transfer by rolling, by stretching, and by twisting.

Practice the balances, remembering our two criteria.
Practice the transitions for smoothness.
Decide the best order.
Ask a friend to critique them.

 Let's use our newly learned computer skills to create a slide presentation of balances and transitions. Your presentation will need to include:

Three balances
A rolling action for transferring out of a balance
A twisting action for transferring out of a balance
A stretching action for transferring out of a balance.

Closure:

What did we study today in our theme of transferring weight?

We transferred weight by three actions. Name them.

Why do we learn different ways to transfer weight in gymnastics?

Reflection:

Do the children have sufficient arm and upper body strength to transfer weight safely onto those parts?

Do they absorb force on the transfer?

What skill, if any, do I need to reteach before application to large apparatus?

Lesson 6

Focus: Transferring weight (on low apparatus)

Subfocus: Jumping and landing, rolling, balancing

Objective: At the end of this lesson the children will have learned to:
combine balancing and transferring weight on low apparatus.

REVIEW CUES: (Posted at stations)

**Materials/
Equipment:** Variety of low apparatus: milk crates, low vaulting box, low table, balance bench, low
balance beam
Dowel rods, plastic bottles (two per rod)
Large charts for posting tasks
Extra mats for surrounding apparatus

**Organization/
Management:** Established protocol for response to signal, listening position
Rotation of stations: independent or controlled
(See Figure 41 for stations)

Introduction:
During this theme, we have studied the skills of transferring weight. You have reviewed rolling plus
jumping and landing.

You have practiced taking weight on your hands and moving into and out of balances by twisting,
curling, and stretching. You have practiced the skills on the mats and then on crates and boxes. Today
we will increase the challenge by applying all these skills to small equipment—tables, benches, balance
beams, and so forth.

The stations are set up according to the component of weight transfer to be used. The tasks for each
station are posted on the large wall charts. (*Record tasks on butcher paper. Tape to walls inside; use
easels outdoors.*) Remember the cues for safety as you work. I will circulate among the stations to
observe and to assist as needed.

Content Development:
1.0   STATION 1: INTO/OUT OF BALANCES
After you finish your practice, please be a spotter for the next person. Stand near the bench facing the
person, for security and to prevent their falling if they become off balance.

Task 1. Balance on your head and hands as in a frogstand. Push with your hands, and slowly roll out of
the balance.

> **CUES:** Rounded back
> Chin tucked
> Strong arms

Task 2. Balance at a low level in a tuck position. Slowly execute a forward roll into a balance with a
new base of support.

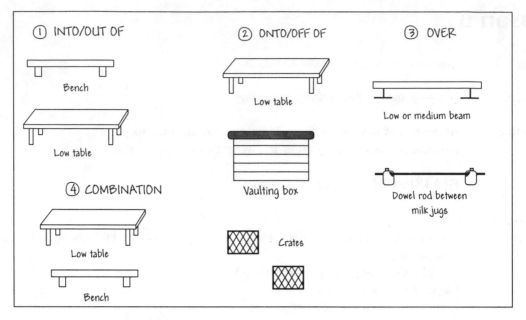

Figure 41 Low Apparatus for Transfers

    CUES: Rounded back
             Chin tucked
             Strong arms

Task 3. Balance on a chosen base of support. Twist free body parts to transfer to a new base of support.

    CUE: Strong arms to absorb force

STATION 2: ONTO/OFF OF EQUIPMENT
Approach the equipment from a distance of approximately ten feet.

Task 1. Use a spring takeoff to transfer weight to a gymnastics balance on the equipment.

    CUE: Soft landings

Task 2. Use a step takeoff to transfer weight onto the equipment.

    CUE: Strong arms to absorb force

Task 3. Use a spring takeoff to transfer weight to hands and knees on the box (crate, table).

    CUE: Head and shoulders erect

(Intratask variation) Use a spring takeoff to transfer weight to hands and head on the equipment.

    CUE: Strong arms to absorb force

Task 4. Jump off the box (table, crate), making a wide shape in the air. Land in a balanced position.

    CUES: Swing and spring for good height on the jump
             Full squash for yielding landing

Task 5. Practice making round, twisted shapes in the air.

    CUE: Head and shoulders erect for good balance

Task 6. Jump and execute a quarter turn. Land on the mats, roll sideways.

> **CUES:** Head and shoulders erect
> Balanced landing, then roll

STATION 3: OVER THE EQUIPMENT

Task 1. Stand two to three feet behind the dowel rod. Transfer your weight by placing your hands on the other side of the rod as you travel from feet to hands to feet.

> **CUE:** Strong arms

Task 2. Transfer weight to hands over the dowel rod; curl your back and roll across the mat.

> **CUE:** Strong arms
> "C & C"

Task 3. Transfer weight from feet to hands on the beam, "vaulting" over the beam.

> **CUE:** Head and shoulders erect

STATION 4: COMBINATIONS

Task 1. Approach the table. Use a spring takeoff to transfer into a balance on hands and knees. Roll out of that balance into a balance on feet only. Jump off the table, making a quarter turn. Roll forward.

Task 2. Approach the bench. Use a step takeoff to transfer into a balance on the bench. Twist into a new balance. Lie on your stomach, reaching your hands to the mat. Roll off the bench into a new balance on the mat.

C   Choose your favorite piece of apparatus that you used today. Create a sequence including the following:

> Takeoff (spring or step)
> Balance
> Transfer out of balance
> New balance
> Transfer off
> Ending balance

 Show your sequence to a friend to be sure you have included all the components. You may then choose to:
record it on paper and show it to me,
videotape it for self-evaluation, or
prepare a computer slide presentation for class.

Closure:

What was different about our lesson today?

Compare your skills of transferring weight today and when we first started this theme.

Compare moving into and out of balances on the mats and on the low apparatus.

Reflection:

Can the children transfer weight onto the apparatus rather than just jumping onto it?

Do they move in and out of balances safely on apparatus?

Can they take weight on their hands in combination with other body parts on low apparatus?

Do they land safely when jumping off apparatus?

Are they ready to apply these skills to large gymnastics apparatus?

> *Transferring weight is a difficult theme for children to master because of its many interrelated skills—balancing, rolling, jumping, and landing—plus the need for strong arms and upper body. At the control level, time is spent on mastering the many components with much concentrated and distributed practice.*

Lesson 7 and Beyond

Focus: Transferring weight (on large apparatus)

Just as children are not ready for transferring weight in relation to low apparatus until they have control of their bodies transferring weight on mats (upper body strength, acceptance of responsibility, mastery of basic transferring weight skills), neither are they ready for the study of transferring weight onto, off, over, and on large gymnastics apparatus until mastery is demonstrated on low apparatus.

At the precontrol level we begin with an exploration of the apparatus, correct ways for getting on, and correct ways of getting off the apparatus—full squash, no crash landings. Safety, body control, and acceptance of responsibility are stressed from the beginning.

The tasks and challenges for transferring weight as well as evaluation examples can be found in *Children Moving,* Chapter 24.

Volleying

Lesson 1

Focus: Volleying (underhand pattern)

Subfocus: Spatial awareness

Objectives: At the end of this lesson the children will have learned to:
1. contact the ball with open palms.
2. be in a forward/backward stance in preparation for striking the ball.

A Note About Cues: Although several cues are listed for the lesson, focus on only one cue at a time. When the children have mastered that cue, then focus on the next one.

CUES: Watch the ball (Watch the ball until it contacts your hand)
Flat palm (Keep your palm flat for contact)
Forward/backward stance (Assume a forward/backward stance for good hits)
Quick feet (Move your feet quickly to always be in position for the contact)

Materials/ Equipment: Plastic balls, 8-1/2-inch (one per child)
Wall space for volleying
Tape lines on wall approximately four feet above floor

Organization/ Management: Established protocol for response to signal (hold ball in hands; place on floor between feet)

Introduction:
Today we are beginning a study of the theme of volleying. When I say the word "volley," most of you immediately think of the sport of volleyball. The skill of volleying is also used as an underhand striking pattern for handball; a volley with feet, head, and thighs in soccer; and a volley as in hacky sack. During your time in physical education, we will study the different types of volley; this theme, however, will concentrate on the underhand striking pattern of a volley.

We will begin the skill with a two-handed pattern, then quickly move to a one-hand volley. Watch as I do the skill (model). The ball is to be hit with open palms, hands touching. Arms are extended. The stance should be forward/backward, the same as you have learned for throwing and other types of striking. Stand around the circle and let's model the skill together. Show me the proper stance: arms extended in front of the body, hands together, palms turned upward and flat.

The volley is a swinging of the arms upward and forward. Pretend you are striking a ball to send it forward; I will move around the circle to observe: flat palms, forward/backward stance.

Content Development:

1.0 Standing approximately six to eight feet from the wall, strike the ball with both hands so it travels to the wall. Catch the ball after it bounces one time (model). The pattern is bounce, hit, bounce, catch.

Watch the ball as it contacts your hands each time.

Keep your hands together, palms flat.

T Continue your single hits as I observe.

I am seeing flat palms. Super! **Don't forget the forward/backward stance.**

Contact the ball so it hits just above the tape line on the wall.

Contact the ball just below the center so it travels forward and slightly upward. When have we used that cue before? Right, kicking a ball to send it upward through the air.

C Continue practicing until you can complete five single hits without a mistake. Catch the ball after each one.

    CUES: Flat palm
            Forward/backward stance

T Ask a friend to watch your single hits. You earn a point for the forward/backward stance and an additional point for hitting with hands together/open palms. (Informal peer assessment.)

Some of you may need to adjust the distance you are standing from the wall; take a step closer if you are not getting the ball to the wall when you hit.

2.0 When you feel confident with your single hits, begin to practice consecutive hits. The skill is the same, but you do not catch the ball after the rebound (model). The pattern is bounce, hit, bounce, hit.

Watch the ball; the hits will come more quickly now.

T To do consecutive hits, you must always be in position to hit the ball. It will not always come directly back to you; you must be ready to move into position behind the ball. Continue your practice, concentrating on always being in position behind the ball.

    CUE: Quick feet

T Try for only two or three consecutive hits when you first begin practicing.

T When you are successful with two or three consecutive hits, try for five with no mistakes.

C Count the number of consecutive hits you can complete without a mistake. Based on that score, set a goal for yourself and try to hit that many consecutive hits without a mistake. It's okay to be working on two or three consecutive hits; set your own goal.

3.0 We have only a few minutes of practice time remaining in our class today. You may choose to practice either your single hits (bounce, hit, bounce, catch) or your consecutive hits (bounce, hit, bounce, hit). Saying the words will help you create the rhythm for the volley.

Don't rush through this lesson. Children need practice on single and consecutive hits to develop the proper skill—flat palms, forward/backward stance, moving into position for each hit. These basic skills are critical to all that follow.

Closure:

What new theme did we begin today?

Name the games or sports that use the volley.

What part of the hand should contact the ball? Show me the correct hand position—open palms, hands together.

What should the position for your feet be—side-to-side or forward/backward stance?

Reflection:

Do the children contact the ball with open, flat palms?

Do they stand in a forward/backward stance in readiness for the contact?

Are they ready for one-hand hits in the next lesson?

The hands-together, palms-up, arms-extended volley is excellent preparation for the bump of volleyball. Depending on the direction of the theme, it can be taught as Lesson 2, or the relatedness can be taught when the class studies the bump (volley) at a later time.

   The two-hand volley can be an introduction to volleying with different body parts with an emphasis on the flat surface, for example, thigh, inside/outside of feet, and head volleys. These can be explored and mastered with different types of balls.

Children's Movement Vocabulary

Ecsta cadite: Tasks completed for additional points (extra credit).

Lesson 2

Focus: Volleying (underhand pattern)

Subfocus: Spatial awareness, partner relationships

Objectives: At the end of this lesson the children will have learned to:
1. volley the ball so it travels forward to the target area (above the tape line on the wall).
2. volley the ball alternately with a partner.

               CUE: Extend (Extend your arms away from the body for a good hit)

               REVIEW CUES: Watch the ball
                                       Flat palms
                                       Forward/backward stance
                                       Quick feet

Materials/
Equipment: Plastic balls, 8-1/2 inch (one per child)
                Wall space for volleying
                Tape lines on wall approximately four feet above floor

Organization/
Management: Established protocol for response to signal (hold ball in hands; place on floor between feet); selection of partners

Introduction:
We began our study of the theme of volleying by concentrating on the underhand striking pattern. Let's review quickly the important cues for hitting the ball correctly for the underhand striking pattern. I will model, and you tell me what I should do. What should I know about the position of my hands? Together or apart? Open palm or closed fist? What should I know about the position of my feet as I prepare to hit? Feet side-to-side or in a front/back stance?

    Good, you seem to have remembered the important cues for the skill. After you select the ball you will be using today, find your space (not less than six feet, not more than ten feet from the wall). Begin your warm-up with single hits as I observe for correct form.

 Teacher Checklist (see Figure 18, p. 97)
     Observation of critical cues:
        Flat palms
        Forward/backward stance

Content Development:
1.0   As I observe your single hits, I am pleased to see the contacts with open, flat palms and your feet in the forward/backward stance. I also noticed that the ball does not always travel where you wish it to go. Continue your practice of single hits for a few more minutes, concentrating on extending your arms forward and away from your body for the contact.

Watch the ball.

Extend your arms to reach for the ball; don't wait for it to come to you.

A ball contacted directly underneath will travel where? Where do I contact the ball to send it forward to the wall?

T   Try to send the ball directly forward to the wall (above the tape line) so it will come directly back to you; you will not have to move from self-space to get the ball.

Reach your arms forward, not upward.

T   This time after you contact the ball for the single hit, "freeze" your arms in that position. Are they directed toward the wall or toward the ceiling? That determines where the ball will go.

T   When you are comfortable with single hits, practice your consecutive hits that you began last time.

Remember: bounce, hit, bounce, hit.

Quick feet to always be in position behind the ball.

C   See if you can equal or better your score from last time. Some of you had four consecutive hits last time; some had ten hits. Try to improve your individual score each day.

2.0   Select a partner whose skills at the underhand volley are similar to your skills. You and your partner will alternate two-hand volleys to the wall, working cooperatively for a score of consecutive hits. Partner "A" hits the ball; the ball bounces one time, then Partner "B" hits.

Spatial awareness is very important when volleying with a partner. After you hit the ball, move out of the way so your partner can get in position.

CUE: Quick feet

"Keep It Going"
Continue cooperative practice with your partner in a game called "Keep It Going." You and your partner will do alternate volleys to the wall. Give yourself one point each time the ball hits the wall above the tape line.

The volley must be with two hands, open palms.

Remember, you are working together for a score. Volley the ball with enough force for a good rebound—not too much, not too little.

Closure:

What did we add to our study of the volley today?

Is it easier to keep the ball going by yourself or with a partner?

What did you learn about extending the arms for the volley? Why is it important that the extension be toward the wall and not toward the ceiling?

Why are quick feet important when alternating volleys with a partner?

Reflection:

Do the children consistently volley with open, flat palms?

Are they beginning to move into position behind the ball for the volley?

Do they extend arms for the volley? Is the extension toward the wall?

Lesson 3

Focus: Volleying (underhand pattern)

Subfocus: Spatial awareness, partner relationships

Objective: At the end of this lesson the children will have learned to:
volley the ball to the wall with one hand.

A Note About Cues: Although several cues are listed for review, with the change of the skill to a one-hand volley the children may need a focus on a single cue as in the beginning. Observation of the total class will dictate review or reteaching for mastery.

REVIEW CUES: Watch the ball
Flat palms
Forward/backward stance
Quick feet
Extension toward target

**Materials/
Equipment:**   Plastic balls, 8-1/2 inch (one per child)
Wall space for volleying
Tape lines on wall approximately four feet above floor

**Organization/
Management:**   Established protocol for response to signal, selection of partners

Introduction:

Thus far in our study of volleying I have confined you to hitting with two hands. Today you will begin the skill many of you have been so eager to do—the one-hand volley. Hitting with one hand will make the games more exciting; it will also require really quick feet for you to always be ready.

I sense some of you are feeling not quite ready for the one-hand hit. No problem. Just as it was your choice of when to move from single hits to consecutive, it will also be your choice of when to move from volleying with two hands to a one-hand volley.

Begin your warm-up today with ten single hits to the wall. Concentrate on extending your arms toward the target so the ball contacts the wall two to three feet above the tape line. After you complete the ten single hits, practice your consecutive hits by yourself, concentrating on those same cues—flat palms, extension of arms, forward/backward stance.

Teacher Observation:

Can the majority of the class execute single hits that travel to the wall above the tape line?

Do they extend arms outward as they contact the ball?

Are they getting into position behind the ball?

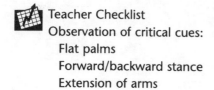 Teacher Checklist
Observation of critical cues:
Flat palms
Forward/backward stance
Extension of arms

Content Development:

1.0   As I observe your consecutive volleys to the wall, I notice we need to add a very important cue. When you were stationary for the single hits, you were in a forward/backward stance. When you are moving into position for consecutive hits, that is not always possible, nor will it be in game situations. Practice getting into position with quick feet, then step forward as you contact the ball (model).

Step forward for the contact. Shifting your weight forward will be very important in game situations.

T   Strike the ball with one hand, sending it to the wall above the tape line. Begin your practice with single hits.

Remember, keep an open palm.

T   As you assume the forward/backward stance for the volley, which foot goes in front? Correct, the foot opposite the striking arm! Where have we heard that before? Continue your practice of the one-hand volley with opposite foot forward.

The arm action is a front-to-back swing; your arm will almost brush your side as you swing.

Observe the children as they continue practice of the one-hand volley, single hits. Individual or group assistance may be needed for swing of the arm front to back, as well as for extension toward the target.

After you feel confident with your single hits, ask a friend to watch and give you a "thumbs up" or "thumbs down" for the following:

Open palm
Back-to-front swing of the arm
Opposite foot forward

Remember, if your partner does not receive a "thumbs up" for a cue, tell him or her how to correct the problem. (Informal peer assessment.)

T   Practice your one-hand volley, concentrating on the ball hitting the wall two to three feet above the tape line.

Extend the striking arm toward the wall.

T   (Intratask variation) Try the volley with your nonpreferred hand.

All cues are the same: flat palm, opposite foot forward, extension to target.

2.0   For those of you who are ready, let's try consecutive hits with one hand, your preferred hand: bounce, hit, bounce, hit.

Quick feet are essential; the ball will not always come directly back to you.

Several minutes of practice will be needed for this task. Permit the children to practice and refine, then provide individual assistance.

T   Always make the volley an underhand hit, a back-to-front swinging action, no sidearm or overhead hits. If the ball rebounds away from your self-space to the side, move your feet quickly to be in position behind the ball for the proper swinging action. If the ball rebounds back to you at a higher level, quickly move your feet backward so contact is at knee to waist height.

C   Challenge yourself to see what is the highest number of consecutive hits you can make without a mistake.

C   What was the highest number of consecutive hits you had with the two-hand volley? Can you better that score with your one-hand volley?

T   Contact each one-hand volley with your preferred hand. This means you must move quickly to either side to always be in position for the volley.

T   Contact the ball for the volley with the preferred hand and then the nonpreferred hand. If the ball rebounds on your right side, contact with your right hand; if it rebounds to your left, use your left hand.

T   Take a few minutes to practice the consecutive volley with two hands, with your preferred hand, then with your nonpreferred hand. Compare your individual scores on each.

Always use an open, flat palm.

Quick feet.

C   Play a cooperative game of "Keep It Going" with a partner using the one-hand volley.

C   If you wish, you may challenge your partner to a competitive game of volleying against the wall. Now, instead of hitting the ball so your partner can return it, volley it to the wall so it will not be easy to return.

> Remember, the ball must contact the wall above the tape line.
> Only one bounce is permitted.
> You will need to determine your back boundaries and sidelines.

Stepping forward for the contact is now very important as you add and take away force to outwit your partner/opponent.

Closure:

Today we continued to work on the skill of the underhand volley. What new component did you practice today?

Compare your single hits to the the hits of the first day. Is your volley better?

What do you need to practice during warm-up next time?

Reflection:

Do the children execute the one-hand volley correctly?

Do they move into position behind the ball?

Is the arm action an extended arm swing from back to front, not sidearm or overhead?

Lesson 4

> Lessons 4 through 6 are designed for classes with a basic mastery of the two-hand and one-hand volley.

Focus: Volleying (underhand pattern)

Subfocus: Spatial awareness, force

Objective: At the end of this lesson the children will have learned to:
strike the ball with the underhand striking pattern, sending it over a line to a partner.

          REVIEW CUES: Watch the ball
                                Flat palms
                                Opposite foot forward
                                Quick feet

Materials/
Equipment: 8-1/2-inch plastic balls
Tape or painted lines on floor five to six feet apart in parallel layout

Organization/
Management: Established protocol for response to signal, selection of partners

Introduction:

In our earlier lessons you learned to volley the ball with two hands, then with one, sending it to the wall. Show me the proper arm and hand position for hitting with two hands. For hitting with one hand. Correct—palms open, arms extended. Show me the correct stance. Correct—forward/backward with opposite foot in front if hitting with one hand.

    Your warm-up activity today will be:

Ten single hits with preferred hand
Ten single hits with nonpreferred hand
Consecutive hits of your choice

Select a ball, find a wall space, and begin your practice.

Teacher Observation:

    Are the children moving into position behind the ball for the volley?

    Do they extend their arms for the contact?

    Are they beginning to step forward as they contact the ball?

Teacher Checklist
Observation of critical cues:
  Flat, open palm
  Stepping forward on contact
  Consecutive hits
  Quick feet

Content Development:

1.0   Today you will change from hitting against the wall to volleying with a partner over a line on the floor (blacktop). Select a partner with whom you would like to work today and a plastic ball for the two of you to share. Stand about three feet from the line, facing your partner. Volley the ball with the under-hand pattern so it crosses the line and bounces in front of your partner. Receiving partner, catch the ball, then volley it back across the line.

Be sure your arm swing is front to back, not sidearm.

 Why is this very important now?

Step forward on the opposite foot as you contact the ball.

T   You may want to use your two-hand volley until you adjust from hitting against the wall to volley-ing over a line.

Adjust the force of your volley. Remember you are only six to eight feet from your partner.

C   Volley the ball across the line five times so it bounces in front of your partner with no mistakes. The pattern is: bounce, volley, partner catch. Use one bounce only.

T   When you complete five single volleys with two hands, then try the skill with the one-hand volley.

2.0   Are you ready for continuous volleys with your partner? Partner "A," volley the ball over the line to your partner. Partner "B," after the ball bounces on your side of the line, volley it back across to your partner.

CUE: Quick feet

T   Cooperate with your partner to see how many consecutive volleys you can hit back and forth over the line.

Volley the ball so it will bounce at a height between your partner's knees and waist. A bounce that is too high or too low is more difficult for your partner.

C   Set a goal for cooperative volleys with your partner. Attempt the skill with a two-hand volley, then with a one-hand volley. Do you need to adjust your goal, higher or lower?

Don't forget the first cue you learned—open palm, flat surface.

T   As you continue your cooperative work with your partner, concentrate on quick feet by doing this: Always use your right hand for the volley if it comes to your right side, your left hand if it comes to your left.

C   Your cooperative partner can now become your competitive partner if you wish. You will play a game of ten points. If you hit the ball outside the boundaries or fail to return the hit, your partner gets a point.

> Determine your back and side boundaries
> One bounce only
> One-hand or two-hand volleys
> Underhand volleys

In a competitive game, sometimes volley the ball for a high bounce, sometimes for a low bounce.

Receiver, if the ball comes to you with a high bounce, wait for it to drop below waist height for a good volley.

In a competitive game, vary the distance of the volley by changing the amount of force you use.

> *Older children may enjoy the challenge of playing different partners in the competitive game. Pair the children for the first game. At the conclusion of each game, match the winners and the non-winners for the next round of games. It is helpful to write partners' names on the chalkboard (flip-chart). The children then circle the winner (no score) and continue to find new partners as above.*
>
>   *Sometimes we have a challenge day so the children can replay or "test the best," including the teacher. Again, the competition is by choice.*
>
>   *This competitive class challenge works equally well for over-the-line and against-the-wall volleying.*

C   You may choose to continue the cooperative game with your partner rather than be competitive. If so, try to get a better score than your last one, or try to get a better cooperative score than the class high, which is _____.

"Two Square"
(This is an adaptation of Four Square for two partners. See *Children Moving,* Chapter 28.)

Closure:

What skill have you been practicing throughout this theme?

How is the skill different over a line compared with against the wall?

Why is varying the height of the bounce and the force of the hit over the line important in the competitive game situation?

Why do I have you practicing "stepping into the volley"?

Reflection:

Do the children volley with a back-to-front arm swing?

Do they now consistently volley with an open palm and flat surface?

Do they move into position behind the ball for the contact?

Do they volley correctly in the gamelike situations?

Does this class prefer cooperative or competitive volley situations?

Lesson 5

Focus: Volleying (underhand pattern)

Subfocus: Spatial awareness, partner relationships, force

Objective: At the end of this lesson the children will have learned to:
volley the ball over a low net using the underhand pattern.

                    REVIEW CUES: Flat palm
                                     Step forward on opposite foot
                                     Quick feet
                                     Extend toward target

Materials/
Equipment: 8-1/2-inch plastic balls
"Nets" suspended approximately three feet above the floor—volleyball, badminton
        nets, stretch ropes between standards, jump ropes between chairs (see Figure 42).

Organization/
Management: Established protocol for response to signal, selection of partners

Introduction:

In our study of volleying you have practiced striking the ball with open palms to send it against the wall and over a line on the floor. You began volleying with two hands and then learned to volley with either the right or the left hand, depending on which side the ball came to you. Let's review the cues for the skill of volleying (Show me, Tell me):

A: Palms?   open, flat surface
    Arms?   extended from the body
    Feet?   quick, to always be in position behind the ball
    Stance?   forward/backward, opposite foot forward, step forward on opposite foot

B: Why open palms? What happens if the contact surface is not flat?
    What happens if arms are too close to the body?
    Why do I need to be behind the ball for contact?
    What does stepping forward as I contact the ball give me?

You know the cues and the reasons for them. You are ready for today! Today's lesson focuses on the underhand volley over a net with a partner. Quickly select a partner whom you have enjoyed practicing with during this theme.

    Let's practice the volley for two or three minutes against the wall for the warm-up. Partner "A," practice your volley to the wall, trying for ten consecutive hits. Partner "B," observe and provide helpful hints or praise. Switch positions. After ten consecutive hits, or three tries for ten consecutive, you may choose to continue your individual practice or to do alternate hits for a cooperative score.

Teacher Observation:

    Do the children demonstrate the important cues as they practice the skill of volleying?

    What cues need more emphasis?

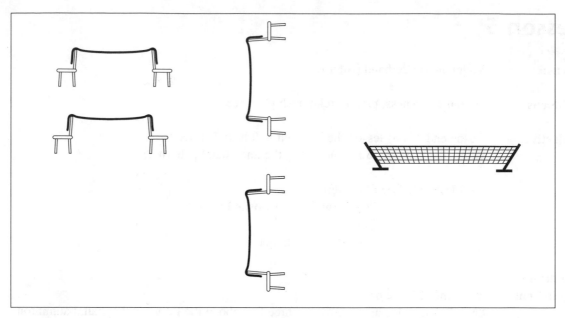

Figure 42   Nets for Underhand Volley

Content Development:

1.0   The work space today is set up with one large station and several small ones. A net or rope is suspended about three feet from the floor. Stand approximately six feet from the net, facing your partner on the other side. Partner "A," bounce the ball one time, then volley it over the net with the underhand action you have practiced. Partner "B," volley it back.

> **Follow through slightly higher for the ball to travel over the net.**

> **Don't forget, step forward as you contact the ball.**

T   If you are having difficulty with the volley, practice single hits to your partner for a few minutes. Partner "A," volley over the net; Partner "B," catch the ball, then volley it back over the net.

> **Remember, quick feet to always be in position.**

T   When you are ready, keep a cooperative score of how many volleys you and your partner can make with no mistakes.

    Remember to hit the ball so your partner can return it—force, placement.

T   Now let's make the partner work. Volley the ball to the right and then to the left so your partner has to alternate hitting with the right and the left hand.

C   See if you can do four volleys alternating right and left hands.

T   Make your partner work again. Vary the amount of force with which you volley the ball. Sometimes hit the ball just over the net so your partner has to run forward to the volley. Sometimes volley the ball so it travels toward the back boundary, forcing your partner to quickly move backward into position.

    Remember to control the volley, even when hitting for distance.

C   Challenge your partner to a game of "Reverse 10." Each of you has ten points. When you make a mistake, subtract one point. Remember to establish your boundaries and discuss any needed rules.

2.0   For the final few minutes today, you may choose to work against the wall, over a line, or over the low net. The small nets can be removed for wall and line space.

You may choose a cooperative situation or a competitive one. The class high score for cooperative volleys is written on the chalkboard and dated.

You may replay an opponent in a competitive challenge or practice with a partner on skills such as placement and change of force.

I will be moving among you to answer questions or help you get started. The one rule is that you must be practicing the skill of our theme—the underhand volley.

Closure:

What new dimension did we add to the underhand volley today?

How is the net skill different?

Which of the three is your preference—against the wall, over a line on the floor, or over a low net? Why?

Reflection:

How do the children's skills compare in the three situations?

How are their skills in dynamic situations?

Are they beginning to place the volley where they wish it to go (distance, height) rather than just over?

Lesson 6

Focus: Volleying (underhand pattern)

Subfocus: Spatial awareness, partner relationships, force

Objective: At the end of this lesson the children will have learned to:
create a game using the underhand volley.

**Materials/
Equipment:**   8-1/2-inch plastic balls
Paper, pencils
Nets suspended approximately three feet above the floor

**Organization/
Management:**   Space for wall volleys, line volleys, net volleys

Introduction:
This theme was designed to practice the underhand striking pattern of the volley. You learned to volley the ball against the wall, over a line, and over a low net. Today you will use that skill in new games you create.

Content Development:
1.0   Make up a game that uses the underhand volley. Include these decisions:

> Choice of partner (or alone)
> Against the wall, over a line, over a net
> Boundaries
> Rules

Remember that the game must use the skill you have been practicing—the underhand volley, open palm.

T   Design your game, try it, make changes. Record it on paper.

> Listed on the flipchart (chalkboard) are the four things that must be on your paper:

> > Name of game
> > How to play—describe the game
> > Boundaries—how much space do you need?
> > Rules

> Some of you may choose to create and play the game, then record it. Others may choose to work through the game on paper before practicing it. I will give you a signal to remind you to begin phase two: the practice if you have been working on paper, or recording on paper if you have been creating/practicing your game. (Figure 43 illustrates one group's volley game.)

 The children's original games (criteria as above) coupled with a daily checklist of critical cues serve as an excellent evaluation of the underhand volley skill.

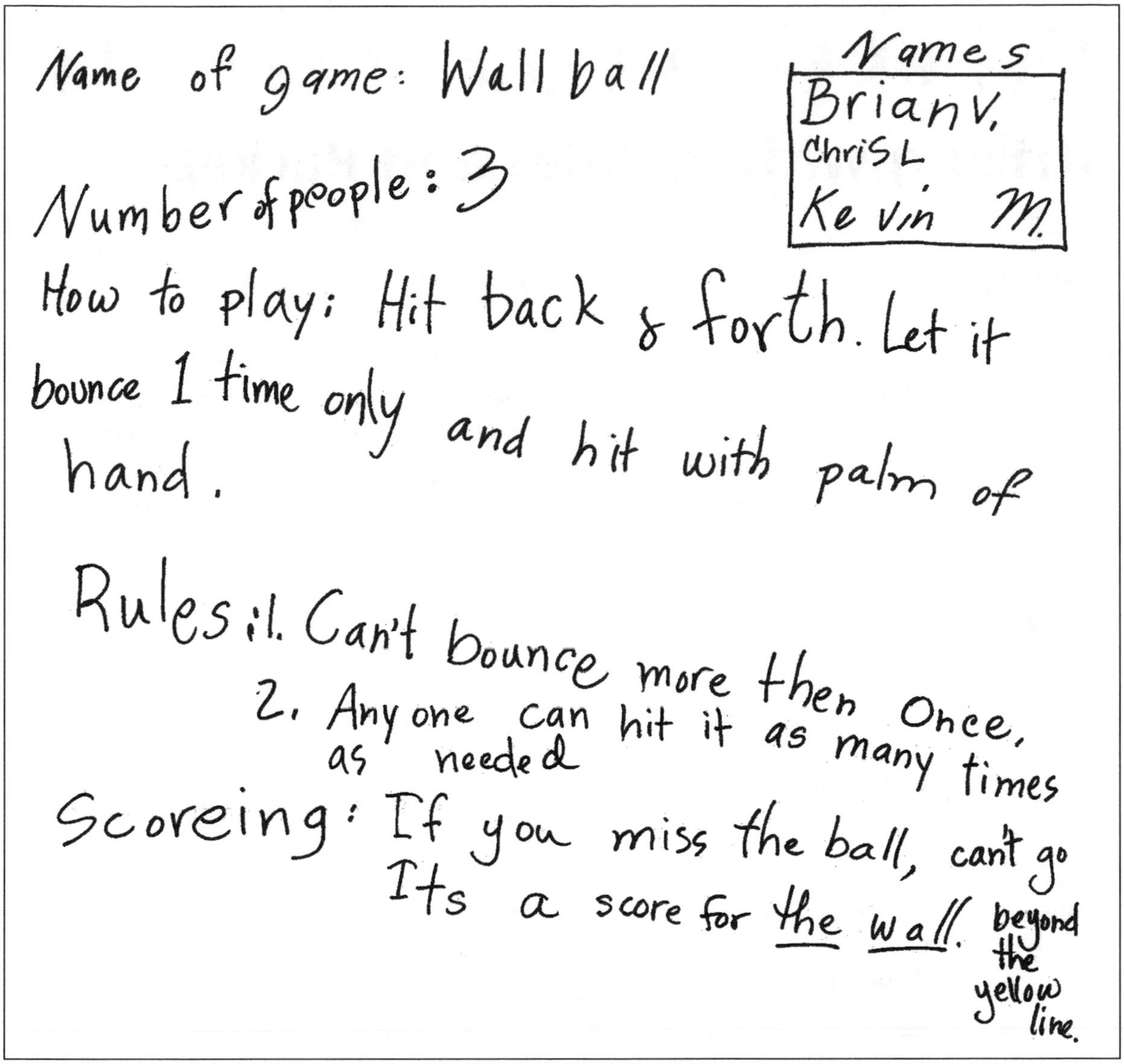

Name of game: Wall ball

Names
Brian V.
Chris L
Kevin M.

Number of people: 3

How to play: Hit back & forth. Let it bounce 1 time only and hit with palm of hand.

Rules: 1. Can't bounce more then Once.
2. Any one can hit it as many times as needed

Scoreing: If you miss the ball, can't go beyond the yellow line. Its a score for the wall.

Figure 43 Children's Game—Underhand Volley

Closure:

Were your games successful? Did you have fun? Did you use the underhand volley in the game you created? Was everyone in the game active?

Evaluate your progress in the skill of volleying. Can you remember your skills on the first day? Have you improved?

When we first began this theme, we discussed the different types of volley— the skills of volleyball, the body part volley of soccer and hacky sack. Which of those skills would you like to study when we revisit volleying?

Reflection:

Are the children executing the volley (underhand striking pattern) correctly?

What adjustments do I need to make in the theme for future teaching?

Striking with Paddles and Rackets

Lesson 1

> It is recommended that striking with implements be taught after children have studied striking with the hand (volleying), especially the underhand pattern. The following lessons are designed with the theme of volleying as a prerequisite.

Focus: Striking with paddles and rackets

Subfocus: Spatial awareness, force

Objective: At the end of this lesson the children will have learned to:
strike a lightweight ball or shuttlecock with a paddle or racket, sending it forward.

CUES: Flat paddle (Keep the paddle surface flat for good contact)
Paddle way back (Bring the paddle way back in preparation for the swing)

**Materials/
Equipment:** Yarn balls, small nerf balls, shuttlecocks
Plexiglas paddles, Ethafoam (lollipop) paddles, short-handled rackets
Colored plastic tape

> This series of lessons is written throughout for interchangeable striking with nerf balls and shuttlecocks. The theme can be taught using only balls, for example, with shuttlecocks used in a revisitation theme. If the two are combined within the lessons, you will need to build in changes from balls to shuttlecocks so the children are equally experienced with each.

**Organization/
Management:** Established protocol for response to signal (place rackets and balls on floor; hold in hand)
Correct way to hold shuttlecock for striking
Tape Xs on the wall, scattered formation, at height of approximately four feet

Introduction:

Earlier in the year we studied a theme called volleying—striking a ball with an open palm to send it to the wall, over a line, and over a low net. Many of the cues that were important for that skill will be important when you practice striking with paddles and rackets.

Select a paddle (or racket) and a ball (or shuttlecock). Standing about six to eight feet from the wall, use the underhand striking pattern to send the ball to the wall. These are single hits; collect the ball or shuttlecock after each hit and begin anew.

276

I will observe to see how much you remember from your work on the underhand volley.

> Teacher Observation:
>
> Do the children swing the racket in a back-to-front action?
>
> Do they stand with opposite foot forward or step forward on the opposite foot as they hit?

Content Development:

1.0 Let's review the key points in striking with one hand or with a racket. The action is the same; the racket is simply an extension of the arm.

> **The arm action is back-to-front, with your arm almost brushing your hip as you swing forward.**

How do you know which foot should be in front for the forward/backward stance? Correct, the foot opposite the paddle/racket arm.

T Practice the underhand hit, keeping these two cues in mind as you hit.

When you first learned to catch a ball, to kick, or to volley, the first cue was "watch the ball." That is still the number one cue: Watch the ball (shuttlecock) until you see it contact your paddle.

T Continue your practice of striking with the paddle. Drop the ball; don't toss it upward.

C See if you can strike the ball (shuttlecock) so it travels to the wall five times. Ask the person beside you to watch you strike the object. He or she will give you a point if you either stand in the forward/backward stance or step forward on the opposite foot as you hit. A second point will be given if the swing of your paddle is with a flat surface.

1.1 In scattered formation on the wall are Xs that will be your targets. Strike the ball (shuttlecock) to the wall, trying to hit an X.

> **Remember when you practiced extending your arm toward the target for the volley; extend your arm as you hit.**

T For the next few minutes, after you strike the ball, freeze your follow-through and see if your arm is extended with racket toward the wall.

T When you think you can do five perfect hits (flat paddle, opposite foot forward, extension of arm), raise your hand. I will come to observe, or a friend can observe for you.

T Let's focus on accuracy for a few minutes. Try to send the ball (shuttlecock) to the wall so it touches within two to three inches of an X.

C Can you be that accurate five times?

2.0 Take a giant step backward. Strike the ball so it contacts the wall at the height of the Xs.

T An increase in distance requires an increase in force. Hit the ball hard!

Really pull your racket back in preparation for the hit; this will give you power.

T When you are successful at hitting or almost hitting an X five times, take another step backward. Continue your practice at this distance.

> **CUE:** Racket way back

> **Step forward as you contact the ball.**

T   Each time you are successful at five hits from a distance, take another giant step backward. Because of the lightweight balls (shuttlecocks), you will soon reach a distance that is maximum for the ball reaching the wall; don't go beyond that distance.

2.1   Return to the first distance of six to eight feet from the wall. Strike the ball (shuttlecock) so it drops to the floor just short of the wall.

Easy does it now.

T   When you can successfully drop the shot just in front of the wall, take a giant step backward and try the drop shot from that distance.

The striking action is the same; the adjustment is the amount of force.

C   Select your favorite distance. Count how many times you can hit the Xs without a mistake. How many times can you drop the ball (shuttlecock) just in front of the wall?

Closure:

What new theme of study did we begin today?

How is this skill similar to the underhand volley?

What makes the difference between a long- and a short-distance hit? What is the cue for increased distance?

Reflection:

Can the children make contact on the ball (shuttlecock) with the racket or paddle?

Do they drop the ball rather than tossing it upward in preparation for contact?

Do they swing back to front?

Do they contact the ball with a forward/backward stance or step forward on the opposite foot?

Lesson 2

Focus: Striking with paddles and rackets

Subfocus: Spatial awareness, force

Objective: At the end of this lesson the children will have learned to:
strike the ball (shuttlecock) with an underhand pattern, sending it forward to a wall.

                  CUES: Follow through to target (Follow through toward the target for accuracy)
                           Racket way back (Pull the racket way back for force and distance)

                  REVIEW CUES: Racket face flat
                                  Opposite foot forward

**Materials/
Equipment:**   Yarn balls, small nerf balls, shuttlecocks
Plexiglas paddles, Ethafoam (lollipop) paddles, short-handled rackets
Colored plastic tape
Hoops for stations (four)
Wall charts with station tasks

**Organization/
Management:**   Group rotation for stations
(See Figure 44 for stations)

Introduction:

We moved quickly in the first lesson of striking with paddles and rackets. That was possible because the skills with paddles are so similar to the underhand volley—striking with an open palm.

    Today you will continue practice of that basic skill of underhand striking with stations designed for practice of accuracy and distance. Our cues help us develop those two parts of the skill:

    Follow through to the target for accuracy.
    Racket way back for force and distance.

During our warm-up today we will concentrate on those two cues. We introduced them last lesson; today we will spend considerable time on them.

    Begin your practice by focusing on the proper arm action of the swing and stepping forward on the opposite foot; you may choose to target the wall within a few inches of an X or try to actually hit an X. I will observe for arm action and foot opposition. On signal, increase your distance from the wall and concentrate on pulling the racket way back for more power. I will then observe for the racket being back each time before you hit. The third practice time will be for the drop shot. I will then move among you to observe, answer questions, and help as needed.

    It's a lengthy warm-up today, but very important. Set your own goals. Do your best.

Teacher Observation:

Is the arm action back to front, rather than sidearm or overhead?

Is the racket face flat for the contact?

Do the children either stand in a forward/backward stance or step forward on the opposite foot?

Are the children beginning to pull the racket way back in preparation for the contact?

Is their follow-through in the direction of the target, for example, the wall?

 Teacher Checklist (see Figure 18, p. 97)
Observation of critical cues:
Arm action back to front
Opposite foot forward for contact

Content Development:

1.0   The four stations set up today are for additional practice of accuracy and distance. I will signal when your group needs to rotate to the next station (Figure 44).

Station 1: Line up beside a partner. Select an X for a target. Say aloud, "I'm going to hit the green X," then try to do so. Repeat task with shuttlecocks.

Station 2: Select two balls for striking. From each marked distance, hit an X with one ball; hit the second ball so it lands inside the hoop on the floor. Repeat with shuttlecocks.

Station 3: How many times can you hit an X with a nerf ball? With the shuttlecock?

Station 4: Stand behind the tape line. Hit the ball (shuttlecock) so it drops inside the first hoop. You may choose five trials or five successful hits. Repeat the task, aiming for the second hoop.

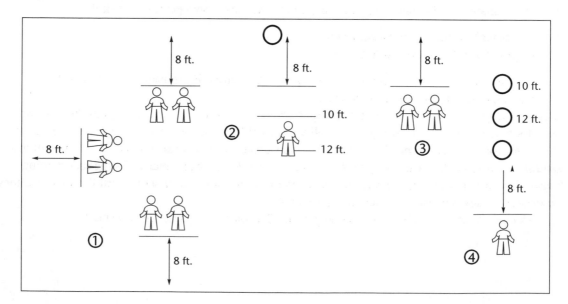

Figure 44   Stations for Striking with Rackets

Closure:

What skill were you practicing at each of the stations today?

What is the key to sending the ball a greater distance? What two things can give you more power?

What are the keys for accuracy? What cues help you when striking for accuracy?

Reflection:

Do the children strike the ball (shuttlecock) so it travels forward rather than upward?

Do they bring the rackets way back, increasing the power of the hit?

Is the follow-through in the direction of the target?

Lesson 3

Focus: Striking with paddles and rackets

Subfocus: Spatial awareness, directions

Objective: At the end of this lesson the children will have learned to: change the swing of the racket to send the ball (shuttlecock) to the left or to the right.

REVIEW CUES: Follow through to the target
Racket way back

Materials/ Equipment: Nerf balls, shuttlecocks
Paddles and/or rackets
Hoops (nine)

Organization/ Management: Tape Xs on the wall
Set of rectangular targets on wall (tape around Xs)
(See Figure 45 for stations.)

Introduction:

During our first two lessons, you were introduced to the skill of striking with a paddle or racket. Using the underhand striking pattern, you practiced for accuracy and distance by hitting to the Xs on the wall. You practiced matching force and distance by sending the ball just short of the wall, as in a drop shot. Today you will practice purposely changing the direction of the ball or shuttlecock, sending it to the right or to the left of an imaginary opponent.

Before you begin practice today, let's review the correct underhand action. Stand in self-space with sufficient room to swing your arm fully. Pretend you are striking a ball. I am observing for:

Back-to-front arm action
Forward/backward stance with opposite foot forward

Good, those beginning cues seem to be well ingrained.

Look at the face of your paddle or racket. If you want to send the ball forward, not upward, how should the face of the racket be when you make contact? Flat and slightly at an angle. Begin your warm-up by concentrating on racket way back in preparation and the follow-through toward the target as you practice hitting the ball (shuttlecock) to the wall.

Content Development:

1.0   Select the X that is to be your target. Practice sending the ball (shuttlecock) straight forward to the target.

Remember, use a back-to-front swing with racket or paddle almost brushing your hip as you swing.

Freeze your follow-through and ask yourself, "Is it toward the target?"

C   Practice until you can hit your selected target five times with no mistakes. You may choose to hit the ball (shuttlecock) directly to the X or within a few inches; set your goal before you begin.

T   Select the distance that is just beyond perfection for you. Practice from this new challenge zone for a goal of five hits.

   CUE: Racket way back

2.0   Now let's pretend that the X on the wall is your opponent. Rather than hitting the ball directly to the X, send the ball about two feet to the left of the X.

   Don't move from your ready position facing the wall. Now the swing of the racket is at an angle, rather than a direct forward/backward swing.

T   Practice purposely sending the ball to the left of the target. Swing your racket backward to your right, then follow through toward the target—to the left.

   Follow through to the target—to the left of the X.

T   Practice purposely sending the ball to the right of the target. Swing your racket backward to your left (slightly behind your back), then follow through toward the target—to the right.

   When you feel comfortable with the swing, or if you are having difficulty, ask a friend to watch and give you an evaluation of your backswing and follow-through. (Informal peer assessment.)

C   Practice until you can send the ball (shuttlecock) to the right, to the left, and on target five times each.

   Placing the ball or shuttlecock where you want it to go rather than just hitting it is often the difference between a skilled player and one who is just so-so. Don't get discouraged; keep practicing.

C   Challenge yourself. Verbally announce the direction—right, left, on target; then hit the ball to that place.

3.0   The stations set up today are designed to give you additional practice on the components of striking we have studied thus far. The stations include: hitting for accuracy, drop shots, distance, and directions—the new one we added today. I will let you choose your first station (no more than five at a station); stay at that station until I signal time to switch (Figure 45).

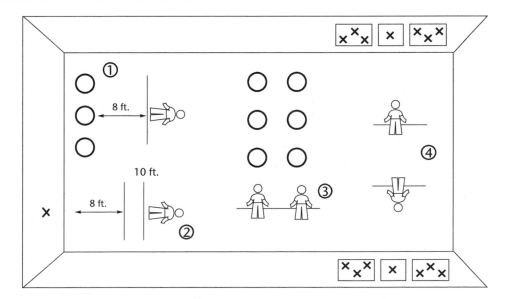

Figure 45   Stations for Distance, Direction, and Accuracy Striking

Station 1: Direction

Stand behind the tape line. Strike the ball (shuttlecock) so it lands inside the center hoop—five trials. For your second turn, target the hoop to the right or to the left of center—five trials. For your third turn, choose the hoop that has not been your target—five trials.

CUE: Follow through to the target.

Station 2: Accuracy

Stand behind the tape line of your choice. Strike the ball or shuttlecock so it hits an X on the wall—five trials. For your second turn, try the drop shot you have been practicing, or take a second turn at an X; this is your choice.

CUE: Step forward on opposite foot.

Station 3: Distance

Hit the ball (shuttlecock) so it drops inside the first hoop. You may choose five trials or five successful hits; then hit to the second or third hoop. Again, your choice.

CUE: Racket or paddle way back.

Station 4: Direction

Standing behind the tape line, strike the ball (shuttlecock) so it hits the center target—five trials. Each time it is your turn, choose a different target—right, left, center.

CUE: Follow through to target.

Targets are made by enclosing three to four Xs with tape. See Figure 46.

Closure:

What new component did we add to our study of striking today?

Describe the arm swing for sending a ball (shuttlecock) directly forward. To the right. To the left.

Of the tasks you have done thus far, what is your favorite? What has been the most challenging?

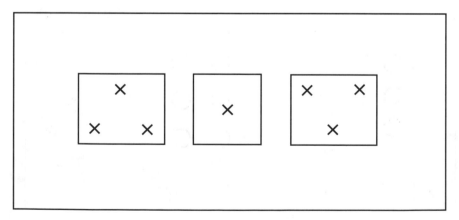

Figure 46 Making Targets

Reflection:

Do the children execute the underhand striking action with the correct arm movement and opposite foot forward?

Can they adjust the amount of force for distance and for drop shots?

Can they purposely send the ball (shuttlecock) to the right or to the left?

Lesson 4

Focus: Striking with paddles and rackets

Subfocus: Spatial awareness, directions, force, partner relationships

Objective: At the end of this lesson the children will have learned to: strike the ball or shuttlecock over a low net.

                REVIEW CUES: Step forward on opposite foot
                                      Follow through to target

**Materials/
Equipment:**   Nerf balls, shuttlecocks
                  Paddles and rackets
                  Net, rope and chair "nets"

**Organization/
Management:**   Established protocol for selection of partners
                  Nets suspended in general space (see Volleying, Lesson 5)

Introduction:

Today we will move closer to a gamelike situation with the theme of striking with paddles and rackets. You will be practicing striking the ball or shuttlecock over a low net. What game or sport can you think of that uses underhand striking over a net with a paddle or racket? Perhaps you will design a new game before we finish this theme!

Thus far in the theme, you have practiced striking with the paddle or racket, sending the ball directly forward to a target, purposely sending the ball (shuttlecock) to the right or to the left, changing the amount of force used for a drop shot. You know best which of these skills need practice. During your warm-up today, choose the skill or skills on which you need to concentrate.

I will circulate to assist as needed and to provide the verbal cues that might help. Remember, I am here to watch your "good shots" as well; let me know when you want me to watch. (*Circulate; provide individual assistance as needed.*)

Content Development:

With your partner decide which net area you wish to use. You will each need a paddle or racket but only one ball or shuttlecock for the two of you. You can change from ball to shuttlecock as you work.

1.0   Stand facing your partner, approximately six to eight feet from the net. Partner "A," strike the ball so it travels over the net. Partner "B," catch or collect the ball or shuttlecock, then hit it back over the net. You will be doing single hits.

      Remember to step forward on the opposite foot as you hit the ball or shuttlecock.

      Hit the ball with such accuracy that your partner can catch it without moving from self-space.

C   Can each of you catch five in a row without moving from self-space?

T   Partner "A," stay in your original position, six to eight feet from the net. Partner "B," move backward two giant steps. Partner "A," hit the ball (shuttlecock) to your partner. After ten trials, switch positions; leave your racket or paddle on the floor to mark the place for your partner.

Remember, racket way back for increased distance.

C   What is the highest score you and your partner can get at this distance? Your partner has to catch without moving from self-space for you to get the point.

T   Partner "B," stay in the mid-court position. Partner "A," hit the ball so it travels over the net and lands in front of your partner. Then hit the ball so it travels over your partner's head, but lands inside the boundary. Five trials to the front, five to the back; switch places with your partner.

T   Pretend your partner is going to hit the ball. Use just enough force to drop the ball beyond reach.

Loft the ball up high for this shot; follow through higher.

T   Partner "B," staying in self-space, try to hit the ball or shuttlecock. If Partner "A" is successful with the drop shot in front of you or the lob over your head, you will not be able to reach the ball. Switch positions after five trials.

Remember, easy does it for the drop shot.

2.0   Let's practice the use of directions you learned earlier. Partner "B," stand in mid-court; Partner "A," hit the ball to the right of your partner so it lands just beyond reach. Now aim to the left. Five trials right, five trials left; switch positions.

Don't forget: follow through in the direction you wish the ball to go.

Use just enough force for the distance to your partner.

C   Can you place five hits to each side of your partner?

C   You may choose to practice hitting to your partner, to the right, to the left, just in front, or over your partner's head. However, you must tell the partner which you are trying to do before you hit.

Closure:

What new component did we add to our theme today?

You had to concentrate on getting height on the ball or shuttlecock to clear the net; then your concentration was on accuracy for travel to your partner or a designated place in relation to your partner. What cues helped you?

Reflection:

Do the children step forward as they strike the ball (shuttlecock) to send it over the net?

Do they follow through in the direction they wish the ball to travel?

Are they beginning to control power and distance?

Lesson 5

Focus: Striking with paddles and rackets

Subfocus: Spatial awareness

Objective: At the end of this lesson the children will have learned to:
strike the ball or shuttlecock over a low net to a partner.

> **CUES:** Quick feet (Move your feet quickly to always be in position behind the ball)
> Racket/paddle back in readiness for contact
> Follow through (Complete the striking action)

Materials/ Equipment: Nerf balls, shuttlecocks
Paddles and rackets
Net, rope and chair "nets"

Organization/ Management: Established protocol for selection of partners
Nets suspended in general space (see Volleying, Lesson 5)

Introduction:

You have worked well on the theme of striking with paddles and rackets. You have practiced sending the ball or shuttlecock for accuracy, varying the distance of the hit, and purposely changing the direction. Then you practiced these skills over a net hitting to a partner; however, I did restrict you by not letting the partner return your hits. Today we will see what happens when the two of you attempt to hit the ball (shuttlecock) back and forth over the net.

During your warm-up, practice for consistency as you hit against the wall. The Xs are still on the wall as targets for your hits. Although you have practiced directions and changes in distance, concentrate just on hitting for accuracy during your warm-up.

Teacher Observation:

Checklist of critical cues:

> Step forward on opposite foot
> Racket way back
> Follow through to target

Provide individual assistance as needed.

Content Development:

1.0   Begin your work today with ten single hits to your partner. Partner "A," hit the ball (shuttlecock) over the net; Partner "B," catch or collect the ball (shuttlecock), then hit it back over the net.

T   When you are ready, you may try for continuous hits with your partner.

Remember, quick feet to be in position behind the ball.

Try a combination of quick feet and slow arm swing; get into position quickly, then swing easy.

T   You and your partner may choose to practice single hits with the partner catching or consecutive hits for a cooperative score, or you may choose to attempt to outwit your partner by hitting where he or she is not. Make the decision with your partner. Let me know if I can help.

> *The emphasis of striking with rackets and paddles at the control level is just that—control. Dynamic game situations can be introduced at a higher level of skill proficiency.*

Closure:

How does striking over a net compare with hitting to the wall? Is it easier or more difficult? Why?

We added working with a partner today. Why do you think we did not begin the theme with hitting with a partner?

Reflection:

What happened to the skill level when the children were asked to do consecutive hits over the net with a partner?

Do they move into position behind the ball for the hit?

Are rackets or paddles pulled back in preparation for the hit?

When we revisit the theme, what skills do I need to reteach?

> *Tennis rackets provide learning experiences for children with a midlength racket. Many of the cues for striking are the same (racket back in preparation, side to target, firm wrist, and follow-through), but several components are specific to the sport of tennis, for example, grips for forehand and backhand and service motion. An excellent resource for teaching tennis skills to children is your local United States Tennis Association. The USTA also provides free in-service to teachers, as well as rackets for students.*

◨ Striking with Paddles and Rackets Evaluation

Focus: Striking with paddles and rackets

Figure 47 provides a sample self-evaluation to be used at the completion of the theme. It is children sharing a personal evaluation just with you as the teacher.

Name _____ Homeroom _____

Striking with Paddles and Rackets Self-Evaluation

I am going to ask each of you to evaluate your skills in this theme. Take your time in completing the paper. There are no right or wrong answers. This paper is a communication between the two of us; no one else will read it. I have listed on the chalkboard all the things we studied in this theme to help you with your self-evaluation.

I most enjoyed doing:

I still need to practice:

I would like my teacher to watch me do these skills:

Additional comments:

Figure 47

Striking with Long Implements

Lesson 1

Focus: Striking with long implements (hockey)

Subfocus: Spatial awareness

Objectives: At the end of this lesson the children will have learned to:
1 strike a hockey puck with a tap-dribble action.
2. stop the movement of the puck with a hockey stick.

CUES: Hands together (Place your hands close together for a proper grip on the hockey stick)
Tap, tap (Tap-dribble the puck so it stays within three to four feet of you)
Trap (Stop the forward movement of the puck by angling your stick over the puck)

Materials/
Equipment: Hockey pucks (yarn balls for introductory lesson)
Hockey sticks

Organization/
Management: Established protocol for response to signal (hockey sticks and pucks on floor). Numbering the pucks will prevent confusion when children are practicing in general space.

Introduction:
When we study striking with long implements, we could use golf clubs, bats, lacrosse sticks, or hockey sticks. For this theme you are going to use hockey sticks. Let's review a couple of important safety rules you learned when we first introduced hockey sticks:

1. Always keep two hands on the hockey stick. The hand on the bottom is the hand you write with; if you write with your left hand, place it beneath the right when you hold the stick.

2. "High sticks" is a violation in hockey. High sticks is called when the stick goes above your shoulders. We are going to say sticks must never go above waist height; that's a rule for safety.

Pretend you are holding a hockey stick. Extend both arms with your preferred hand lower, as if holding a stick. The action of the tap-dribble in hockey is a wrist action. Move your wrists back and forth; don't swing your arms very much. This is a major switch from hitting with paddles and rackets; we emphasized a firm wrist for those skills. For hockey: arms extended—wrist action (model).

Content Development:

1.0 Travel throughout general space, tapping the puck as you go.

Keep your hands together on the stick.

Two hands always!

T Tap the puck so it stays "within reach." Where have you heard that before? Correct, just like the soccer dribble—keep the puck within three to four feet of you for good control.

Striking with too much force will result in the puck getting away from you, out of control.

Tap, tap.

T Continue to tap-dribble the puck as you travel throughout general space, concentrating on keeping it within reach.

Watch out for others as you travel.

C Here are two challenges for points. On signal, begin to travel and tap-dribble the hockey puck without bumping others. Give yourself ten points if you have not had a collision when I give the signal to stop. Begin the tap-dribble again, this time concentrating on keeping the puck within reach at all times; you are the best judge of that control. Give yourself an extra ten points if you were successful.

T Most of you were moving cautiously, controlling the distance of the puck and avoiding others. Increase your speed slightly this time.

Keep arms extended, wrists loose for the hit.

T Travel throughout general space so you cover every corner of our work space.

Quick feet, gentle taps.

 Monitor all activity for safety and no high sticks.

C I will time you for two minutes. See if you can travel to every open space of the work area before the signal is given to stop.

Remember, keep the puck within reach at all times.

Arms extended.

C I am very pleased with no collisions. Let's refine the control with an even bigger challenge. This time tap-dribble with such control of stick and self that not only do you not bump another person, neither does your puck. Ready? Begin.

> How many had no collisions?
> How many kept both hands on the stick?
> How many traveled with your puck never bumping another puck?

Let's try for an additional two minutes.

2.0 As I observe your travel and tap-dribble, I am very pleased to see both hands on sticks, pucks within three to four feet, and no high sticks. (*If observation does not reveal all of these elements, continue practice of the component.*) The tap-dribble looks good; now let's focus on stopping the puck. This time as you travel, practice stopping the puck by placing your stick in its path while it is moving.

Angle the hockey stick slightly over the puck to trap it.

T   Continue your independent practice of the tap-dribble, combined with stopping the puck. Establish a rhythm: tap, tap, tap, trap; tap, tap, tap, trap.

Arms extended, wrist action for the tap.

Angle the stick for the trap.

T   Increase the speed of your travel; don't concentrate on stopping so much that you are not moving very well.

Keep the rhythm: tap, tap, tap.

T   Begin traveling in general space, tap-dribbling the puck. When you hear the drumbeat, stop the puck quickly.

Remember, block and angle.

T   As you increase the speed of your travel and the travel of the puck, you will find it helpful to absorb the force of the puck when stopping it by "giving" with the stick just like you did when catching. This way the puck will stop, not rebound off the hockey stick.

T   Continue your travel and tapping of the puck. On signal, try to stop the puck within three seconds. (*Continue for two to three minutes of travel, with frequent signals for stopping.*)

T   Travel in general space at a speed with which you feel in control of the dribble. Each time you meet another person, stop the puck quickly, then continue to travel. The action will result in quick starts and stops.

The skill is the same: tap, tap, tap.

Starts and stops. No collisions.

"Plus and Minus"
I will time you for thirty seconds. Travel throughout general space at a moderate speed, tap-dribbling the puck as you go. When you hear the drum, stop the puck quickly. I will count 1-2-3; try to stop the puck before you hear the "3."

For each thirty seconds you travel with no collision of person or puck, give yourself one point. Each time you stop the puck within three seconds, give yourself an additional point.
Guess what happens if you have a collision? What happens if you fail to stop the puck within the three seconds? Subtract one point for a collision, one point for failure to stop.

Closure:

What new theme did we begin today?

Why do we have a rule about high sticks?

Show me the correct hand position on the hockey stick. The correct swinging action.

Why do you need to keep the puck "within reach"?

How do you correctly stop the puck?

Reflection:

Do the children maintain two hands on the hockey stick when traveling and striking?

Do they keep the puck within reach when traveling at a slow speed?

Do they strike the puck with a wrist action rather than a full arm swing?

Are they beginning to stop the puck by placing the stick in its pathway at a slight angle?

Lesson 2

Focus: Striking with long implements (hockey)

Subfocus: Directions, pathways

Objective: At the end of this lesson the children will have learned to:
purposely change the direction of the puck.

                 CUES: Hands together (Place your hands close together for a proper grip on the
                     hockey stick)
                    Tap, tap (Tap-dribble the puck so it stays within three to four feet of you)
                    Trap (Stop the forward movement of the puck by angling your stick over the
                     puck)

**Materials/
Equipment:**   Hockey sticks, pucks

**Organization/
Management:** Established protocol for response to signal (hockey sticks and pucks on floor).

Introduction:

During our last lesson you practiced striking a puck with the hockey stick. We called the striking a tap-dribble because you tried to keep the puck within three to four feet at all times. You also practiced stopping a moving puck correctly by trapping it with your stick. We discussed "giving" with the stick for stopping, similar to pulling in a ball when catching, and creating an angle over the puck with the stick so the puck would not rebound off the stick.

    Select a hockey stick and puck for today. Travel throughout general space tap-dribbling the puck. Travel at different speeds, and practice stopping the puck frequently.

Teacher Observation:

     Do the children keep both hands on the hockey sticks?

     Do they keep the hockey sticks below waist height?

     Do they keep the puck "within reach" as they travel?

     Do I need to reteach or provide additional practice before moving forward with this lesson?

Content Development:

1.0   Last time when you practiced the tap-dribble, I asked you to concentrate on the wrist action, with arms extended and keeping the puck within reach, always under control. This time as you tap-dribble, sometimes travel with the puck slightly to your left. Tap the puck with either side of your stick rather than running around the puck to get into position. Skilled hockey players are able to tap on the right or the left, just as basketball players dribble with either hand.

      Remember, keep your wrists in action.

T   Pretend you are dribbling around opponents, switching to the right and to the left side as you go.

Is the puck within reach on either side?

2.0   Tap-dribble as you travel at a moderate speed. Each time you meet someone, change the direction of your travel—to the right, to the left, or backward. Then continue to tap-dribble in any direction you choose until you meet another person.

Decrease your speed slightly when you begin to change your direction.

T   Each time you hear the drumbeat, change your direction as if you just met an opponent—quickly. Continue your tap-dribble, listening for the next drumbeat.

T   Practice checking the forward motion of the puck by placing your hockey stick on the other side, stopping the forward progress as you begin to change directions.

That looks much better. I see good control of pucks, sticks, and bodies. You are now ready for a challenge.

C   Tap-dribble in general space, changing directions each time you hear the drumbeat. Challenge yourself to complete the two minutes without ever bumping into another person or letting the puck get away from you.

If you had a perfect score, increase your speed this time.

3.0   Another excellent strategy for changing directions is traveling in different pathways. This time as you tap-dribble, travel in curves and zigzags as well as straight pathways.

Remember, keep the puck within reach.

T   Travel in zigzag pathways the length of our work area.

Don't forget, alternate the sides of your hockey stick.

T   Map out a pathway strategy against imaginary opponents. Travel using those pathways.

Closure:

What new component did we add today?

Name the directions you traveled today in floor hockey.

Why do you need to be able to change directions as you tap-dribble?

Will you always travel a straight pathway in a games situation of floor hockey? What can you do to avoid an opponent?

Reflection:

Do the children continue to keep both hands on sticks when switching sides for the tap-dribbles?

Can they combine striking with changes of direction?

Can they travel different pathways?

Is the tap-dribble under control when moving at a moderate speed? Is the class ready to progress to striking for distance—to a goal, to a partner?

Lesson 3

Focus: Striking with long implements (hockey)

Subfocus: Spatial awareness, force

Objective: At the end of this lesson the children will have learned to:
swing the hockey stick with sufficient force to send the puck a distance of twelve to
    fifteen feet.

      CUES: Gentle taps/hard hits (Tap-dribble the puck gently; strike it hard to send to a
        partner or the goal)

**Materials/
Equipment:** Hockey sticks, pucks
       Marker cones

**Organization/
Management:** Established protocol for response to signal

Introduction:
Thus far in our theme of striking with hockey sticks we have concentrated on "soft" hits so the puck
would always be within the distance of the stick for a quick stop. Today you will begin to strike the
puck with more force so it will travel a greater distance—to a partner, to the goal.

    Let's begin the activity today by practicing the "soft" hits, the tap-dribble. During the next few
minutes, practice dribbling as you travel at a moderate speed, then increase your speed but keep control
of the puck. Practice stopping the puck, hitting on either side, and changing directions. I will observe
for safety: two hands on the stick and the stick below waist height. I will also observe for arm extension
and wrist action and quick stopping of the puck. Ready? Begin.

Teacher Observation:

    Do the children keep the puck and the stick under control when traveling at moderate and
    faster speeds?

    Are they beginning to tap-dribble on both left and right sides of their bodies?

    Can they change directions without losing control of the puck?

 Teacher Checklist (see Figure 18, p. 97)
Observation of critical cues:
   Arm extension/wrist action
   Angle trap of puck

Content Development:
1.0   Stand approximately ten to twelve feet from a wall. Strike the puck with sufficient force to send it
to the wall.

    Watch out for high sticks!

Extend your arms with a slight back swing, then follow through to the target—the wall.

T   Let's focus for a few moments on the action of the hockey stick. It does not change to a golf swing; the stick still remains below waist height. Continue your practice with only a slight back-swing and a low follow-through.

Adjust your force. Do you need more or less?

C   Try for ten hits with no mistakes—no missed shots, no stray pucks to one side.

1.1   Travel throughout general space, tap-dribbling as you go. On signal, quickly tap-dribble to the outside boundary and strike the puck with enough force to send it to the wall. Retrieve your puck and continue the tap-dribble, listening for the next signal.

Use a slight backswing, then follow through to the wall.

When you first combine the tap-dribble and shooting for the goal, you may need to stop the puck before you hit it to the wall.

T   On signal, quickly travel to the boundary and hit the puck to the wall as one continuous motion; pause, but don't stop.

Slow the forward progress of the puck before you shoot, but don't completely stop the puck. You did this "checking" in an earlier lesson.

C   You may choose to stand still with the puck in front of you and hit to the wall, or you may choose to tap-dribble in general space and then hit to the wall. Visually locate a wall space that will be your target; see if you can hit that target ten times.

1.2   (*Scatter marker cones around the outside boundaries to serve as goals. Space each set four to five feet apart.*) Travel throughout general space controlling the puck as you tap-dribble with either side of your hockey stick. As you approach a set of cones, strike the puck hard, sending it between the cones. Continue the tap-dribble until you come to another set of cones; shoot for the goal. The pattern will be: tap-dribble, shoot for the goal; tap-dribble, shoot for the goal.

Remember, the tap-dribble is always within reach.

Sticks are below waist height when shooting for the goal.

Be sure you have a clear pathway when you strike the puck hard, sending it between the cones.

T   Pretend other persons are opponents. Vary your speed, change directions and pathways as you move toward the side boundary to shoot for a goal.

Remember, you can use either side of your stick.

> *Discarded hoops, cut apart to make a half circle and placed on the floor between two marker cones, are excellent "goals" for floor hockey. When the puck hits inside the goal, it travels around the half circle and rebounds back into the play area. The harder the drive of the puck to score the goal, the faster the rebound action. Children really enjoy the challenge of this one.*

"Total Score"
(*Divide the children into five or six groups, depending on space available, with an equal number of skilled and semiskilled in each group. Each group needs one hockey stick and one puck.*) "Total Score" combines the tap-dribble and shooting for a goal that you have been practicing. The first person in each

group will tap-dribble as he or she travels toward the marker cones (Figure 48). At any point after you pass the colored tape line, you may shoot for the goal—striking the puck to send it between the cones. After you shoot for the goal, move quickly outside the side boundary and tap-dribble back to your group for another turn. I will time you for three minutes, and we add all the points for our total score.

Remember, keep the puck within reach as you tap-dribble; I might hit the drum to signal a stop!

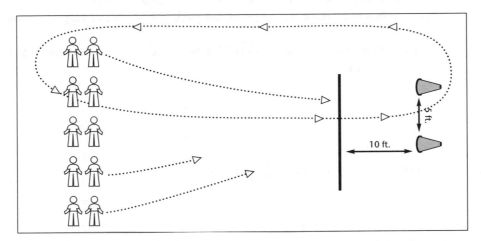

Figure 48   Total Score

You are not racing against anyone; you are trying to tap-dribble and shoot to earn a point for the class.

If your first shot for the goal misses, you may choose to continue shooting for the goal until you are successful, or you may tap-dribble back to your group. It's a strategy of point versus time.

Don't forget to use the sideline areas for the tap-dribble back to your group.

Closure:

What new component did we add to the theme today?

What is the difference between the tap-dribble and striking for distance?

What two cues are important when striking for distance and accuracy?

Reflection:

Do the children maintain control of the tap-dribble in a dynamic activity?

Do they control the puck as they switch from the tap-dribble to shooting for the goal?

Do they change directions and pathways to avoid others as they travel?

Lesson 4

Focus: Striking with long implements (hockey)

Subfocus: Spatial awareness, partner relationships

Objective: At the end of this lesson the children will have learned to:
tap-dribble and increase force to send the puck to a partner at varying distances.

              CUE: Gentle taps/hard hits (Tap-dribble the puck gently; hit the puck hard to send it to a partner)

**Materials/
Equipment:**   Hockey sticks, pucks

**Organization/
Equipment:**   Established protocol for selection of partners

Introduction:

During our last lesson, you practiced striking the puck with increased force to send it to the wall or to score a goal. Today you will combine force and accuracy to send the puck to a partner.

Let's review the individual skills before working with partners. After you select your hockey stick and puck, travel in general space as if you were in an imaginary game. Move with changes of speed, direction, and pathways, as if you are dodging and outwitting opponents.

Teacher Observation:

Can the children travel with changes of speed and direction yet keep the puck within reach at all times?

Can they do these skills and avoid collisions with others?

Are they in control of the puck rather than being controlled by it?

Which individuals need assistance regarding arm extension, wrist action, alternate sides of stick, stopping the puck, and so forth?

Content Development:

"Plus and Minus"

Your practice of dribbling plus striking the puck for distance will be a different version of "Plus and Minus." I will time you for thirty seconds as you travel in general space. You are going to travel from where you are now to the farthest distance in the work area, using all the skills of tap-dribble and changing directions. On signal, tap-dribble quickly to a side boundary and strike the puck hard—shooting for a goal. Give yourself "+" for no collisions, for keeping the puck within reach, and for striking the wall. Give yourself "–" only if you made a mistake in one of those areas. Remember, "+" and "–" will cancel each other, leaving you with zero!

Keep two hands on the stick at all times.

Keep sticks always below waist height.

300

C   Calculate your score based on the number of "+"s and "−"s you earned. Let's repeat "Plus and Minus," trying to better your score or to maintain a perfect record with all "+"s.

1.0   Stand approximately ten feet from your partner with open space between you. You will need only one puck. Strike the puck with sufficient force to send it to your partner. Receiving partner, stop the puck, then send it back.

Hit the puck to your partner; adjust the force of your hit.

Follow through in the direction of your partner so the puck travels straight to him or her.

C   Let's concentrate just on sending the puck to the partner. See if you can pass the puck ten times directly to the partner.

T   Now let's concentrate on the partner receiving the puck and stopping it correctly. Continue your practice of passing but be very sure you stop the puck each time before you send it back to your partner.

Remember to "give" slightly and angle your stick over the puck.

T   Shorten the distance between you and your partner. Accuracy may increase, but how about stopping the puck?

Easy does it.

T   Increase the distance by two giant steps.

T   With a distance of no more than fifteen feet between partners, send and receive the puck without either person moving from self-space.

2.0   Partner "A," remain in self-space. Partner "B," stand approximately fifteen feet from your partner. Tap-dribble the puck, changing directions, alternating sides of the stick; then pass to your partner who has remained stationary.

T   Repeat with Partner "B" stationary and Partner "A" moving before the pass.

Remember to have the puck in control before you pass.

Receiving partner, stop the puck before you begin to tap-dribble.

3.0   Move throughout general space with your partner. Combine the tap-dribble with passing as you travel.

Now you must use stops and changes of direction to avoid others and their pucks.

Remember our earlier work on "open spaces." Send the puck slightly ahead of your partner so he or she does not stop to receive the pass but actually receives the puck while "on the move."

4.0   We have only a few minutes of class time left today for striking with hockey sticks. You may choose to practice alone or with your partner. By yourself you can travel while changing speed, directions, and pathways. You can practice scoring a point by setting up marker cones as a goal.

With a partner you may choose to practice passing to each other stationary or moving, or you may choose to have one partner trying to shoot for a goal while the other partner assumes the defensive position, trying to block the shot. If you have other ideas for your activity, let me know. At the conclusion of the activity, we will share our ideas.

> *Dynamic game situations involving striking with long implements are beyond the control level of skill proficiency. Children are content to pass to a partner and usually choose to do so within the context of self-space. Playing-the-game to children means making some choices on their own, using the hockey sticks and pucks.*

Closure:

During this theme, you used hockey sticks and pucks. What skills did we try to improve?

Will we always have the rule about high sticks? Why?

Why is it important to be able to change directions and pathways as you tap-dribble?

The puck should always be how close to your stick? Why?

How is passing to a partner like hitting to the goal? How is it different?

Reflection:

Do the children tap-dribble with a mature pattern?

Do they maintain the correct action when moving with a partner in general space?

Are they ready for partners as obstacles as a revisitation theme?

Revisitation to Hockey
Offensive/defensive goalie versus tap-dribble player; one-on-one offensive and defensive player in general space with open goal; one-on-one hockey with third person as goalie; two-on-two hockey for practice of tap-dribble, passing, receiving, and shooting for the goal.

◪ Striking with Long Implements Evaluation

Focus: Striking with long implements (hockey)

The evaluation of the theme, striking with long implements (hockey), may be done throughout the theme or as a culmination to the theme. Each child has a task sheet with skills to be evaluated. A partner will observe each skill and initial it for verification. If completed throughout the theme, it is helpful to date each as it is completed (see Figure 49).

The task sheet is an excellent communication to parents regarding the skills studied and their child's progress. A brief paragraph should be attached, explaining the process and the theme of study.

Children's Movement Vocabulary
A "soon" day: Kindergarten children come to me for physical education two times per week. At the end of the lesson and our discussion of the day, I always try to give a hint of the next lesson. As I was doing so, David began waving his hand high above his head. His question: "Is that a 'soon' day?" MAY ALL YOUR DAYS OF TEACHING PHYSICAL EDUCATION TO CHILDREN BE "SOON" DAYS!

Name ———————————————————— Homeroom ————————————

Striking with Long Implements (Hockey) Evaluation

	I can tap-dribble the puck keeping it within 3–4 feet of my hockey stick.
	I can stop the puck on signal—3 second count from partner.
	I can tap-dribble the puck with either side of my stick.
	I can tap-dribble changing directions from side to side as I travel.
	I can strike the puck, sending it between the cones from a distance of 10 feet. (Cones 6 feet apart.)
	I can pass the puck to a partner in self-space from a distance of at least 6 feet.

Why is it called a tap-dribble?

Why is "high sticks" a violation?

Figure 49 Evaluation Form for Striking with Long Implements

Notes on Dance

Dance experiences compose one-third of the physical education curriculum at Linden Elementary. These learning experiences fall into three categories: creative dance, folk dance, and rhythmical experiences. Creative dance experiences range from a few minutes (A Moment of Dance) to a full theme of study (People in Motion); these and other creative dance experiences are found throughout *Children Moving*, 5th edition, and within the lesson plans of *On the Move*.

Examples of rhythmical experiences are lummi sticks, tinikling, and Chinese ribbons. After being introduced to the basic patterns and the cultural context of the activity, the children design new patterns. Creativity, again, receives a strong emphasis.

Folk dances from various countries are studied throughout the elementary years. Linden Elementary is blessed with children from many countries; they enjoy the introduction of a dance from their native countries. We also enjoy studying the cultural heritage of the dance. A list of folk dances we enjoy at Linden follows. After the children learn folk dances from different countries, they begin to see common patterns and skills within them. They then design a new folk dance, putting together the skills, formations, and floor patterns they choose. After experiencing American square dance, we often do "Scatter Square Dance," a very informal combining of skills within a free formation.

Dance experiences provide children with excellent opportunities to express themselves with no fear of failure, opportunities to learn of other countries and heritages, opportunities for creativity and decision making, and opportunities for social interaction in a very positive, noncompetitive environment. I would encourage you to make dance a strong component of your curriculum; it will be a very rich, rewarding experience for the children and for you.

Suggested Folk Dances for Children, K–6

Kindergarten, Grade One
Singing Games
Muffin Man
Looby Lou
Lassie
Bluebird
Carrousel
Chimes of Dunkirk
Danish Dance of Greeting

Grade Two, Grade Three
Hopp Mor
A Hunting We Will Go
Kinderpolka
Shoemaker's Dance
Paw Paw Patch
Jump Jim Joe
Bleking
Cshebogar
Hansel and Gretal
Circassian Circle

Grade Four
Seven Jumps
Troika
Greensleeves
Norwegian Mountain March
Bingo
Little Brown Jug
Oh, Suzanna

Grade Five, Grade Six
Seven Jumps (with creative shapes)
Troika (with partner change)
Polka Step
Kavelis
Virginia Reel
Red River Square
Teton Mountain Stomp

Grade Six
Little Man in a Fix
Red River Square
Mayim, Mayim

PART FOUR
Fitness Concepts

Physical Fitness

Physical fitness is the *product* of a quality program of physical education. Physical fitness comes as a result of competence in movement skills and confidence in oneself. Enjoyment of physical activity is perhaps the number one determinant for continuing participation in activity, the development of competence through practice, and the resulting self-confidence it brings.

Physical fitness at the elementary school level is not formal exercises and calisthenics or required running of laps. For elementary-age children, the focus for physical fitness in the physical education curriculum is the introduction to the concepts of fitness, an awareness of the components, and enjoyment of activity. The physical fitness lesson plans that follow are designed to do just that. The first is an introduction to the concept of fitness and the components of fitness. The second lesson plan is designed to increase children's awareness of cardiovascular fitness and the specificity of exercise and activity. Lessons 3 and 4 focus on the role of nutrition and physical activity in overall health and wellness.

Physical fitness is a *process* attained through quality instructional physical education, participation in physical activity, and a knowledge of fitness components coupled with an appreciation for good health. Teaching fitness includes planning all lessons for maximum active participation, planning and providing opportunities for physical activity beyond the instructional physical education program, and providing individual assistance to those youngsters whose fitness levels are below what is needed for good health and wellness.

> *The fitness lessons that follow are not designed to be taught as a unit;*
> *they are to be distributed throughout the school year within the curriculum.*

Lesson 1

Focus: The concept of fitness

Objectives: At the end of this lesson the children will have learned to:
1. define physical fitness.
2. count their pulse rates.
3. discuss the effects of exercise and activity on fitness.

Introduction:

What is fitness? What does a person look like who is physically fit? Name someone that you think is physically fit. Why do you think that person is physically fit? (*Discuss for several minutes, building on children's answers to define fitness in terms of good health, wellness, absence of disease, energy to meet daily chores, recreational activities, and emergencies.*) Today we are going to learn about fitness. We will focus on three areas of fitness—cardiovascular fitness, muscular strength, and flexibility.

Content Development:

1.0   Cardiovascular—that's a big word! Can anyone tell me what it means? Right, it has to do with the heart. This part of physical fitness has to do with fitness of the heart and lungs.

T   Can you hear your heart beating? When the room is very quiet, just before you go to sleep at night, you can "hear" your heart beating. Another way to "listen" to your heart is by counting your pulse. Let's count our pulse while we are seated in our resting position around the circle. (*Teach the children to count the pulse for ten seconds and then multiply by six.*) That's how many times your heart beats in one minute.

Repeat an additional time for practice.

Don't worry if the pulse count is not accurate. The increase of the pulse during activity is the focus, and that increase will be obvious to the children.

What do you think will happen to your heart rate when you run around the track, when you jump rope? Right, your heart will beat faster. Why does the heart beat faster when you exercise?

T   Standing in your self-space, let's do our magic jump rope for thirty seconds. Magic rope is jumping without the rope; it's magic because you never make a mistake. Jump up and down on two feet until I give the signal to stop. On signal, sit down quickly and position your fingers ready to count your pulse.

T   Now let's recheck our heart rates. What happened? Why is exercise for your heart good for you?

 What is this type of fitness called?

2.0   The second fitness component for today is muscular strength and endurance. (*Briefly discuss the difference between strength and endurance.*) Who is the strongest person you know? What makes them strong? We build a strong heart muscle by exercising the heart—running, swimming, jumping rope. We build strong leg muscles when we run. We build strong abdominal muscles when we do curl-ups. How can we build strong arm muscles? Right—push-ups and pull-ups will help us. What are some other ways?

T   Let's all learn to do a push-up correctly.

Demonstrate correct push-up, modified according to fitness standards.

T   Now let's learn to do a belly-up! They are much more fun.

Demonstrate correct belly-up (inverted push-up). (See Children Moving, *Chapter 4, for description.)*

Let's do three to five belly-ups for arm strength. Many of the older boys and girls do these at home each evening to build strong arm muscles.

3.0   The third area of fitness introduces another new word—flexibility. What do you think flexibility means? (*Demonstrate with a rubber band and a pencil.*) Can a rubber band stretch and bend? How about the pencil? Which one is flexible? Flexibility—the ability to stretch and bend. Who can tell me the sports or physical activities in which flexibility is very important? Do we need to be flexible for good health and wellness?

T   Seated in a V-position in your self-space, gently stretch toward your toes. Follow this with gentle stretching and then repeat the activity.

Discuss with the children the importance of stretching—the warming up of the muscles to prevent injury and to perform better.

T   Seated in the V-position, place your fingers on your knees. "Walk" your fingers forward to touch your socks. Rest. Now walk them forward to touch your shoelaces. Rest. Now walk them forward to your toes and beyond. Isn't it easier when we approach with a gentle stretch?

T   Stretch your back forward as well as to the sides.

T   Extend your right hand upward and reach behind your back to touch your left hand (*Aerobics Institute shoulder stretch*). Repeat with left hand upward and reaching.

Discuss the importance of flexibility in each of these areas.

Culmination and Assessment:

Grades K–2 (*butcher paper, crayons or markers*) Draw a picture of a person who is strong and healthy, a person who is physically fit.

Grades 3–4 (*pencil, journal*) Write in your journal a paragraph describing a physically fit person. What does it mean to be physically fit?

Closure:

Today we talked about physical fitness. Tell your neighbor what fitness means.

We talked about physical fitness in three areas. We did activities in each of the areas. Let's name the three components of fitness we introduced today.

How do we improve our fitness?

How do we make our muscles stronger?

How do we become more flexible?

Reflection:

Do the children understand the concept of fitness?

Can they define and discuss fitness?

Can they identify the components of health-related fitness?

Lesson 2

Focus: Cardiovascular fitness

Concept: Active participation is necessary to increase cardiovascular efficiency.

Objective: At the end of this lesson the children will have learned to:
identify an exercise or physical activity that improves cardiovascular fitness.

**Materials/
Equipment:**   playground balls (one per child)
jump ropes (one per child)

Introduction:

Earlier in the year, we discussed the concept of fitness and why fitness is important for good health. Who can tell me what physical fitness means? Today we are going to focus on one component of fitness—-cardiovascular fitness. Cardiovascular is a really big word for the heart. Does the human heart look like this? (*Show valentine heart.*) No, the human heart is a muscle that looks like this. (*Show model.*) Like all muscles it becomes stronger by exercise and physical activity. Today we will analyze different activities to determine if they are good for the heart.

Content Development:

1.0   When we did our lesson on fitness you learned to count your pulse. Let's practice counting our pulse for a few seconds. Remember to place two fingers just to the sides of your neck and listen for the beat. Let's count our resting pulse while we are seated—before we begin moving. (*Have the children count their pulses while you time them for ten seconds, then multiply by six.*) That is your pulse rate for one minute. Repeat for another count.

Don't be overly concerned if the children's count of the pulse rate is not accurate; the number will increase with the exercise or activity. The goal is to have the children realize the level of activity needed to increase the pulse rate.

Have the children do the following activities as a group. Stop after each activity; check the pulse rate.

2.0   "Sticky Popcorn." Stand in your self-space. On signal, begin jumping up and down in that self-space (thirty seconds). On signal, jump carefully toward another person; touch shoulders with that person and continue jumping up and down. Continue jumping with your partner (thirty seconds). On signal, the two of you jump carefully to "stick" with two other persons; now four are jumping together. Continue jumping as a group of four (thirty seconds). On signal, the four jump to "stick" with another four, forming a group of eight. Continue jumping until the signal is given to stop.

  Jumping alone—thirty seconds

  Partner—thirty seconds

  Groups of four—thirty seconds

  Groups of eight—thirty seconds.

T   Sit down quickly and listen for the signal to count your pulse. Ready? Begin the count.

3.0 "Sit and Reach." Sit down in your self-space, with legs in a "V," a comfortable distance apart. Keeping your legs flat on the floor, walk your fingers from your knees to your socks, shoelaces, or toes, gently stretching as far as you can reach. Hold for four counts. Move your legs closer together and repeat. Move legs together, bend one leg upward with foot flat on floor and walk your fingers up the extended leg. Now bend and stretch the other leg. Hold for four seconds.

T   Check pulse rate.

4.0 Select a playground ball for dribbling. On signal, begin dribbling the ball in your self-space, using either your preferred or alternate hand. Stay in your self-space. I will time you for two minutes of dribbling. Move from your self-space only if you lose control of the ball. On signal, place the ball between your feet for safekeeping and be ready for the pulse rate signal.

T   Check pulse rate.

5.0 This time you will dribble while traveling in general space. We will dribble for two minutes. When you hear the signal to stop, place the ball between your feet and be ready for the pulse rate. (*Dribble for two minutes while traveling.*)

T   Check pulse rate.

6.0 Put away the playground balls and select an individual jump rope. Stand in your self-space with sufficient room for safe jumping. On signal, begin jumping your rope; you may use any type of jump you wish, but do not stop jumping until you hear the signal.

Children who have difficulty jumping can do "Magic Rope."

We will jump for one minute then count our pulse.

T   Check pulse rate.

Closure:

Let's discuss the different activities we did today and how each affected our pulse rates. What does pulse rate mean? How is it measured?

Which activities caused the pulse rate to increase?

What type of activity is necessary to increase pulse rate?

What does this tell us about exercising for a healthy heart?

Reflection:

Can the children discuss the link between cardiovascular fitness and good health?

Can they identify activities that contribute to cardiovascular fitness, as well as those that do not?

Lesson 3, Part 1 (in the classroom)

Focus: Nutrition

Concept: The body needs food for energy; the body needs energy to do well in physical activity.

Objectives: At the end of this lesson the children will have learned to:
1. discuss good nutrition as a component of wellness.
2. categorize foods according to the "Food Guide Pyramid."
3. discuss the relationship between nutrition and good performance in sports and physical activities (Part II).

Introduction:

Designed by the classroom teacher to introduce children to the concept of nutrition, the importance of good nutrition, and ways to attain good nutrition within children's busy schedules.

Can you remember what you ate for dinner last evening? How about snacks? Did you have a treat before bedtime? Today we are going to look at the foods we have eaten in a one-day period of time. We will then compare our eating with the Food Guide Pyramid to see if we have a strong base, a balanced food intake for one day.

Content Development:

1.0   (*On a selected day, have the children record answers to the following questions.*) What did you eat for dinner last evening? What did you have for breakfast this morning? What will you have for lunch today? Don't forget snacks. Record all of those foods in your journal.

2.0   (*Use a prepared block diagram sheet, Figure 50.*) Record each food item—one per block on your blank block diagram sheet. List only one food item per block.

Some children may need assistance in breaking down certain items, for example, a sandwich, into the components.

T   After you have completed a block for each food item you ate, cut the blocks apart. You may color and/or decorate if you wish.

3.0   Build a personal food pyramid (four tiers) using the building blocks of your food choices: breads, cereals, pastas on the bottom; fruits and vegetables on the next tier; dairy products, meats, beans, and eggs on the next tier; and sweets on top. Cut and paste your food pyramid to show your eating for the day.

T   After you have completed your food pyramids, we will compare them with the Food Guide Pyramid (Figure 51) recommended for good health.

Discuss nutrition and its relationship to good health and wellness.

4.0   Write a personal goal for nutrition in your journal; be sure to date the entry. We will take another look at our eating habits later in the year and see how we are doing on achieving our personal goals for good nutrition. Remember, foods are not "good" or "bad"; balance is the key.

Closure:

Were you surprised at the types of food you ate during a single day?

Was your personal food pyramid balanced with a solid, wide base of breads, pastas, and cereals?

Why is good nutrition important when you are eight or nine years old? (*Use the correct ages for the children involved in the discussion.*)

Reflection:

Do the children understand the role of nutrition in good health?

Can they analyze their food intake in relation to the Food Guide Pyramid?

Write the name of each food eaten in a box: remember, record only one food per box.

After you record your food choices, cut apart the blocks to build your food pyramid.

Figure 50 Food Pyramid Building Blocks

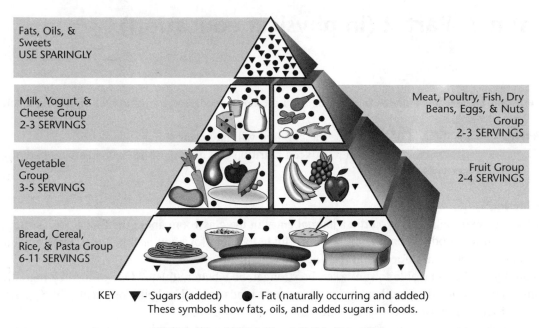

Figure 51   USDA Food Guide Pyramid

Source: From *Dietary Guidelines and Your Health* by U.S. Department of Agriculture, 1992, Rockville, MD.

Lesson 3, Part 2 (in physical education)

Focus: Nutrition

Concept: The body needs food for energy; the body needs energy to do well in physical activity.

Objective: At the end of this lesson the children will have learned to:
discuss the relationship between nutrition and good performance in sports and physical activities.

Introduction:

Earlier this week/month/year, you did a journal entry in the classroom about the foods you ate for a day. You compared the foods you ate with the Food Guide Pyramid for good health. Today we are going to look at that same journal information for "fuel for activity" purposes.

Would you like to be able to run faster, be stronger, be a better athlete? One of the key ingredients to being a good athlete is good health, eating the right foods as well as being physically fit. Our lesson today will focus on nutrition for us as athletes.

People who participate in sports, gymnastics, and dance need a special focus on proteins, carbohydrates, fats, and water. Each of these is important for our work in sports and physical fitness.

Content Development:

1.0   Essential nutrients:

Carbohydrates are the main fuel source for muscles. They supply energy to muscles during exercise.

1.1   What foods provide us with carbohydrates? Breads, cereals, fruits, and vegetables.

1.2   Do you eat toast for breakfast? How many eat cereal? What is your favorite fruit? Name one vegetable that you like.

All of these supply us with carbohydrates to give our muscles energy during physical activity.

Proteins are the building blocks of body tissues. They form the important parts of muscles, bones, and blood. They help in tissue repair.

1.3   What foods provide us with proteins? Meat, fish, poultry, eggs, milk products, and dried beans.

1.4   How many of you had some protein in your diet yesterday? Name the food that provided your protein.

Fats supply energy and insulate and cushion organs. Yes, we all need some fat!

1.5   Is some amount of fat needed? Why? To cushion organs, to keep us warm, to supply energy.

Water is the coolant for the body; it helps maintain adequate blood volume, lubricate joints, and maximize muscle strength.

1.6   Why do you get thirsty when you exercise vigorously?

1.7   How much water do you need each day?

1.8   Do you need more water when you exercise and play in a sport? Why?

1.9   Is drinking a soda the same as drinking water?

2.0   Remember the Food Guide Pyramid you studied in the classroom. (*Post the Food Guide Pyramid on the wall.*) Which category of foods should we partake of the most in a given day? What category should we eat the least of? Are all the categories needed for good health and to be physically active?

3.0   Let's brainstorm a typical day—what foods do you normally eat? I will list them on the board (flipchart). We will then compare our listing of foods with the Food Guide Pyramid and with the categories of food that we need for good health and energy for activity.

Use responses in general from the class to avoid focusing on a single child and what are often very poor eating habits.

Remember, athletes can improve their performance with good nutrition.

Closure:

Why is good nutrition important for athletes?

Why do I need to drink lots of water when I play in a soccer game, play chase with my friends, ride my bike?

Does it matter what foods I eat?

How can nutrition help me be a better athlete?

Reflection:

Can the children discuss the relationship between nutrition and good performance in physical activities?

Can they identify the food groups important for good health and performance in physical activity?

Lesson 4

Focus: Physical activity

Concepts: Physical fitness is improved with regular physical activity.
                   Daily physical activity has positive health benefits.

Objectives: At the end of this lesson the children will have learned to:
                   1. discuss the positive benefits of regular physical activity.
                   2. analyze different types of activity for health and fitness benefits.

Introduction:

Thus far in our discussions of fitness concepts we have defined physical fitness and discussed the benefits of being physically fit. We have discussed cardiovascular fitness, muscular strength, and flexibility as major components of fitness. Throughout our physical education lessons we have been involved in activities to foster a healthy level of each of these components. We discussed nutrition and its positive benefits on our physical activity and sports performances, as well as nutrition for good health. Today we are going to look at the different activities we do at home, in our recreational time, and when we play. Are they all of the same benefit for physical fitness and good health? Do they all strengthen the heart? Why is daily physical activity important?

Content Development:

1.0   Take a moment to list in your journal the activities you choose when you go home after school: riding your bike, soccer league, delivering the paper, walking the dog, playing outside with friends, playing video games, using the computer, and so forth.

T   Let's brainstorm all the different activities we like to do. I will list them on the board (flipchart) as you name them. When we finish our listing, we will have all the physical activities we do after school and before going inside for the evening.

2.0   (*Post the "Physical Activity Pyramid," Figure 52, p.* 322.) Let's categorize our activities according to the Physical Activity Pyramid; we did an activity very similar to this with the Food Guide Pyramid. This time, we will code them as a group:

Level 1: outdoor play with friends; family walks

Level 2: jogging, swimming, biking, sports, dance, gymnastics clubs

Level 3: flexibility exercises, strength training exercises

Level 4: rest, computer games, inactivity

Just like the Food Pyramid, the Physical Activity Pyramid should have a solid base with the greatest number of activities in this category; this is level 1. The tip of the pyramid, rest and activity with very little total body movement, should have the least emphasis; this is where we should spend the least amount of our time. Good health and fitness are attained only if we are physically active, preferably every day.

T   Look at the activities you listed in your journal. Code your activities according to the categories listed. Where do you spend the greatest amount of your time? Are you physically active or inactive? Is your favorite activity outdoor play with your friends or computer games and videos?

Older children can benefit from knowing the amount of emphasis recommended for each level of activity; the emphasis for younger children is recognizing more and less from level 1 to level 4.

Remember, all categories are needed. You need periods of rest and quiet time each day; however, they are not the base of the pyramid, only the tip . . . small amounts, please.

T   Write a personal Physical Activity goal for yourself. Is there a category you wish to increase? Is your activity pyramid balanced with a strong base of physical activity?

Remember, physical activity and good nutrition are *the* team for good health and well-being. A combination of physical activity and good nutrition every day provides the body with what is needed to be physically fit, to be healthy, and to perform well in school and at play.

3.0   This balance of activity and good eating habits also plays an important role in the fourth component of fitness—body composition. We haven't discussed this fitness component yet. Who can remember the components of fitness we learned earlier in the year? Cardiovascular fitness, muscular strength, and flexibility. The fourth component is body composition. What could those words possibly mean? Body composition is the balance of lean tissue and fat within the body. We talked earlier about the role of fat in protecting the body from injury and supplying energy. Yes, we all need some fat; we also need lean tissue. Being physically active every day and practicing good nutrition will give us the balance of fat and lean tissue needed for good health and good performance in activity.

Remember, physical activity every day—just like brushing your teeth!

Closure:

What did we learn about physical activity and fitness today? Is physical activity important only for fitness? Tell your neighbor two reasons why physical activity is important.

Why does physical activity provide the broad base for the pyramid rather than inactivity? What would happen if inactivity was the base of the pyramid? Would the person be healthy? Would he or she be fit?

What are the four components of physical fitness? Is a person physically fit if he or she is very strong but not flexible? How about able to run very fast but with very little muscular strength? What was our original definition of fitness? Why does it take all four to be truly fit?

Reflection:

What do the children's journal entries tell me about their fitness, their activity levels, their self-concepts, and their personal concerns?

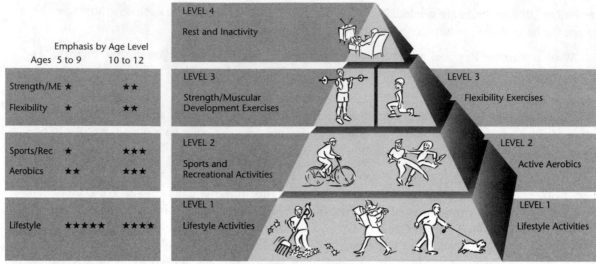

Emphasis by Age Level

	Ages 5 to 9	10 to 12
Strength/ME	★	★★
Flexibility	★	★★
Sports/Rec	★	★★★
Aerobics	★★	★★★
Lifestyle	★★★★★	★★★★

NOTE: This table is designed to indicate physical activity including in and out of school.

★★★★★ greatest emphasis
★★★★ considerable emphasis
★★★ moderate emphasis
★★ some emphasis
★ little emphasis

Figure 52 Physical Activity Pyramid

Source: Physical Activity for Children: A Statement of Guidelines, 1998, Reston, VA: NASPE.

PART FIVE

Integrated Projects

Integrated Projects

In recent years much has been written about integrated physical education. Professional journals, such as *Teaching Elementary Physical Education* and *Journal of Physical Education, Recreation, and Dance*, carry articles on the theory as well as the application of the integrated curriculum. Entire texts have been devoted to the topic (Cone et al., 1998*). Integrated curriculums tend to fall within two categories. The first is the integration of other subject areas into physical education—for example, critical thinking, social and personal responsibility, and fitness concepts. This internal approach to an integrated curriculum results in extending physical education beyond the development of motor skills. The second approach to an integrated curriculum, referred to as an external integration, is the integration of physical education into other subject areas within the broader school curriculum—for example, social studies, math, and so forth.

A third type of integrated curriculum is the thematic approach to curriculum development, in which the entire school or grade level within the school focuses on a theme with content development in all disciplines centered around the selected theme. The lesson plans that follow illustrate a thematic approach to the integration of physical education for elementary children. The first series of lesson plans, "People in Motion," demonstrates the integration of art, music, and physical education for upper elementary students. The second example, "The Rain Forest," demonstrates a total school approach to a selected theme. Each example is designed to show an integrated curriculum that does not compromise the content of physical education, force integration, or sacrifice the existing curriculum.

*Cone, T. P., Werner, P., Cone, S. L., & Woods, A. M. (1998). *Interdisciplinary teaching through physical education*. Champaign, IL: Human Kinetics.

People in Motion

Focus: Locomotor skills and body shapes

Subfocus: Levels, directions, time
Stretching, curling, twisting actions

Objectives: At the end of this series of lessons the children will have learned to:
1. travel with different locomotor skills.
2. balance in different body shapes.
3. move to the beat of a designated rhythm.
4. analyze a favorite sport and/or physical activity to determine movements and shapes that illustrate that activity.
5. combine shapes and actions into a creative dance that portrays a favorite sport and/or physical activity.

Phase I:

This integrated project began in art class with the children learning to draw the human body with correct proportions—for example, arms and legs at proper length in relation to the trunk. The imagery for the activity was the children's favorite sport and/or physical activity. After each child chose a favorite activity, he or she selected four or five different body positions that depicted various segments of the activity: the volleyball player's serve, spike, set, and high and low positions; the sky diver's jump, free fall, and aerial maneuvers; the runner's start, middle, and ending postures and stretches. Using combination media, the children completed paintings with a focus on correct body proportions, alignment, and positioning.

Phase II:

Following completion of their art projects depicting "People in Motion," the children created the music to accompany movement sequences of shapes and actions. Working with partners and in small groups in music class, rhythmic accompaniment was designed with the use of Orff instruments. The music was purposely designed in ABA form. The A representation provided a faster beat for the actions of the physical activity; the B representation was a slower beat for the shapes of the activity. Both the A and the B segments of the music contained distinct phrases to accompany the different movement actions and shapes. Each class recorded their music on cassette tape for easy transfer to the gymnasium for the design of the movement sequences.

Phase III:
The final portion of the "People in Motion" project was the design of movement sequences and creative dances combining shapes and actions to portray children's favorite sports and/or physical activities. The physical education experiences were designed as four lessons, culminating in each child presenting a brief description of his or her painting and performing the dance with the musical accompaniment. The videotaping of the children's dances was done in two parts: Each child's dance was videotaped individually with verbal description and visual representation, then the group dances were performed with the paintings serving as a backdrop. As with all creative dance lessons for children, the lesson plans were not designed for a full thirty to forty-five minutes but for the completion of a segment of the development—the fulfillment of an idea. (See *Children Moving*, Chapter 20, for further discussion of teaching dance to children.)

Lesson 1

Focus: Body shapes

Subfocus: Stretching, curling, twisting actions; levels

Objectives: At the end of this lesson the children will have learned to:
1. balance in wide, narrow, curled, and twisted shapes.
2. match body shapes to sports and physical activity positions.

**Materials/
Equipment:** Paper, pencils

Introduction:

Today we begin work on a project that you actually started in art class. Remember when you did the drawings and paintings of "People in Motion." You chose your favorite sport or physical activity and then painted shapes that represented that motion. You then created in music class the music that would accompany the shapes and actions of that activity. Your musical creation included a fast and a slow segment, with a repeat of the fast; the music was in ABA form.

Today we begin to add the final phase of that project—the shapes and actions that portray your "People in Motion." Your first decision is the size of your group—whom you choose to work with on this project. You may work alone, with a partner, or in a group of three or four.

Content Development:

1.0   Written on the board (flipchart) are the steps we need to complete today. After your group is given paper and pencil, write the name of the project at the top of your paper, "People in Motion." To the right side, record the inventors of the dance—the names of the people in your group. On the left side of your paper, record the sport or physical activities each of you did.

T   In art class you did excellent drawings and paintings of the shapes that represent your sport or physical activity. Choose four of those shapes to draw on this project paper. Many of you had more than four shapes; you must select only four for the dance. Some of you had less than four shapes; you will hold one shape for a longer period of the music. Each person in your group, using stick figures, will draw the four shapes of his or her sport or activity.

2.0   After you complete your drawings, explore the body shapes that will represent those drawings. Ask yourself the following questions as you make the body shapes:

Will the shape be wide, narrow, curled, or twisted?

Will you be at high, medium, or low level?

How will you use arms, legs, bends, and stretches to make the shapes?

T   After you explore body shapes to represent the drawings, choose the best shape for each drawing and show them to the group. Ask your group to evaluate your shapes to help you achieve your best.

T   As you practice your four body shapes to represent your sport or activity, begin to think about the order of the shapes:

What is the best for 1-2-3-4?

How can you use curling, twisting, stretching actions as transitions between the balances?

Practice to make them flow together like a sequence.

Closure:

What movement concepts did we study today?

Analyze your favorite sport or activity and tell your neighbor four body shapes that are important to that sport or activity.

Why are transitions important in a sequence?

Reflection:

Are the children able to match body shapes to sport or physical activity to portray images of that activity?

Can they use movement to create the image of the sport or activity without doing only pantomime?

Lesson 2

Focus: Body shapes

Subfocus: Stretching, curling, twisting actions

Objectives: At the end of this lesson the children will have learned to:
1. balance in wide, narrow, curled, and twisted shapes.
2. match body shapes to sports and physical activity positions.
3. combine shapes into sequences with smooth transitions between shapes.

**Materials/
Equipment:** Paper, pencil
Music recorded on cassettes earlier in music class
Triangle (cymbals) for signal

Introduction:
Last time we began our project, "People in Motion." You chose the people to be in your group and selected your drawings from the ones you did in art class. We call them stick figures; your art teacher refers to them as *pictographs*. That is a new word for us to learn and know how to spell. Today we will complete the shapes portion of our sequences.

Content Development:
1.0   Complete the pictographs that represent your drawing in art class. You may wish to make some changes after practicing the shapes for stillness.

T   Show your pictographs to your group. They will evaluate the drawings and the body shapes you made to represent the drawings. Remember, your shapes must match the drawings—wide, narrow, curled, bent, stretched, twisted.

T   After your group has checked your drawings and shapes for accuracy and has given you some "pointers" to make your shapes even better, show them to me.

2.0   We are now ready to add the rhythmical accompaniment you created in music class. We will be using the slow music as you demonstrate the shapes of your sport or activity. Find your self-space and the music will begin. Hold each shape absolutely still, just like you did in gymnastics sequences. I will touch the triangle when you are to change to your next shape.

T   The shapes look really good. They are memorized. You are holding them very still. Now you will need to add a beginning shape to start the sequence and an ending shape for the completion of this segment. (*Create and practice with music for several minutes.*)

T   Remember when we worked on transitions in gymnastics. Who can tell me what a transition is? Right, it is the movement between shapes, the smooth action between stationary shapes. Purposely move from one shape to the next with a smooth transition. Begin with your first shape; explore ways to move from that stillness to your next shape. When you are satisfied with that transition, work on the next one. Continue this exploration and refinement until you have smooth transitions between each shape, as well as after the beginning and before the ending shapes.

Closure:

What did you add to your movement sequences today?

What new word did we learn? What does *pictograph* mean?

What are transitions? Why are they important in a sequence?

Reflection:

Are the children able to use body shapes to represent the positions of the sport or physical activity they have chosen?

Is their focus on the movement quality rather than on the mirror image of the sport?

Do they use bending, stretching, and twisting actions as transitions between the balances?

Do the sequences flow from beginning to ending shape?

Lesson 3

Focus: Locomotor skills with stretching, curling, twisting actions

Subfocus: Pathways, directions

Objectives: At the end of this lesson the children will have learned to:
1. move in self- and general space representing two actions of a chosen sport or physical activity.
2. match movements to sports and physical activity actions.
3. combine locomotor skills with stretching, curling, and twisting actions to portray the chosen sport or physical activity.

**Materials/
Equipment:**   Paper, pencil
Music recorded on cassette tapes

Introduction:

Last time we learned a new word in physical education. Who can tell me the new word? Pictograph. What does that mean? You completed pictographs to represent the paintings you did in art class, the pictographs of your favorite sport. You then created the body shapes to match those drawings and practiced them to the slow music created earlier in music class. Today we add the next segment of the project—the actions of the sport.

Content Development:

1.0   Select your two favorite actions from your sport or physical activity. The actions will be done in general space to the fast music you created. Remember, you created music with ABA form: fast, slow, fast. Each of the A segments also had ABA phrases within the segment; thus the fast music contains three phrases. A will be the first action of your sport or activity; B will be the second action. A will then be repeated.

T   Select, practice, and refine your actions. I will play the music so you can begin to practice for matching of rhythm and length of sequence.

T   After you have chosen your actions and practiced them several times, show them to another person within your group. This partner will give you suggestions to make your actions even better!

2.0   After you have completed the action portion of your movement sequence and shown it to a partner, record it on your paper. On the left of your paper, list A-B-A. You may choose to write or draw the first action you selected; that is A. Then write or draw your second action; that is B. The third A is simple; it is a repeat of the first action.

T   Give your paper to your partner and let him or her watch to see if you have recorded the actions correctly, that is, if you are doing what your paper says for each action.

3.0   Your actions create a floor pattern as you move. This floor pattern will be repeated each time you do your sequence, just like the actions are repeated. Draw the pathways that create your floor pattern on your paper.

Closure:

The new word for today is *choreographer*. Each of you is a choreographer—the creator of a dance. When we did games, you were inventors. When we create shapes and actions for this project, you are choreographers, just like Bruce Ewing with the Oak Ridge Ballet. Next time we will put everything together for our "People in Motion" dances.

Reflection:

Are the children able to portray the actions of the sport or physical activity in a creative, abstract manner without the sequence becoming strictly pantomime?

Do their actions match the actions of the sport or activity they have chosen?

Do they use a variety of locomotor skills, as well as stretching, curling, and twisting actions?

Does each phrase of their sequence match the phrase of the rhythmical accompaniment?

Lesson 4

Focus: Combining shapes and actions

Subfocus: Locomotor skills, actions, shapes, levels, directions, pathways, body shapes

Objective: At the end of this lesson the children will have learned to:
combine shapes and actions into a creative dance portraying a favorite sport or physical activity.

**Materials/
Equipment:** Paper, pencil
Music on cassette tapes
Triangle

Introduction:
Your movement project is almost complete. You have drawn pictographs and written descriptions of actions. You have created body shapes and movement actions. What was the word we used for creators of the dance? Choreographers—each of you is a choreographer. Today we put the finishing touches on the dances.

Content Development:
1.0   We will begin our work today with practice of the actions of our "People in Motion" dance. Remember the music is in ABA form. The A portion is faster for the actions; the B portion is slower for the shapes. Let's begin our practice with the A portion of the music—the actions of your dance.

You selected two actions to portray your sport or physical activity. The fast music has three phrases; you will do the first action with the first phrase and the second action with the second phrase, followed by a repeat of the first action. (*Practice with the music.*)

T   The B portion of the music is slower for the shapes that represent positions within your sport or activity. Remember you created four different shapes; I will touch the triangle for your transition to the next shape.

T   The final A portion of the music is a repeat of the first A; your actions will be a repeat.

2.0   Remember the beginning and ending shapes that you worked on earlier in our lessons. You are now going to use them for the beginning and the ending of your dance. Select your self-space, assume your beginning shape and wait for the music to begin. When the music ends, assume your ending shape and hold very still for three seconds. (*Allow several minutes for practice of entire sequences: ABA, three actions, four shapes, three actions.*)

T   Wow! Everything looks great. Actions are clear, transitions are smooth, and shapes are held very still. Let's have a final practice from beginning to end.

3.0   When you are ready, I will videotape your "People in Motion" dances so you can see them, so the videotape can be seen by other classes, so you and I can watch the tape together to evaluate your sequence, and so the videotape can be a part of your portfolio for final evaluation and to be shared with your parents.

Closure:

What movement skills and concepts did we use for our "People in Motion" dances?

What is the difference between creative dance and pantomime?

Tell your neighbor two things you liked best about this project.

Write in your journal the things you would like me to know about your work on this project.

Reflection:

Were the children able to abstract the sport or physical activity skills into dance form?

Did the sequences flow from beginning to end?

What did I learn about this project from reading the children's journals?

The Rain Forest

The second integrated project is a schoolwide thematic approach to curriculum development, with all grade levels and all special area classes focusing on a selected theme (the rain forest).

Phase I:
The theme began with a schoolwide decoration of hallways, classrooms, and entryways depicting the rain forest. Classroom teachers centered reading, mathematics, and other subject areas around the theme. The librarian featured books on the rain forest; early morning announcements included a child giving a brief statement of facts about the rain forest. Classroom activities centering around the theme continued for a four-week period of time.

Phase II:
For special area classes the theme began in art class, with the children painting animals of the rain forest. Whereas the younger children were free to draw from their imagination of animals in the rain forest, the older children researched books and the Internet for descriptions and pictures of the animals.

Phase III:
In physical education class the theme featured children's movement sequences of the animals in the rain forest. The sequences began with daybreak in the rain forest and the animals awakening from their sleep. Body shapes and actions illustrated the animals' movements; three actions were highlighted. The sequence ended with the animals assuming positions for their midafternoon nap. Actions centered around the following:

- How would the animal move?

- Would the movements be fast or slow?

- At what level does the animal move?

The children returned to their classrooms from physical education class each time with questions to be researched. Each return to physical education was an addition to their sequence based on the research and reading done in the classroom. (*The lesson plans were developed in similar style to those of the earlier integrated theme, with a movement focus for each and the development and refinement of the sequences over time—written work, peer assessment, videotaping, and evaluation.*)

Phase IV:
Following the painting of the rain forest animals in art class and the development of a movement sequence in physical education, the children created the rhythmical accompaniment in music class. The music created featured the dawning of a new day in the rain forest—gentle, soft accompaniment; music for action and moving—a variety of rhythms; and finally music for the slow pace of midafternoon and the approaching nap.

Culmination:
The integrated project culminated with the children performing their sequences in physical education, accompanied by their musical creations. Each child was videotaped individually, and then the entire class performed "A Day in the Rain Forest."

PART SIX
Children Moving Challenges

Children Moving Challenges

Physical activity plays an important role in the development of good health and wellness for children. Its role is established in the prevention of degenerative diseases whose symptoms are seen in physically inactive children as young as ages eight and nine. At the same time that research indicates the need for large-muscle physical activity for children, national surveys indicate an increasingly alarming decline in physical activity among children. Beginning in early elementary school and increasing through adolescence, youngsters, for a variety of reasons, are less active at home, at school, and at play. These activity patterns, established in childhood, become the physical activity lifestyles of adulthood.

With the obesity rate for children increasing and the activity rate for children decreasing, physical education for elementary school boys and girls would appear to be the answer to the problem. Daily, quality programs of physical education taught by qualified, certificated physical education specialists would indeed address the issue in a most positive manner; however, not all schools have daily physical education for children. Some have no physical education specialist; some have no physical education! The combinations of these factors led to the creation of *Children Moving* Challenges.

The *Children Moving* Challenges presented in this section are written for the classroom teacher. They are designed to provide children with meaningful physical activity during recess or play break. They are designed for maximum participation for all children, with tasks that foster skill development. *Children Moving* Challenges are designed for the classroom teacher. They require minimum advance preparation and single-task presentation. The classroom teacher may choose to become involved in the teaching by observation and presentation of learning cues, or the teacher may choose to supervise only.

The *Children Moving* Challenges are divided by grade level for easy reference and progression, although children do not learn in closed steps. Children who are less skilled may still need practice on those challenges listed for an earlier level. Children with more advanced skills should be encouraged to broaden their skill base, assist others with their skills, and/or create new challenges. This expansion of skills is preferable to moving to a higher grade-level series of tasks.

If your school has a physical education specialist, the challenges will complement the instructional program of physical education. If you are the specialist responsible for physical education, you are encouraged to share the *Children Moving* Challenges with your classroom teachers. If you are the classroom teacher, you are encouraged to use the *Children Moving* Challenges for your students. I welcome your input on their usefulness to you and your children. Working together, we can make a difference in encouraging children to be physically active for a lifetime of good health and wellness.

Each year classroom teachers invest in playground equipment for youngsters to use, only to find within a couple of months that the amount of equipment has been reduced to less than adequate. One of the best ways we have found to collect, store, transport, and maintain equipment for the playground is the use of a "muck" bucket, a large plastic bucket with rope handles on two sides. Two children are assigned the duty of carrying the muck bucket to and from the playground, a rotating classroom duty. The rule for the playground is: If you use it, you are responsible for returning it to the bucket. Stock the muck bucket with the following, introducing the equipment as it is needed for the new activity that day or week:

four or five good playground balls for dribbling (not to be used for kicking)

four or five 8-1/2-inch rubber balls for kicking/soccer dribbling

variety of small balls

four or five inexpensive 8-1/2-inch plastic balls

six to eight whiffle balls

four to six beanbags (primary grades)

four or five individual jump ropes sized appropriately for age of children

one long jump rope

two sets of balance cans (primary grades)

four to six scoops for catching

carnival supply balloons (primary grades)

Beaver tail rackets (primary grades)

short-handled rackets/paddles (intermediate grades)

badminton shuttlecocks

Kindergarten

Locomotor Skills

Task: Hop on one foot across the play yard without losing your balance or bumping into another person. When you tire of hopping on that foot, switch to the other foot and continue hopping across the play area.

Equipment: None

Setup: Any space, indoors or outdoors, free of obstacles

Development: Have the children hop across the play yard, staying on one foot for several hops. They can switch feet when they tire, when you give the signal, after a certain number of hops, or when they reach the far side of the area.

Criteria: Hopping on one foot four or five times, moving forward, without losing balance or returning to both feet on the ground

Cue: One foot up—hop, hop, hop . . .

Task: Gallop across the play yard like a horse. Remember to keep the same foot in front at all times.

Equipment: None

Setup: Large open space, free of obstacles

Development: Have the children gallop across the play yard. Remind them to keep the same foot in front at all times. The gallop can be across the play area, around a circle, or just free gallop in open space.

Criteria: Galloping in general space, keeping the same foot in front at all times

Cue: Same foot forward—gallop, gallop, gallop . . .

Locomotor Skills (continued)

Task: Jump on two feet like a kangaroo as you travel across the play yard. Jump like: Tigger the Tiger; a frog; you are on a pogo stick.

How high can you jump?

How far can you jump?

Equipment: None

Setup: Large open space, free of obstacles

Development: Have the children jump up and down as they travel across the play yard, taking off on two feet and landing on two feet. Use different imagery, but always focus on the two feet to two feet movement.

Criteria: Taking off and landing on two feet (a less mature pattern is leading with one foot)

Cue: Two to two—jump, jump, jump . . .

For Further Development: Jumping for height and jumping for distance involve swinging the arms upward (height) and forward (distance). At the beginning levels of jumping and landing, the focus is on using both feet for the takeoff and the landing.

Skipping can be introduced to kindergarten children. However, great emphasis should not be placed on skipping correctly. Skipping is one of the last locomotor skills to be mastered. The focus for kindergarten boys and girls is on enjoyment and active participation, not on mastery.

Bounce/Catch (Dribble)

Task: Bounce the ball and catch it after each bounce.

Equipment: 8-1/2-inch playground balls for bouncing

Setup: Large open space, smooth surface

Development: Have the children stand in self-space, not touching anyone, and drop or bounce a playground ball and catch it after the first bounce. Although they are trying to stay in their self-space, some children will find the task easier to complete if they walk as they bounce and catch.
Challenge: Can you bounce the ball and catch it five times?

Criteria: Dropping or bouncing the ball so it does not land on the toes; bouncing the ball so it comes upward to where the child is standing

Cue: Bounce, catch . . . bounce, catch . . .

For Further Development: Can you keep the ball going without catching it each time? This is called dribbling, like a basketball player. Can you dribble the ball five times before you catch it?

Catching

Task: Catch the ball tossed to you by the teacher.

Equipment: 8-1/2-inch soft foam balls, for example, volleyround balls; inexpensive plastic balls

Setup: Large open space

Development: Standing approximately six feet from the children, toss the ball so the child can catch. Use an underhand toss, targeting the child's chest; most will catch with a "cradle" catch, that is, the ball touches the chest and the arms close around the ball. As the child tosses the ball back to you, model "ready hands" by placing your hands in position ready for the catch prior to the child throwing the ball.

Note: The development of catching for young children comes from an adult or older child tossing the ball. Young children do not have sufficient control of force or direction to practice throwing for another child to catch.

Criteria: Catching the ball before it bounces; catching the ball without turning the head to the side or closing the eyes

Cues: Ready hands
Watch the ball

For Further Development: Can you catch the ball with your hands only?

Balance

Task: Stand on one foot for five seconds.

Equipment: None

Setup: Any space, indoors or outdoors, free of obstacles

Development: In self-space, not touching anyone, have the children stand on one foot for a five-second count: one thousand one, one thousand two. . . . Repeat with the other foot.
Note: Remind the children that extending the arms outward to the sides will help them stay balanced.

Criteria: Standing on one foot for five seconds without letting the other foot touch the ground or floor; standing still without extreme waving of arms

Cue: Extend the arms for good balance

Task: Walk the balance beam or tape lines like a tightrope walker in the circus.

Equipment: Low balance beam, lines painted on the asphalt, tape (masking, plastic) lines on the floor

Setup: Sufficient space for children to walk lines without touching others

Development: Have the children walk the balance beam or tape line without stepping off. Walk alternating feet, one foot in front of the other—left, right, left, right.
Note: Remind the children that extending the arms outward to the sides will help them stay balanced.

Criteria: Walking the balance beam or tape line without stepping off and without extreme waving of the arms

Cue: Extend the arms for good balance

For Further Development: Can you walk backward on the beam?

Balance (continued)

Task: Walk on the balance cans across the play yard

Equipment: Balance cans (commercial purchase or homemade from large coffee cans with ropes attached)

Setup: Large open space or smooth surface for children to walk on balance cans without touching others

Development: Have the children walk on the balance cans across the play yard (between the start and finish lines).
                 Challenge: Walk around the cone and return to the start space.
                               Zigzag around the marker cones as you walk across the space.
                 Note: The key to walking on the balance cans is keeping the attached ropes taut.

Criteria: Walking on the balance cans a short distance without stepping off

Cue: Heads up (Watch where you are going)

Balance cans: Using a handheld can opener, cut two holes in each side of the bottom of a large can. Push the rope through the openings, tying the rope in a secure knot. The can's plastic cover serves as a pad on the bottom of the can as it contacts the floor (Figure 53).

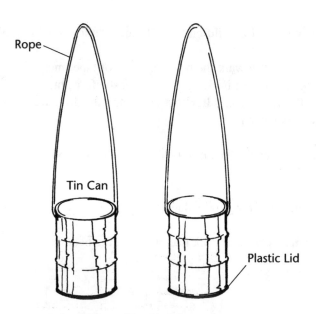

Figure 53   Balance cans

Jump Rope

Task: Jump rope either forward or backward five times.

Equipment: Individual jump ropes

Setup: Large open space or smooth surface for children to jump rope without the rope hitting others

Development: Have the children stand with the rope behind them. On signal, they will throw the rope over their heads; with the rope in front of them, they will then step over the rope. Repeat the process: Throw the rope over the head, step over. The children will tend to step over the rope, step jump over the rope leading with one foot, or jump over the rope with two feet.

Challenge: Can you do that five times?

Can you jump your rope backward?

When you are ready, you can keep your arms turning the rope so you jump without stopping.

Criteria: Completing five single jumps (swing the rope, jump over; swing the rope, jump over)

Cue: Throw, jump . . . throw, jump . . . throw, jump

Grade 1

For first-grade children who did not have guided movement (recess, physical education) during kindergarten, refer to the kindergarten-level *Children Moving* Challenges for appropriate activities.

Locomotor Skills

Task: Hop on one foot across the play yard without losing your balance or bumping into another person. When you tire of hopping on that foot, switch to the other foot and continue hopping across the play area.

Equipment: None

Setup: Any space, indoors or outdoors, free of obstacles

Development: Have the children hop across the play yard, staying on one foot for several hops. They can switch feet when they tire, when you give the signal, after a certain number of hops, or when they reach the far side of the area.

Criteria: Hopping on one foot eight to ten times, moving forward, without losing balance or returning to both feet on the ground

Cue: One foot up—hop, hop, hop . . .

Task: Gallop across the play yard like a horse. Remember to keep the same foot in front at all times.

Equipment: None

Setup: Large open space, free of obstacles

Development: Have the children gallop across the play yard. Remind them to keep the same foot in front at all times. The gallop can be across the play area, around a circle, or just free gallop in open space.
Challenge: Can you gallop leading with your other foot?

Criteria: Galloping in general space, keeping the same foot in front at all times

Cue: Same foot forward—gallop, gallop . . .

Task: Jump on two feet like a kangaroo as you travel across the play yard. Jump like: Tigger the Tiger; a frog; you are on a pogo stick.

Equipment: None

Setup: Large open space, free of obstacles

Development: Have the children jump up and down as they travel across the play yard, taking off on two feet and landing on two feet. Use different imagery, but always focus on the two feet to two feet movement.

Challenges: Jump high in the air like a basketball player. Swing your arms upward to jump really high.

Jump as far as you can. Swing your arms forward to jump really far.

Criteria: Taking off and landing on two feet (a less mature pattern is leading with one foot)

Cues: Two to two—jump, jump, jump . . .
Soft landings

For Further Development: Jumping for height and jumping for distance involve swinging the arms upward (height) and forward (distance). At the beginning levels of jumping and landing, the focus is on the use of both feet for the takeoff and the landing.

Task: Skip across the play yard as if very happy and carefree

Equipment: None

Setup: Large open space, free of obstacles

Development: Have the children skip in general space throughout the play space. Skipping is best accomplished by just the suggestion; do not try to analyze the action . . . just enjoy.
Note: Children progress from a gallop to skipping on every other foot to a mature skipping pattern. As with kindergarten children, do not be overly concerned with first-graders who cannot skip.

Criteria: Skipping with a lift of the knee and a step-hop on each foot

Cue: Life your knees . . . swing your arms

Dribbling

Task: Dribble the playground ball like a basketball player—with one hand.

Equipment: 8-1/2-inch playground balls

Setup: Large open space, smooth surface

Development: Have the children stand in self-space, not touching anyone, and bounce the ball and catch it after the first bounce. Repeat the task without catching the ball, without stopping it between bounces.

Note: Some children will dribble with two hands, others with only one. The progression is usually from bounce/catch to two hands to only one hand.

Challenges: Can you dribble five times?

                  Can you dribble ten times?

                  Can you dribble as we say the alphabet? How many times will we dribble if we complete all the letters?

Criteria: Dribbling the ball with one hand; dribbling the ball with beginning control—that is, the child controlling the ball, not the ball controlling the child

Cue: Push the ball . . . don't slap

For Further Development: Can you walk as you dribble? Basketball players rarely stand still and dribble; they move about. Travel across the play area as you dribble the ball.

Throwing and Catching

Task: Throw and catch the ball with your teacher.

Equipment: 8-1/2-inch soft foam balls, for example, Volleyround balls; inexpensive plastic balls

Setup: Large open space

Development: Standing approximately eight to ten feet from the children, toss the ball so the child can catch. Have the child throw the ball back to you. Repeat the task.
Note: For first-graders it is important to begin to use the overhand throw or chest pass with two hands; children will model the type of throw you use. As the child throws the ball back to you, model "ready hands" by placing your hands in position ready for the catch prior to the child throwing the ball.

Criteria :   Catching the ball before it bounces; catching with hands only

Cues: Ready hands
Watch the ball

For Further Development: Standing in self-space, toss the ball upward and catch. Remember to catch with hands only.

Task: Catch the ball in the scoop.

Equipment: Whiffle balls, scoops (made from one-gallon plastic milk containers)

Setup: Large open space with sufficient room to toss and catch without bumping others

Development: Have the children stand in self-space and toss the ball upward and catch it in the scoop. They may choose to let the ball bounce one time before they catch it or catch it with no bounce.

Criteria: Catching the ball in the scoop after one bounce or with no bounce

Cue: Watch the ball

Scoops can be made from plastic milk jugs by cutting the bottom from the jug, leaving the scoop with handle for catching (Figure 54).

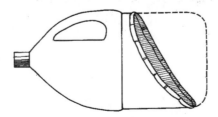

Figure 54   Scoops

Striking with Paddles

Task: Strike the ballon or ball upward with your paddle.

Equipment: Lightweight paddles (beaver tail, made from hangers and knee-high hose, or commercial plastic); balloons, small foam balls

Setup: Large open space with sufficient space to strike balls or balloons upward without hitting another person

Development: Have the children stand in self-space and strike the ballon or ball, sending it upward.
Challenges: Can you make the balloon or ball travel upward and back down to you so you do not leave your self-space?
Can you strike the ball twice before stopping?

Criteria: Making contact with the balloon or ball

Cues: Flat paddle (Keep the paddle flat)
Watch the ball

Note: Heavy-duty balloons (carnival supply) are a most enjoyable way of introducing striking with paddles to young children. Their lightness creates a low descent and therefore maximum time for visual tracking.

Beaver tail paddles can be made from coat hangers and knee-high hose. Pull the coat hanger into the extended shape of a paddle and fold the hook toward the neck of the hanger. Pull the knee-high over the hanger, wrap the extended hose around the neck of the hanger, use masking tape to secure the hose around the neck (Figure 55).

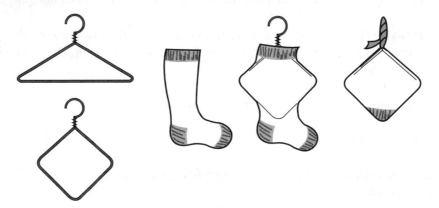

Figure 55 Beaver tail paddles

Jump Rope

Task: Jump rope five times forward and five times backward.

Equipment: Individual jump ropes

Setup: Large open space or smooth surface for children to jump rope without the rope hitting others

Development: Have the children turn their individual ropes, jumping over with each turn. Some children will choose a step jump (like running); others will choose a two-foot takeoff and landing. Either is quite correct.

                   Repeat the skill, turning the rope backward rather than forward.

Criteria: Taking five consecutive jumps forward (swing of rope and jumping five times without a mistake); taking five consecutive jumps backward

Cues: Ready, jump
Small, bouncy jumps

Task: Jump a long rope

Equipment: A long jump rope

Development: Have the children jump a long rope, beginning inside the rope. An adult or older student will assist as one of the turners.

Criteria: Completing five successive jumps with an adult assisting with the turning of the rope

Cue: Jump (When young children are first learning to jump a long rope, the best cue is a verbal "jump" by the teacher just prior to their need to do so.)

Grade 2

Locomotor Skills

It is hoped that children will achieve a mature pattern of the basic locomotor skills and balance tasks presented earlier by the completion of Grade 2. Review of these skills, especially with music, provides excellent classroom movement activity for second-grade children.

Development: Hop on one foot five times
Jump on two feet as you travel across the space
Run and jump with a one-foot takeoff as if leaping over a puddle
Gallop across the play space
Skip across the play space

Balance on one foot for five seconds. Balance on the other foot.
Walk the low or medium balance beam forward. Walk backward.

Dribbling

Task: Dribble the playground ball with one hand like a basketball player.

Equipment: 8-1/2-inch playground balls

Setup: Large open space, smooth surface

Development: Have the children stand in self-space, not touching anyone, and dribble the playground ball. Tell them to dribble as if they were going to dribble until the end of the school day . . . forever!

Challenges: Dribble in self-space, without moving from that space.

Count the number of times you can dribble. Try for 25, 50, 100.

Criteria: Dribbling the ball with one hand, staying in self-space

Cue: Push the ball, don't slap

Task: Dribble the ball as you travel through the general space, weaving among other boys and girls but never touching anyone.

Challenges: Dribble across the play area, from one side of the blacktop area to the other side.

Dribble in curved and zigzag pathways as you travel.

Dribble with a gentle jog, not walking, not running full speed.

Dribble as you travel behind a chosen partner, going wherever he or she goes.

Criteria: Dribbling and traveling with control of ball and body

Cues: Push the ball, don't slap

Dribble the ball slightly to your side and in front when you travel

For Further Development: Practice dribbling in self-space without looking down at the ball. When you look "over" the ball, you will still be able to see it. Look at another person, a spot on the playground. Can you travel and look over the ball rather than down at the ball? This skill will be important for basketball and dribbling games.

Throwing and Catching with a Partner

Task: Throw and catch the ball with a partner.

Equipment: 8-1/2-inch playground, plastic, and foam balls

Setup: Large open space

Development: Have the children stand approximately eight to ten feet from a chosen partner and throw and catch with their partners.

Note: Some children will need to be at a shorter distance from partners for successful throwing and catching. Encourage the children to throw "so the partner can catch"; I have found a two-hand chest pass* provides success for both partners. Remind them of "ready hands" for catching.

Challenges: Stand at the distance from your partner at which you are most comfortable for throwing and catching. Throw and catch five times with your partner.

If you are successful on all five catches, each of you will take a giant step backward and repeat the task.

Continue the challenge of five catches and a giant step backward until you reach your maximum distance for throwing and catching without a mistake.

If either of you does not catch the ball:
- take one giant step forward to shorten the distance and continue the challenge
- return to your starting distance and begin again.

Criteria for Throwing: Throwing to a partner—not over the head, not at the feet
Criteria for Catching: Catching with hands only

Cue for Throwing: Two hands on the ball—push
Cues for Catching: Ready hands
Watch the ball

For Further Development: Throw and catch with your partner using different types of balls.

---

*Chest Pass: Two hands on the ball, holding it at chest height. Push the ball forward as you step forward, sending the ball to your partner. Target: throw to partner at chest height.

Catching

Task:　　　　Standing in self-space, toss the ball upward and catch.

Equipment:　　A variety of small balls for catching—whiffle balls, foam balls, rubber balls; beanbags

Setup:　　　Large open space with sufficient room to toss and catch without bumping others

Development:　Have the children stand in self-space and toss the ball upward and catch it.
　　　　　　　Challenges:　Catch the ball at a height above your head.
　　　　　　　　　　　　Explore catching different types of balls.

Criteria:　　Catching the ball with hands only—no "cradle" catches

Cue:　　　　Venus Flytrap (Heels of hands together; close your fingers around the ball)

For Further Development:　After children have been introduced to catching small balls with the cue of closing hands around the ball, they can practice catching different sizes and types of balls, including playground balls. The criteria is still catching with hands only; the difference is the lack of closing fingers around the larger balls.

Striking with Short Rackets or Paddles

Task:　　　　　Strike the ball or badminton birdie (shuttlecock) upward with your racket or paddle.

Equipment:　　A variety of lightweight, short-handled rackets and paddles (inexpensive, commercial solid-surface paddles, stringed rackets, etc.); badminton birdies (shuttlecocks), whiffle balls, foam balls

Setup:　　　　Large open space with sufficient space to strike balls upward and forward without hitting another person

Development:　Have the children stand in self-space and strike the ball, sending it upward.
　　　　　　　　Challenges:　Strike the ball or shuttlecock so it travels upward and back down to you without leaving your self-space.
　　　　　　　　　　　　　　Can you strike the ball or shuttlecock twice before stopping?

Criteria:　　　Making contact with the ball or shuttlecock

Cues:　　　　Flat paddle (Keep the paddle flat for contact)
　　　　　　　　Watch the ball

Task:　　　　　Strike the shuttlecock so it travels to your partner.

Setup:　　　　Large open space with sufficient room for partners to stand approximately eight to ten feet apart and strike the ball or shuttlecock without hitting anyone

Development:　Have the children stand approximately eight to ten feet from a chosen partner and strike the ball or shuttlecock, sending it forward to their partner.
　　　　　　　　Note:　When children work on striking with partners, sufficient space is *very* important. They move to the side without realizing they have done so and are unaware of the nearness of others.
　　　　　　　　Challenges:　Keep the ball or shuttlecock going back and forth to your partner.
　　　　　　　　　　　　　　How many hits can you make without a mistake?

Criteria:　　　Making contact with the ball or shuttlecock to send it forward to a partner; making contact with the ball or shuttlecock when it comes from a partner

Cues:　　　　Watch the ball (Watch the ball until it leaves your racket)
　　　　　　　　Rainbow swing (Swing your racket from back to front so the ball or shuttlecock travels through the air in a high arch, like a rainbow)

Jump Rope

Task: Jump rope ten times forward and ten times backward.

Equipment: Individual jump ropes

Setup: Large open space or smooth surface for children to jump rope without the rope hitting others

Development: Have the children turn their individual jump ropes, jumping over with each turn. Repeat the skill, turning the rope backward rather than forward.
Challenges: Jump with a step jump (like running, but not going anywhere).
Jump with a two-foot jump (two feet for takeoff and landing).
Count the number of times you can jump without a mistake.

Criteria: Taking ten consecutive jumps forward (swinging rope and jumping ten times without a mistake); taking ten consecutive jumps backward

Cue: Small, bouncy jumps

For Further Development: Skier: Using a two-foot takeoff and landing, jump side to side like you are snow skiing.

Task: Jump a long rope

Equipment: Long jump ropes

Development: Have the children jump a long rope, beginning inside the rope. Two partners are turning the rope.
Note: Turning a long rope is a skill to be mastered, just like jumping rope. Two partners turning for a first and second jumper, who then become the turners, has proven successful.

Criteria: Making five successful swings of the rope; completing five successive jumps.

For Further Development: As third-graders you will work on turning a long rope plus being able to "run in." Can you start on the outside of the rope and "run in" after the turning has begun? Let's practice front door (rope turning toward the person who is running in).

Special Notes

1. Encourage second-graders to work or play with partners, expanding their listing of "best friends" as they select new partners. Practicing skills with a partner (counting the number of dribbles, number of jumps, etc.) also helps when the amount of equipment is limited.

2. When selecting games for second-graders to play, choose games that promote maximum participation for all children, avoiding elimination games. Most games can be easily adapted to avoid children being "out" and to maximize participation. Active play for all and practice for those both skilled and less skilled is the focus of games play for young children.

Grade 3

Dribbling

Task: Dribble the playground ball in self-space without losing control of the ball.

Equipment: 8-1/2-inch playground balls

Setup: Large open space, smooth surface

Development: Have the children stand in self-space with their feet in a forward/backward stride and dribble the playground ball. See how many times they can dribble without losing control of the ball or moving from their space.

Challenges: Count the number of dribbles you can complete without a mistake. That is your personal best. Try again for an even higher score. Practice each day to better your personal best.

Standing four to five feet from a friend, look at that person while you dribble, keeping your head up. Keeping your visual contact with your partner, continue to dribble the ball. If you look down, you partner will say your name as a reminder to keep your head up while dribbling

Dribble in self-space using your nonpreferred hand. If you have been dribbling with your left hand, now use your right. What is your personal best with this hand?

Criteria: Dribbling the ball with one hand; looking "over," not down at, the ball

Cues: Push the ball, don't slap
Heads up (Look over the ball)

Task: Dribble as you travel across the play area, controlling both your body and the playground ball you are dribbling.

Challenges: Run at a medium speed as you travel and dribble.
Set an imaginary target for yourself at a point somewhere on the play space. Dribble as quickly as possible to that space without bumping another person or losing control of the ball. Repeat with another visual target.

Criteria: Dribbling the ball with control and traveling at a faster-than-walking speed

Cues: Heads up (Look over the ball)
Dribble the ball slightly to your side and in front of you when you travel

361

Kicking

Task: Kick the ball to your partner.

Equipment: Old partially deflated playground balls, large plastic or foam balls

Setup: Large open space with sufficient room to kick balls without hitting someone

Development: Standing approximately fifteen feet from your partner, kick the ball so it travels across the play yard to your partner. Begin your kick with the ball placed on the ground and you standing behind and slightly to the side of the ball.

Challenges: Place the ball on the ground and execute a running kick by approaching the ball for the kick rather than standing behind it.

Have your partner roll the ball across the open space to you and then kick the ball when it comes to you.

Criteria: Making contact with the ball so it travels forward

Cues: Watch the ball

Contact *behind* the ball for travel across the ground; contact slightly *under* the ball for travel through the air

For Further Development: With your partner, join another set of partners, forming a group of four. Practice rolling the ball to the kicker. The person kicking may kick along the ground or in the air; the fielders retrieve or catch the ball. Rotate positions after two or three kicks so everyone plays each position and gets lots of practice.

Dribbling (with feet)

Task: Dribble the ball (playground or soccer) by tapping it gently with the inside of your foot, alternating your right and your left feet. This is a soccer dribble.

Equipment: Old playground balls, soccer balls, plastic or foam balls

Setup: Large open space with sufficient room for dribbling the ball with the feet and not bumping others on the playground

Development: Tap-dribble the soccer (playground, plastic) ball like a soccer player. Gently tap the ball with the inside of your foot, sending it forward a short distance. Alternate tapping the ball with your left and right feet as you travel across the play area.

                     Challenges: Tap-dribble the soccer ball across the play area, from one side of the playing field to the other side.

                                  Tap-dribble in general space, weaving among other boys and girls, but never touching anyone.

                                  Tap-dribble with a gentle jog . . . not walking, not running full speed.

Criteria: Dribbling the ball with the feet, alternating for contact

Cue: Tap, Tap (Gently contact the ball with the inside of the feet for the dribble)

Note: Within any class of children, there will be boys and girls with no previous soccer experience, as well as boys and girls who play in soccer leagues. After the introduction of the basic skill of dribbling, children can then have a choice of:

- practice of the basic skill;

- cooperative work with a partner or small group, no more than four, for a game of soccer they design;

- a child's invented version of soccer with skills matched to the more advanced level of those with experience in the game.

Throwing and Catching with a Partner

Task: Throw and catch the ball with a partner.

Equipment: Whiffle balls, softball-size rubber balls, playground balls

Setup: Large open space

Development: Have the children stand approximately fifteen feet from a chosen partner and throw and catch with their partners. The focus is on throwing with a one-hand, overhand throw and catching with hands only.

Note: The longer distance is needed to encourage children to use the overhand throwing pattern. At a shorter distance, they often choose an underhand, scooping action.

Challenges: Throw so your partner can catch ten times in a row.

How many times can you and your partner throw and catch without a mistake?

Throw so your partner can catch without moving from his or her space.

Criteria for Throwing: One-hand, overhand throw—not two hands, not underhand
Criteria for Catching: Catching with hands only

Cues for Throwing: Side to target (Turn so your nonthrowing arm is toward your partner as you prepare to throw)

Opposite foot forward (Step forward on your nonthrowing side as you throw to send the ball really far)

Cues for Catching: Watch the ball

Ready hands for larger balls

Venus Flytrap for smaller balls

For Further Development: In small groups of three or four, play a game of "Monkey in the Middle," practicing your throwing and catching. Rotate positions after five throws so everyone plays each position.

364

Catching

Task: Standing in self-space, toss the ball upward and catch.

Equipment: A variety of small balls for catching—whiffle balls, foam balls, rubber balls; beanbags. A variety of objects to catch with—scoops, commercial scoops, Velcro gloves, and so forth.

Setup: Large open space with sufficient room to toss and catch without bumping others

Development: Have the children stand in self-space and toss the ball upward and catch it. Some will be catching with a scoop or glove; others will be catching with hands only.
Challenges: Toss the ball really high and catch.
                   Catch the ball high above your head.
                   Catch the ball at low level—just before it touches the ground.

Criteria: Catching the ball with hands only or in the scoop

Cues: Thumbs together (Ball above the head)
                   Thumbs apart (Pinkies together for ball at low level)
                   Venus Flytrap (Close fingers around the ball)

                   For catching with a scoop or glove: Watch the ball

For Further Development: Play a game of "Keep Away" with a group of three or four, or design a game of throw and catch with a partner or a small group.

Jump Rope

Task: Jump a single rope continuously for one minute without stopping.

Equipment: Individual jump ropes; stopwatch for teacher

Setup: Large open space or smooth surface for children to jump rope without the rope hitting others

Development: Have the children practice jumping rope counting to themselves or with a partner for a count of sixty seconds. They may choose to jump either forward or backward, double bounce, single bounce, or step jump.

Criteria: Jumping for sixty seconds without stopping or making a mistake (Use a stopwatch to time individuals or a group for task completion.)

Cue: Bounce, bounce (Small jumps, very little height)

For Further Development: Jump rope with a partner—facing each other with one rope; side by side with two ropes, alternating turns or turning together.

Task: Jump a long rope with "running in."

Equipment: Long jump ropes

Development: Have the children jump a long rope, starting outside the rope and running in.
Note: Some children may need to begin inside the rope; the ability to "run in" is a difficult skill to master.
Challenges: Jump ten times
                 Jump as you turn around
                 Jump and touch the ground
                 Jump with your partner

Criteria: Successful jumping of the rope

For Further Development: Introduce the children to a couple of jump rope rhymes or to a new one if they already have a favorite.

Grade 4

Dribbling (hand)

Task: Dribble a playground ball across the blacktop without losing control of the ball or bumping into anyone else. Challenge yourself to see how fast you can travel as you dribble.

Equipment: 8-1/2-inch playground balls for dribbling

Setup: Large open space, smooth surface; distance marked for starting and stopping

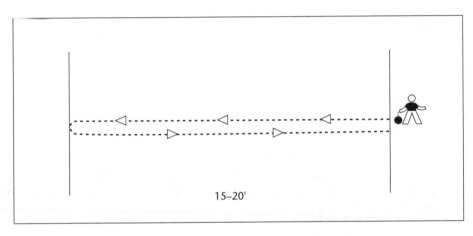

15–20'

Figure 56 Setup for dribbling (hand)

Development: Have the children practice dribbling a playground ball with one hand as they travel in a forward direction across the blacktop. When they arrive at the opposite line (fifteen–twenty feet), they are to turn and continue dribbling back to the starting line.

           Challenges: How many times can you travel and dribble without a mistake?

                     How fast can you travel and dribble to the line and back?

                     Design three tricks for dribbling and ball handling. We will then write them on a challenge chart for other fourth graders to try, for example, dribble behind your back, through your legs.

Criteria: Dribbling and traveling without losing the ball or bumping into another person

Cues: Finger pads (Use the pads, not the palms, for dribbling)

                Heads up (Keep your head up to watch for open space; don't watch the ball)

For Further Development: Design a game of "Dribble Keep Away" with your friends, using the skill of dribbling combined with throwing and catching. If your playground has a basketball goal, you may choose to add shooting baskets to your game.

367

Dribbling (feet)

Task: Dribble the ball (playground or soccer) in and out around the cones; when you reach the last cone, kick the ball across the line (between the cones) to score a goal.

Equipment: Old playground or soccer balls for dribbling; plastic marker cones (two-liter plastic bottles with sand for weighted bottoms)

Setup: Large open space for safety (playground or blacktop)
Set the cones in a line with approximately eight feet between each; after the last cone, set two cones six feet apart as a goal (Figure 56).

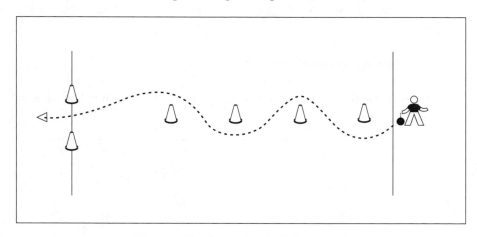

Figure 57   Setup for dribbling (feet)

Development: Have the children practice dribbling the ball with their feet as in soccer. They are to zigzag around the cones, using the right and the left foot, as they dribble and travel. After they pass the last cone, they are to kick the ball hard, sending it between the cones (over the line) to score.

Criteria: Dribbling the cones without bumping a cone

Cues: Tap, tap (Gently contact the ball with the inside and/or outside of either foot for the dribble)
Kick hard (Kick the ball really hard—contact behind the ball—to score a goal)

For Further Development: Challenge a friend to a game of one-on-one soccer, using your skills of dribbling and zigzagging to avoid your friend getting the ball. You may chose to play "Soccer Keep Away" or combine the skill of dribbling with shooting for a goal.

Throwing and Catching with a Partner

Task: Throw and catch with your partner with a goal of 100 percent accuracy.

Equipment: Variety of balls (types and sizes) for throwing and catching

Setup: Large open space for safety; distance of fifteen feet marked by chalk or permanent lines

Development: Have the children practice throwing and catching with a partner, using a variety of balls. The focus of the task is throwing so your partner can catch and achieve 100 percent accuracy on the catches.

                  Challenges: Throw to your partner at a high level so he or she must catch above the head.

                            Throw to your partner with your partner in a catcher's position—at low level.

Criteria: Each partner making ten consecutive catches

Cues for catching: Watch the ball
                                Thumbs together (at high level)
                                Thumbs apart (at low level)

Cues for throwing: To the target (Throw so your partner can catch)
                                Overhand, underhand, two hands, one hand

For Further Development: Design a game of "Keep Away" with your friends, using the skills of throwing and catching and adding traveling.

Paddle Dribbles

Task: Using a lightweight paddle, repeatedly strike the ball downward.

Using a lightweight paddle, repeatedly strike the ball so it travels upward.

Equipment: Lightweight rackets, short-handled tennis rackets; tennis balls (old tennis balls are better for children; new ones are too lively); stopwatch for the teacher

Setup: Large open space or smooth surface; sufficient room for children to practice safely

Development: Have the children practice striking the ball with the racket so the ball travels downward and bounces again upward to their racket. When they first practice the skill, have them count the number of consecutive dribbles they can execute properly.

Have the children practice striking the ball with the racket so the ball travels upward approximately two feet and returns downward to the racket.

Criteria: Dribbling continuously downward (upward) for thirty seconds—no stopping, no losing control of the ball

Cues: Flat paddle (Keep the racket face flat for a good rebound downward or upward)

Firm wrist (A firm wrist helps keep the racket face flat)

For Further Development: "Racket Two Square" or "Minitennis" with a friend. Introduce the proper forehand grip to children and have them play short-court tennis or two square using a sidearm striking action. (Proper grip: Lay the racket down flat on the ground; pick it up with a natural grip. That is the correct grip for striking on the forehand side.)

Volleying the Ball

Task: Volley the ball (beach ball, lightweight plastic) upward in your group so it does not touch the ground.

Equipment: Lightweight plastic or beach balls

Setup: Large open space for safety; groups of three (Figure 58)

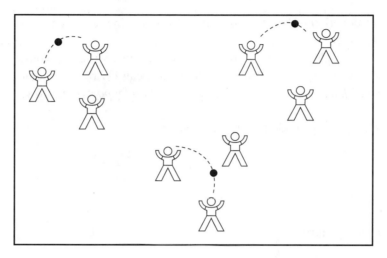

Figure 58   Setup for volleying the ball

Development: Have the children stand shoulder-to-shoulder (triangle) facing each other, then take a giant step backward. They are to strike the ball with both hands, overhead volley (finger pads), sending the ball upward to another person in the group. The challenge is to complete ten volleys without a mistake; everyone in the group must volley the ball at least three times.*

Criteria: Making ten volleys without a mistake, ball traveling upward above the head (One individual cannot volley two consecutive times; volley must alternate players.)

Cues: Quick feet (Move your feet to always be in position to hit the ball)
                    Crab fingers (Curl your fingers to use the pads; don't slap the ball)

For Further Development: Design a game of one-on-one or two-on-two volleyball with a friend or friends. Challenge yourself to see how many volleys you and your partner or friends can complete without a mistake.

*Adapted from: PE Central Challenge, "Keep It Up," http://www.pecentral.org

371

Jump Rope

Task: Jump a single rope continuously either forward or backward.

Equipment: Individual jump ropes

Setup: Large open space or smooth surface for children to jump rope without the rope hitting others

Development: Introduction of basic jump rope skills, following progression from American Heart Association.

Note: Educational kits, including wall charts and descriptions of jump rope skills, are available from local chapters of the American Heart Association. *(You do not have to be a skilled jumper to teach or provide these opportunities to youngsters.)*

Criteria and Cues: Provided by the AHA manual

Task: Jump a long rope continuously.

Equipment: Long jump rope

Development: Have the children jump a long rope, running in after the turners have begun turning the rope.

Challenges: Jump the rope five, ten, fifteen times
Jump with a friend
Jump to your favorite jump rope rhyme

Criteria: Successful jumping of the rope

Cues for running in: Stand to the side of one of the turners
Begin running when the rope hits the floor

For Further Development: Have the class design a booklet of jump rope rhymes to accompany long rope jumping. Each rhyme can include the directions for jumping, the words of the rhyme, and illustrations.

Grades 3 and 4

Children in Grades 3 and 4 are beginning to establish peer relationships beyond the single best friend of Grades 1 and 2. Physical activity provides a rich environment for positive small-group interaction, the widening of the social circle, and acceptance of others. The activities listed under "For Further Development" are designed to encourage children in these important areas, as well as in skill development.

Beyond Grade 4

Beginning in Grades 5 and 6, and continuing through adolescence, group acceptance and social interaction are of major importance to both boys and girls. The playground, physical education, and sports become arenas for "testing" social skills. A solid base of physical activity skills can be a tremendous asset as children seek acceptance among their peers. Equipped with the skills for successful participation in physical activity, recess or play break can be an excellent time for the development of positive social skills. Opportunities are abundant for demonstrating respect for others and acceptance of responsibility. Groups should be encouraged to create and adapt games, to establish rules of play, and to deal with conflict as it arises. Through opportunities for acceptance of responsibility, as well as demonstration of respect for self and others, students gain these critical life skills.